JIM MANTHORPE wrote the first edition of this book. He has trekked in many of the world's mountainous regions from Patagonia to the Himalaya and Scandinavia to the Canadian Rockies. Since 1999 he's been a freelance travel writer, photographer and lecturer. He is the author of three other Trailblazer guidebooks, *Tour du Mont Blanc*, *Pembrokeshire Coast Path* and *Scottish Highlands – The Hillwalking Guide*. He has also researched and updated *Offa's Dyke Path*, *West Highland Way*, *Cornwall Coast Path* and the *Coast to Coast Path* in the British Walking Guide series as well as *Trekking in Ladakh* and *Trekking in the Annapurna Region*.

If he's not criss-crossing the country on foot you'll find him editing other guidebooks or out climbing hills from his base in Knoydart on the west coast of Scotland. He is also passionate about wildlife photography and film-making. See www.jimmanthorpe.com.

This **fourth edition** of *South Downs Way* was researched and updated by Bryn Thomas, Nicky Slade and Henry Stedman.

Authors

South Downs Way

First edition: 2004, this fourth edition 2012

Publisher Trailblazer Publications
The Old Manse, Tower Rd, Hindhead, Surrey, GU26 6SU, UK
info@trailblazer-guides.com, www.trailblazer-guides.com

British Library Cataloguing in Publication Data
A catalogue record for this book is available from the British Library

ISBN 978-1-905864-42-3

© **Trailblazer** 2004, 2007, 2009, 2012: Text and maps

Series Editor: Anna Jacomb-Hood
Editor: Nicky Slade **Cartography**: Nick Hill
Layout: Bryn Thomas **Index**: Jane Thomas
Photograph opp p17: © Jim Manthorpe
Photographs (flora): C3 Bottom right, © Jane Thomas
All other photographs: © Bryn Thomas unless otherwise indicated

The maps in this guide were prepared from out-of-Crown-
copyright Ordnance Survey maps amended and updated by Trailblazer.

Acknowledgements

We're grateful to everyone who helped us with information and advice along the way, in
particular Andy Gattiker & Tim Squire; Tim Muddle, Steve Lord, Lucy Ridout & Chris
Scott for company on the trail; Ben Slade for identifying the 'ugly derelict building' on Map
25 and to Trudi & Andy Rintoul on the path near Jevington. Thanks also to all those read-
ers who've written in with comments and suggestions, in particular, Stuart Blackburne, Tim
Cook; Diana Deal; Rodney Duggua; Alison Field; John Gallagher, Michael Hoey; Jane
Major; Richard Marshall; Steve, Heather, Graham & David Oxley and Nick Price.
   Thanks, as always, to everyone at Trailblazer: Nicky Slade for research, writing and
editing; Henry Stedman for research, Nick Hill for the maps and Jane Thomas for the index.

A request

The author and publisher have tried to ensure that this guide is as accurate and up to date
as possible. Nevertheless, things change. If you notice any changes or omissions that should
be included in the next edition of this book, please write to Trailblazer (address above) or
email us at ☐ info@trailblazer-guides.com. A free copy of the next edition will be sent to
persons making a significant contribution.

Warning: coastal walking and long-distance walking can be dangerous

Please read the notes on when to go (pp13-15) and outdoor safety (pp68-70). Every effort
has been made by the author and publisher to ensure that the information contained herein
is as accurate and up to date as possible. However, they are unable to accept responsibility
for any inconvenience, loss or injury sustained by anyone as a result of the advice and information given in this guide.

Updated information will be available on: ☐ **www.trailblazer-guides.com**

Photo opposite and front cover: Beachy Head Lighthouse © Bryn Thomas

Printed on chlorine-free paper by D'Print (☎ +65-6581 3832), Singapore

South Downs
WAY

WINCHESTER TO EASTBOURNE

60 large-scale maps & guides to 49 towns and villages
PLANNING – PLACES TO STAY – PLACES TO EAT

JIM MANTHORPE

FOURTH EDITION RESEARCHED AND UPDATED BY
BRYN THOMAS, NICKY SLADE
& HENRY STEDMAN

TRAILBLAZER PUBLICATIONS

INTRODUCTION

About the South Downs Way

PART 1: PLANNING YOUR WALK

Practical information for the walker

Budgeting 27

Itineraries

What to take

Getting to and from the South Downs Way

PART 2: THE ENVIRONMENT & NATURE

Flora and fauna

Conservation of the South Downs

PART 3: MINIMUM IMPACT WALKING & OUTDOOR SAFETY

Minimum impact walking

Outdoor safety and health

Contents

Contents

ABOUT THIS BOOK

This guidebook contains all the information you need. The hard work has been done for you so you can plan your trip from home without the usual pile of books, maps, guides and internet research.

When you're all packed and ready to go, there's comprehensive public transport information to get you to and from the trail and 60 detailed maps and town plans to help you find your way along it.

The guide includes:

● All standards of accommodation with reviews of campsites, camping barns, hostels, B&Bs, guesthouses and hotels
● Walking companies if you want an organised tour and baggage-carrying services if you just want your luggage carried
● Itineraries for all types of walkers
● Answers to all your questions: when to go, degree of difficulty, what to pack, and how much the whole walking holiday will cost
● Walking times in both directions and GPS waypoints
● Cafés, pubs, tearooms, takeaways, restaurants and food shops
● Rail, bus & taxi information for all villages and towns along the path
● Street plans of the main towns both on and off the path
● Historical, cultural and geographical background information

MINIMUM IMPACT FOR MAXIMUM INSIGHT

Nature's peace will flow into you as the sunshine flows into trees. The winds will blow their freshness into you and storms their energy, while cares will drop off like autumn leaves. **John Muir** (one of the world's earliest and most influential environmentalists, born in 1838)

Why is walking in wild and solitary places so satisfying? Partly it is the sheer physical pleasure: sometimes pitting one's strength against the elements and the lie of the land. The beauty and wonder of the natural world and the fresh air restore our sense of proportion and the stresses and strains of everyday life slip away. Whatever the character of the countryside, walking in it benefits us mentally and physically, inducing a sense of well-being, an enrichment of life and an enhanced awareness of what lies around us.

All this the countryside gives us and the least we can do is to safeguard it by supporting rural economies, local businesses, and low-impact methods of land-management, and by using environmentally sensitive forms of transport – walking being pre-eminent.

It is no surprise that, since the time of John Muir, walkers and adventurers have been concerned about the natural environment; this book seeks to continue that tradition. There is a detailed section on wildlife and conservation as well as a chapter devoted to minimum impact walking with ideas on how we can broaden that ethos.

Break clear away, once in awhile, and climb a mountain or spend a week in the woods. Wash your spirit clean. **John Muir**

About this book

INTRODUCTION

The South Downs are a 100-mile (160km) line of chalk hills stretching from the historic city of Winchester, in Hampshire, across Sussex to the Pevensey Levels by Eastbourne. For centuries travellers and traders have used the spine of the Downs as a route from one village to the next.

Today that route is still used by walkers, outdoor enthusiasts and others who simply need to escape from box-like offices in congested towns and cities. London, Brighton, Southampton and other urban areas are all within an hour or two of the South Downs, making these beautiful windswept hills an important recreational area for the millions who live in the region.

A traverse from one end to the other following the national South Downs Way trail is a great way of experiencing this beautiful landscape with its mixture of rolling hills, steep hanging woodland and windswept fields of corn. Add to this the incredible number of pretty Sussex and Hampshire villages with their friendly old pubs, thatched cottages and gardens bursting with blooms of roses, foxgloves and hollyhocks and one begins to understand the appeal of the Downs as a walking destination.

The Way takes you through, or close by, numerous pretty English villages such as Amberley with their thatched cottages, village greens and ancient churches.

The start of the South Downs Way: Winchester Cathedral ...

... and the end – Eastbourne.

The South Downs Way begins in the cathedral city of Winchester from where it heads across rolling hills and the Meon Valley with its lazy, reed-fringed chalk-bed river and charming villages. At Butser Hill the Way reaches the highest point of the Downs with views as far as the Isle of Wight and, in the other direction, the North Downs. Continuing along the top of the ridge the Way passes through ancient stands of mixed woodland, past the Roman villa at Bignor and on towards the sandstone cottages of Amberley. Close by is the fascinating town of Arundel with its grand cathedral and even grander castle rising above the trees on the banks of the River Arun. Then it is on to Chanctonbury Ring with its fine views across the Weald of Sussex. The next stretch climbs past the deep valley of Devil's Dyke and over Ditchling Beacon to Lewes with its crooked old timber-framed buildings and the famous Harvey's Brewery. Finally, the path reaches the narrow little lanes of Alfriston with more historic pubs than one has any right to expect in such a small village. The walk's grand finale includes the meandering Cuckmere River and the roller-coaster Seven Sisters chalk cliffs – before reaching the final great viewpoint of Beachy Head, overlooking the seaside town of Eastbourne.

Walking the Way can easily be fitted into a week's holiday but you should allow more time for excursions to the many nearby places of interest such as Arundel, Lewes and Winchester itself ... not to mention the lure of all those enchanting village pubs that are bound to make the trip rather longer than intended!

Arundel Castle, 90 minutes on foot or five minutes by train from Houghton Bridge (see p116).
© Jim Manthorpe

History

There has been a long-distance route running along the top of the South Downs for far longer than walking has been considered a leisure activity. The well-drained chalk hilltops high above the densely forested boggy clay below were perfect for human habitation and were certainly in use as far back as the Stone Age.

From this time onwards a complex series of trackways and paths developed across the land and it is believed that by the Bronze Age there was an established trade route along the South Downs. All along the crest of the Downs escarpment there is evidence of Iron Age hill-forts and tumuli (ancient burial grounds), many of them very well preserved, particularly the Old Winchester hill-fort site in Hampshire.

In more recent times the land was cleared and enclosed, and the flat hilltops were put under the plough. Although this process erased many of the lesser

❑ Geology

It helps to examine the geology of the region as a whole in order to understand how the South Downs reached their present-day form. South-East England is made up of three bands of rock and sediment, the deepest layer being sandstone, the one above clay and the top layer chalk. Over time these three layers were pushed up, probably due to tectonic plate movements, with Africa nudging into Europe. Through the ensuing millennia the soft chalk was eroded through weathering, exposing first the clay and then the more resistant sandstone. The North and South Downs are all that remains of the chalk that lies over the deeper clay and sandstone layers. They are still being eroded today.

One interesting feature of the Downs is the lack of streams. Chalk is highly permeable so streams flow only very briefly during periods of very heavy rainfall. It is worth remembering this when walking on a hot day.

The chalk cliffs between Cuckmere and Birling Gap are known as the Seven Sisters.

A peaceful place to rest your legs:
St Peter's Church in Southease.
© Henry Stedman

Famous local landmarks, the two
windmills above Clayton are
known as Jack and Jill (see p138).
© Jim Manthorpe

tracks the most significant of them remained; the one which ran east–west along the edge of the escarpment. It was not until 1972, amid rapidly growing public interest in walking, that the Countryside Commission designated the 80 miles from Eastbourne to the Sussex–Hampshire border the first long-distance bridleway in the UK. Later, the final section through Hampshire was added bringing the length of the South Downs Way to one hundred miles and giving it a spectacular start in the historic city of Winchester. Today the route is growing in popularity with walkers, cyclists and horse-riders alike, all of whom tend to mingle with ease.

How difficult is the path?

The South Downs Way is one of the most accessible and easiest of Britain's long-distance paths. Those on foot will find the route usually follows wide, well-drained tracks in keeping with its designation as a long-distance bridleway, catering for cyclists and horse-riders as well as walkers. If anything walkers may, on occasion, crave a few more lightly trodden paths since the route always sticks to the well-beaten track.

The South Downs Way is one of the most accessible and easiest of Britain's long-distance paths.

This one-hundred-mile walk can be conveniently divided into sections starting and stopping at any of the numerous little villages that sit at the foot of the escarpment or in a fold in the hills. One thing to note, though, is that because the Way generally follows the high ground along the top of the South Downs, to reach the villages offering accommodation, pubs and shops you usually have to descend steeply off the Downs and climb back onto them to continue, which can make pub lunches less attractive! When calculating the day's timings you need to bear in mind this extra walking time involved.

(Opposite) South Harting (see p99) from Harting Down. © Jim Manthorpe

How long do you need?

Walkers will find that the whole route can be tackled over the course of a week but it is well worth taking a couple of extra days to enjoy the beautiful down-land villages that are passed along the Way. It is also worth taking time to explore the former capital of Saxon England, Winchester, a historic town with a beautiful cathedral. At the

The whole route can be tackled over the course of a week

Looking east from Beacon Hill (see p85). © Jim Manthorpe

other end of the walk Eastbourne, to be polite, is perhaps a little less interesting but will keep those who like to sit on a windy seafront happy for hours.

The practical information in this section will help you plan your walk and design an itinerary to meet your particular preferences.

See pp28-32 for suggested itineraries covering different walking speeds

When to go

The south-east of England has probably the best climate in a country maligned for its fickle weather. By best climate I mean not too much rain and more hours of sunshine than other parts of the UK. The route can be followed at any time of year but clearly the chances of enjoying good weather do depend on the season.

SEASONS

Spring

A typical spring is one of sunshine and showers. From March to May a day walking on the Downs may involve getting drenched in a short sudden shower only to be dried off by warm sunshine a few minutes later. However, the weather can vary enormously from year to year, sometimes with weeks of pleasantly warm sunny weather and in other years days of grey drizzle. In general this is a great time to be on the Downs. Walker numbers are low and the snowdrops, bluebells and primroses decorate the bare woodland floors.

❑ MAIN FESTIVALS & EVENTS

May
● **Winchester Mayfest** (🖥 www.winchestermayfest.co.uk) Well-known international folk, jazz and blues acts perform at venues across the city. One weekend in mid-May.
● **Charleston Festival** (☎ 01323-811626, 🖥 www.charleston.org.uk) Held in Charleston Manor (see p156) in the last week or two of May. Arts and literature abound.

July/August
● **Winchester Hat Fair** (☎ 01962-849841, 🖥 www.hatfair.co.uk) Originally a buskers' festival, now a celebration of street arts and community; all events are free but contributions are welcome – just put your money in the hat. First weekend of July.
● **Goodwood Festival of Speed** (☎ 01243-755055, 🖥 www.goodwood.co.uk) Held on the Goodwood Estate a few miles south of Cocking; see box p102. Horse racing takes place at Goodwood Race Course between May and October.
● **Winchester Festival** (🖥 www.winchesterfestival.co.uk) A two-week festival in mid-July which includes classical and choir music in the cathedral, folk music in the pubs, dancing in the street, art exhibitions, comedy events and plenty more.
● **Lewes Guitar Festival** (🖥 www.lewesguitarfestival.co.uk) Held in the last week of July/first week of August with guitarists from around the world.
● **Arundel Festival** (🖥 www.arundelfestival.co.uk) takes place over the last ten days of August in the castle's grounds featuring folk, rock and classical music as well as plays (Shakespeare) and comedy.

November
● **Lewes Bonfire Celebrations** (🖥 www.lewesbonfirecouncil.org.uk) Largest bonfire-night celebrations in the country, held on 5 November unless it's a Sunday.

Leafy lane near Buriton on a hot summer's day.
© Jim Manthorpe

Summer

It can get surprisingly hot and sunny from June to September but again the weather can vary from one year to the next. Always be prepared for wet weather but also be confident of enjoying some balmy summer days too. Occasionally it can be a touch too hot for walking. This can be a problem as there is not much water on the Downs so bring plenty of full bottles. Visitor numbers are high at this time of year, as you might expect, so it can be a little difficult to enjoy a solitary day on the Way. The hills are colourful in summer with wild flowers in bloom in the meadows, red poppies among the corn and fields of bright yellow oil-seed rape. Hay-fever sufferers may not agree that this is such a good thing. However, everyone seems to be in a good mood and the pubs are brimming with all sorts of folk, from fellow walkers to country gents. The big advantage of summer walking is that it remains light until well after nine in the evening so there is never any rush to finish a day's walk.

Autumn

Autumn is probably the season when you can reliably expect to be rained on. The weather from September to November tends to be characterised by low-pressure systems rolling in from the Atlantic one after another, bringing with them prolonged spells of rain, mist and strong winds. On the positive side those who enjoy a bit of peace and quiet will find very few fellow walkers out and about at this time of year. Furthermore, it is not all rain and wind. Sometimes the weather can surprise you with a day of frost and cold sunshine that can make a day on the Way a real treat. It's important to remember that some businesses shorten their opening hours at this time of year or even close all together.

Snowy days are rare and can be magical. One reader opted for contrasting seasons and did half in the winter and half in the summer.
© Steve & David Oxley

Winter

Southern England doesn't experience as many cold snowy winters as it used to some ten to twenty years ago. From December to February these days it's usually relatively mild with wet weather and occasional spells of colder, dry weather. Any snow that does fall is usually during January and February. It is more likely the further east you go since it is the south-east corner that gets caught by the snow showers that roll in from the North Sea, when the wind is from the north or east. Many walkers will appreciate winter walking for the wilder weather it offers and the days of solitary sauntering along the high windswept crest of the Downs. The best days are the cold, frosty ones when the air is clear and the views stretch for miles. Bear in mind that in winter many businesses, particularly in the more remote villages, are closed. It is always wise to call a guesthouse or pub before turning up expecting a bed or dinner.

TEMPERATURE

Generally, temperatures are comfortable year-round. In winter, warmer clothes will be needed as the temperature drops towards and, on occasion, just below freezing. Summer is usually pleasantly warm with temperatures around 16°C to 23°C but temperatures as high as the low thirties Celsius do occur on at least a few days during July or August which can make walking on exposed sections of the Way uncomfortable.

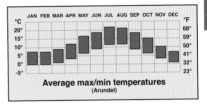

Average max/min temperatures
(Arundel)

RAINFALL

The weather in England is affected mostly by the weather systems that come from the south-west. These are usually low-pressure systems that contain a lot of rain. Rain can and does fall in any month of the year but dry weather is usually more likely in the early summer.

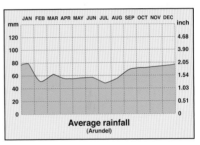

Average rainfall
(Arundel)

DAYLIGHT HOURS

If walking in autumn, winter and early spring, you must take account of how far you can walk in the available light. Also bear in mind that you will get a further 30-45 minutes of usable light before sunrise and after sunset depending on the weather.

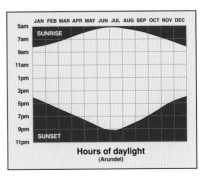

Hours of daylight
(Arundel)

Practical information for the walker

ROUTE FINDING

There is very little opportunity to get lost along the Way. It would be an easy route to follow even without the waymark posts, which are

usually marked with the National Trail 'acorn' symbol. An acorn on a **yellow** chevron indicates that this route is a footpath, ie exclusively for pedestrians. A **blue** background indicates that the trail is a bridleway and can therefore also be used by horses and cyclists. A **purple** background quaintly adds a pony and trap. A **red** or **white** background warns that the route can also be used by motorbikes. Bear in mind that other footpaths may be indicated on the waymark posts so **follow the acorn**.

Nevertheless, it is hard to go astray. Should you find yourself erring from the path the chances are a fence on one side or the steep Downs escarpment on the other will deflect you back in the right direction. In addition there are usually other walkers around who you can ask for directions.

Using GPS with this book

Given the above, modern Wainwrights may scoff while more open-minded walkers will accept that GPS technology can be an inexpensive, well-established if non-essential navigational aid. In no time at all a GPS receiver with a clear view of the sky will establish your position and altitude in a variety of formats, including the British OS grid system, to within a few metres.

The maps in the route guide include numbered waypoints; these correlate to the list on pp182-5, which gives the latitude/longitude position in a decimal minute format as well as a description. Where the path is vague, or there are several options, you will find more waypoints. You can download the complete list of these waypoints for free as a GPS-readable file (that doesn't include the text descriptions) from the Trailblazer website: 💻 www.trailblazer-guides.com (click on **GPS waypoints**).

(Opposite): A hot summer's day and classic South Downs rolling landscape: the view towards Truleigh Hill (see p135).

It's also possible to buy state-of-the-art digital mapping to import into your GPS unit, assuming that you have sufficient memory capacity, but it's not the most reliable way of navigating and the small screen on your pocket-sized unit will invariably fail to put places into context or give you the 'big picture'.

Bear in mind that the vast majority of people who walk the Way do so perfectly well without a GPS unit. Instead of rushing out to invest in one, consider putting the money towards good-quality waterproofs or footwear instead.

ACCOMMODATION

The South Downs lie in a populous area so there are plenty of villages and towns within easy reach of the Way, most of which offer accommodation for the walker. However, the Way generally follows the high ground along the top of the South Downs escarpment while the villages lie at the foot of the hills. This tends to leave the walker with a small detour to reach a bed at the end of each day. Bear this in mind when calculating times and distances from the maps in Part 4. As a general rule it is a good idea to allow an extra hour each day for the walk to and from your accommodation.

Camping

Unfortunately, there is little to no opportunity for wild camping on the South Downs so campers will have to rely on organised campsites of which there are few. Refer to the itinerary chart for campers on p32 to organise a schedule. Most of these campsites charge from £5 per camper. Some of the more complex, organised sites have showers and washing facilities while others are merely a place to pitch a tent in the grass.

It is difficult to arrange a camping trip along the length of the Downs without being forced into more solid accommodation for one or two nights. Those who have the urge to camp in greater isolation where there is no recognised site may find it worthwhile asking a landowner for permission to set up camp.

Those who do camp will certainly appreciate the experience: the pampered comforts of a bed and breakfast are outweighed by the chance to sleep under the stars and be woken by the sun, should it happen to be showing.

Hostels and camping barns

There are five youth hostels within easy reach of the Way but all are between Arundel and Eastbourne.

Despite the name, anyone of any age can join the YHA. This can be done at any hostel or by contacting the **Youth Hostels Association of England and Wales** (YHA; ☎ 0800-0191 700 or ☎ 01629-592700, 🖳 www.yha.org.uk). The cost of a year's membership is currently £15.95 (£9.95 for anyone under 26). Having secured your membership, YHA hostels are easy to book, either online or by phone. The hostels also offer a booking service and will reserve a bed at the next stop on the path for you.

Each hostel has a drying room, shower and a fully equipped kitchen. Telscombe (see p154) is self-catering only but has a small shop. The others offer breakfast, a packed lunch and an evening meal. Arundel and Alfriston have wi-fi.

❏ **Booking accommodation**
You should always book your accommodation in advance because of the competition for beds in summer and the distinct possibility that the place may be closed in winter. It is often possible to book online but if not phone the establishment. When booking check the rate and facilities and always let the owner know if you need to cancel so that they can free the bed for someone else. You may be asked to pay a deposit, usually 25-50%.

If you are having problems finding accommodation some tourist information centres (see p40) still provide a booking service. The majority charge for this and take a 10% deposit towards the cost of the first night's accommodation, though the deposit is then deducted from the bill.

There's an **independent hostel** located near East Meon called Wetherdown Hostel (p92) and a **camping barn** run by the National Trust near Bignor Hill, which goes by the charming name of Gumber Bothy (p114).

Bed and breakfast

Some B&Bs can be quite luxurious and come at a price but in our experience all the Downs walker really wants is a warm bed and a hot bath. For this reason most of the B&Bs listed in this guide are recommended because of their usefulness to the walker and convenience to the Way, not for how many stars the tourist board has awarded them.

Bed and breakfast owners are often proud to boast that all rooms are **en suite**. This enthusiasm for private facilities has led proprietors to squeeze a cramped shower and loo cubicle into the last spare corner of the bedroom. Not having an en suite room is sometimes preferable as you may get sole use of a bathroom across the corridor and a hot bath is just what you need after a day's walking – and you will also probably save a few pounds.

You may find it hard to find establishments with **single** rooms. **Twin** rooms and **double** rooms are often confused but a twin room usually comprises two single beds which can either be pushed together for a couple or kept separate. A double room has one double bed. **Family** rooms are for three or more people and usually consist of a double bed and a single or three single beds.

Most B&Bs do of course provide a hefty cooked **breakfast** as part of the rate though some now also offer a lighter continental-style breakfast. Some also provide a packed lunch or an evening meal but you will need to give them advance warning and there will be an extra charge. Most B&Bs, however, are close enough to a pub or restaurant but if not the owner may give you a lift to and from the nearest eating place.

Rates B&Bs in this guide vary from around £40 for two sharing a room and for the most basic accommodation to over £70 for the most luxurious, en suite places. Most charge around £50 per room. Remember that many places do not have single rooms and deduct between £5 and £15 for single occupancy of a double or twin room. Prices can be less during the winter months and if you are on a budget you could always ask to go without breakfast which will usually result in a lower price.

Guesthouses, hotels, pubs and inns

Guesthouses are usually more sophisticated than bed and breakfasts, offering evening meals and a lounge for guests; rates are around £30-40 per person.

Pubs and inns offer bed and breakfast of a medium to high standard and have the added advantage, of course, of having a bar downstairs, so it's not far to stagger back to bed. However, the noise from tipsy punters below your room might prove a nuisance if you want an early night. Prices usually range from £30 to £40 per person per night.

Hotels are usually aimed more at the motoring tourist rather than the muddy walker and the price (£40-60 per person) is likely to put off the budget traveller. A few hotels have been included in the trail guide for those feeling they deserve at least one night of luxury during their trip.

FOOD AND DRINK

Breakfast and lunch

If staying in a B&B, guesthouse or hotel you'll be served a full cooked breakfast which may be more than you are used to. Ask for a lighter continental breakfast if you can't stand so much food first thing in the morning; alternatively, ask to have a packed lunch instead of breakfast, particularly if you are planning an early start. Many B&Bs and youth hostels can also provide you with a packed lunch at an additional cost.

Alternatively, breakfast and packed lunches can be bought and made yourself. There are some great cafés and bakeries along the Way which can supply both and if you are lucky you will be in town on the day of a farmers' market (see box p22); they are great places to pick up fresh food and try something from the local area. Remember that certain stretches of the walk are devoid of places to eat so check the information in Part 4 to ensure you don't go hungry.

Evening meals

The **pubs** that grace the pretty flint villages of the Downs rank as some of the most authentic country inns in England. Many of them date from the 14th or 15th centuries and have fascinating histories. Food can vary from cheap traditional bar food to high-quality cuisine served in a pub restaurant. For the serious 'connoisseur' drinker the best thing about the downland pub is the range of real ales on offer (see box opposite).

While evening meals in the villages are often limited to whatever the local pub is serving, some of the larger towns such as Winchester, Eastbourne, Petersfield and Midhurst are home to some quality **restaurants** with specialities ranging from fish to Italian fare. Those on a budget, or walkers who stumble into town late in the evening, will find a number of late-night **takeaway** joints offering everything from kebabs and pizzas to Indian and Chinese and, of course, traditional fish and chips.

❏ LOCAL FOOD AND DRINK

Food

Food in Hampshire and Sussex is varied and tasty. Local farm produce concentrates on beef and pork but there is also a variety of local cheeses and other dairy products. Look out for traditional English dishes such as steak and ale pie, shepherd's pie and ploughman's lunch which can all be found on pub menus.

Fruit farms are a common sight in the south. Most of them invite people to '**pick your own**'. That is not an invitation to get off their land and pick your own elsewhere but to help yourself to their strawberries, raspberries, blueberries and other fruit growing in the fields. Once you have picked enough, you take the fruit to be weighed and paid for.

Hampshire has also long been well-known for its **watercress** beds, particularly around Warnford, Overton and Hurstbourne Priors. The large-scale propagation of watercress in these areas dates back to the 19th century and is much aided by alkaline water provided by the chalky streams of Hampshire. Some of the original watercress beds are still used today.

Cream teas can be ordered in many of the cafés along the South Downs Way. Partaking in this quintessentially English activity is usually done in the mid-afternoon and involves a pot of tea accompanied by scones, clotted cream and jam.

Drink

There's a plethora of local breweries for the real-ale connoisseur to get excited about. Probably the most famous Sussex brewery, and certainly the oldest, is **Harvey's** of Lewes which dates from 1790. Beers to look out for include their Sussex Best and Armada Ales while in September they release their seasonal Southdown Harvest Ale which they proudly describe as the 'taste of the South Downs'.

There are also several newer local breweries. Of particular interest are **Rectory Ales** of Plumpton Green, a tiny brewery set up in 1996 by the rector of Plumpton to raise funds for the local parish, a once-common tradition. Their most popular brews are Rector's Pleasure (4%) and Rector's Revenge (5%). On tap at the The Five Bells at Buriton is real ale from **Ballard's Brewery**, which was founded on a farm near Petersfield in 1980. Finally, there is the **Gribble Brewery** from Chichester whose ales deserve awards not just for flavour but for decorating beer pumps with some of the quirkiest names. Look out for Pig's Ear and the dangerously named Plucking Pheasant but go steady on the Winter Wobbler which, at 7.2%, is probably one of the most dangerous concoctions ever to drip from a beer tap.

PLANNING YOUR WALK

Self-catering supplies

If you are camping, fuel for the stove and other equipment is an important consideration. Supplies can be found at any of the outdoor shops in Winchester and Eastbourne, whilst en route there are outdoor shops in Petersfield, Lewes and Arundel. Check Part 4 for more detailed information about these shops.

Drinking water

Depending on the weather you may need to drink as much as 3-4 litres of water a day. If you're feeling lethargic it may well be that you haven't drunk enough, even if you're not feeling particularly thirsty.

❑ **Farmers' markets**

Farmers' markets are held in a number of towns and villages throughout Hampshire and Sussex. These give local farmers a chance to showcase their produce and give consumers the opportunity to purchase locally grown stuff in the knowledge that they are helping not just the local economy but the environment too. Buying local produce helps cut down on the wasteful long-distance carriage of food both nationally and internationally – plus, of course, the food is much fresher.

To find out more about farmers' markets near the South Downs Way check out the websites 🖥 www.localfoods.org.uk, 🖥 www.hampshirefarmersmarkets.co.uk and 🖥 www.westsussex.info/farmers-markets.shtml and 🖥 www.eastsussex.gov.uk.

The following farmers' markets are all close to the South Downs Way:

● **Winchester** The biggest of its kind in the UK. Held on Middle Brook St on the second and last Sunday of the month; also in the Cathedral grounds on the third Saturday of the month
● **Petersfield** On the first Sunday every month (Mar to Dec) in Market Square
● **Midhurst** In Capron House car park on the fourth Saturday of every other month starting in January
● **Arundel** In Market Square on the third Saturday of every month
● **Pulborough** In the village hall on the last Saturday of every month from February to November (Pulborough is just one stop on the train from Amberley)
● **Steyning** In the main car park off the High St on the first Saturday of every month
● **Lewes** On Lower High St by the river on the first Saturday of the month
● **Eastbourne** On Ocklynge Rd on the last Saturday of the month

Although drinking directly from streams and rivers can be tempting, it is not a good idea. Streams that cross the path tend to have flowed across farmland where you can be pretty sure any number of farm animals have relieved themselves. Combined with the probable presence of farm pesticides and other delights, it is best to avoid drinking from these streams. Drinking-water taps are marked on the route maps. Where these are thin on the ground you can usually ask a friendly shopkeeper or pub barman to fill your bottle or pouch for you – from the tap, of course.

MONEY

While Eastbourne and Winchester at each end of the Way have plenty of banks and ATMs (cashpoints/cash dispensers), the villages in between do not. Bear in mind that some of these ATMs charge up to £1.75 per withdrawal. However, if you find yourself without a penny on the Way it is only a short detour to some of the larger towns; banks with cash dispensers can be found in Petersfield, Midhurst, Arundel, Storrington, Steyning, Lewes and Meads Village. Nevertheless, it is worth having more cash than you think you might need since small local shops will require you to pay in cash, as will most B&Bs, camping barns and campsites, though they will probably all accept a cheque if you have a debit card. Shops that do take cards, such as supermarkets, will sometimes advance cash against a debit card (a transaction known as 'cashback') as long as you buy something for at least £5 at the same time.

Using the Post Office for banking

Several banks have agreements with the Post Office allowing customers to make cash withdrawals free of charge using a debit card at branches throughout the country. Given that many towns and villages have post offices this is a very useful facility. However, check with the Post Office Helpline (☎ 08457-223344, 💻 www.postoffice.co.uk) that the post offices en route are still open and that your bank has an agreement with the post office. If using the website click on Counter services, then Counter money services, then Pay in and withdraw money under Use your bank account for a full list of banks offering withdrawal facilities through post office branches and for a list of the branches with an ATM.

OTHER SERVICES

Most villages and all the towns have at least one public **telephone**, a small **shop** and a **post office**. Post offices can be used for receiving mail – if you know where you are going to be from day to day – or for sending unnecessary equipment home which may be weighing you down. In Part 4 mention is given to other services that may be of use to the walker such as **banks**, **cash machines**, **outdoor equipment shops**, **laundrettes**, **internet access**, **pharmacies** and **tourist information centres** which can be used for finding and booking accommodation among other things.

WALKING COMPANIES AND BAGGAGE CARRIERS

There are a number of holiday companies who will arrange all your accommodation and baggage transport for you. Some of the best are listed below.

Guided holidays
● **Footpath Holidays** (☎ 01985-840049, 💻 www.footpath-holidays.com, Wiltshire) Offers 'highlights' itineraries.
● **Ramblers** (☎ 01707-386800, 💻 www.ramblerscountrywide.co.uk, Welwyn Garden City) Offers itinerary for five nights along sections of the way.
● **HF Holidays** (☎ 020-8732 1250, 💻 www.hfholidays.co.uk, Elstree, Herts) This long-established company runs at least one guided walk of eleven nights along the length of the trail (Winchester to Eastbourne) in summer.

Self-guided holidays
● **British & Irish Walks** (☎ 01242-254353, 💻 www.britishandirishwalks.com, Cheltenham) Offers itineraries along part of the way.
● **Celtic Trails** (☎ 01291-689774, 💻 www.celtic-trails.com, Chepstow) Offers set itineraries and walks tailored to individual requirements.
● **Contours Walking Holidays** (☎ 01629-821900, 💻 www.contours.co.uk, Derbyshire) Has a variety of South Downs packages from short three-night sections to the whole walk.
● **Explore Britain** (☎ 01740-650900, 💻 www.explorebritain.com, Durham) Offers a selection of self-guided trips with luggage transfer and accommodation in inns, from two-night excursions around Alfriston to the entire route.

PLANNING YOUR WALK

● **Footpath Holidays** (☎ 01985-840049, 🖳 www.footpath-holidays.com, Wiltshire) Offers itineraries for the whole way or part of it.
● **Footprints of Sussex** (☎ 01903-813381, 🖳 www.footprintsofsussex.co.uk, West Sussex) Does seven- to ten-night self-guided holidays with accommodation and baggage transfers. Also organises an annual, supported rather than guided, South Downs Way Walk each June (🖳 www.southdownsway.com).
● **Freedom Walking Holidays** (☎ 07733-885390, 🖳 www.freedomwalking holidays.co.uk, Goring-on-Thames) Can accommodate variations of requirements within holiday packages.
● **Load Off Your Back** (🖳 www.loadoffyourback.co.uk, Welwyn Garden City) Offers a variety of options for the whole way.

❏ **Information for foreign visitors**

● **Currency** The British pound (£) comes in notes of £100, £50, £20, £10 and £5, and coins of £2 and £1. The pound is divided into 100 pence (usually referred to as 'p', pronounced 'pee') which comes in silver coins of 50p, 20p, 10p and 5p, and copper coins of 2p and 1p.

● **Money** Up-to-date **rates of exchange** can be found on 🖳 www.xe.com/ucc, at some post offices, or at any bank or travel agent. **Travellers' cheques** can be cashed only at banks, foreign exchanges and some of the large hotels; it is probably better to use a debit card or bring cash.

● **Business hours** Most shops and main post offices are open at least from Monday to Friday 9am-5pm and Saturday 9am-12.30pm but many shops open earlier and close later, some open on Sunday as well. Occasionally, especially in rural areas, you'll come across a local shop that closes at midday during the week, usually a Wednesday or Thursday, a throwback to the days when all towns and villages had an 'early closing day'. Many supermarkets remain open 12 hours a day; the Spar chain usually displays '8 till late' on the door. Banks typically open at 9.30am Monday to Friday and close at 3.30pm or 4pm, but of course ATM machines are open all the time (if they are outside). Pub hours are less predictable; although many open daily 11am-11pm, often in rural areas, and particularly in winter months, opening hours are 11am-3pm and 6-11pm Mon-Sat, 11am/noon-3pm and 7-11pm on Sunday.

● **National holidays** Most businesses are shut on 1 January, Good Friday (March/April), Easter Monday (March/April), first and last Monday in May, last Monday in August, 25 December and 26 December.

● **School holidays** State-school holidays in England are generally as follows: a one-week break late October, two weeks over Christmas and the New Year, a week mid February, two weeks around Easter, one week at the end of May/early June (to coincide with the bank holiday at the end of May) and five to six weeks from late July to early September. Private-school holidays fall at the same time, but tend to be slightly longer.

● **Documents** If you are a member of a National Trust organisation in your country bring your membership card as you should be entitled to free entry to National Trust properties and sites in the UK.

● **EHICs and travel insurance** Although Britain's National Health Service (NHS) is free at the point of use, that is only the case for residents. All visitors to Britain should be properly insured, including comprehensive health coverage. The European Health Insurance Card (EHIC) entitles EU nationals (on production of the EHIC card so ensure you bring it with you) to necessary medical treatment under the NHS while on a temporary visit here. For details, contact your national social security institution.

● **Macs Adventure** (☎ 0141-530 8886, 🖥 www.macsadventure.com, Glasgow) Operates a number of self-guided walks lasting seven to nine nights; can tailor-make to suit.

● **Sherpa Walking Holidays** (☎ 020-8577 2717, 🖥 www.sherpa-walking-holidays.co.uk, Middlesex) Offers eight-day and ten-day self-guided inn to inn walks from Eastbourne to Winchester covering 9-11 miles per day.

● **Sherpa Van Project** (☎ 01609-883731, 🖥 www.sherpavan.com, North Yorkshire) offers an accommodation-booking service.

● **Walk & Cycle** (☎ 0844-870 8648, 🖥 www.walkandcycle.co.uk/southdowns, Petersfield) Offers a wide selection of walking and cycling holidays and short breaks for the South Downs Way, accommodation in top hotels and inns.

However, this is not a substitute for proper medical cover on your travel insurance for unforeseen bills and for getting you home should that be necessary.

Also consider cover for loss and theft of personal belongings, especially if you are camping or staying in hostels, as there will be times when you'll have to leave your luggage unattended.

● **Weights and measures** The European Commission is no longer attempting to ban the pint or the mile: so, in Britain, milk can be sold in pints (1 pint = 568ml), as can beer in pubs, though most other liquid including petrol (gasoline) and diesel is sold in litres. Distances on road and path signs will continue to be given in miles (1 mile = 1.61km) rather than kilometres, and yards (1yd = 0.9m) rather than metres. The population remains divided between those who still use inches (1 inch = 2.5cm), feet (1ft = 0.3m) and yards and those who are happy with millimetres, centimetres and metres; you'll often be told that 'it's only a hundred yards or so' to somewhere, rather than a hundred metres or so.

Most food is sold in metric weights (g and kg) but the imperial weights of pounds (lb: 1lb = 453g) and ounces (oz: 1oz = 28g) are frequently displayed too. The weather – a frequent topic of conversation – is also an issue: while most forecasts predict temperatures in Celsius (C), many people continue to think in terms of Fahrenheit (F; see the temperature chart on p15 for conversions).

● **Smoking** The ban on smoking in public places relates not only to pubs and restaurants, but also to B&Bs, hostels and hotels. These latter have the right to designate one or more bedrooms where the occupants can smoke, but the ban is in force in all enclosed areas open to the public – even if they are in a private home such as a B&B. Should you be foolhardy enough to light up in a no-smoking area, which includes pretty well any indoor public place, you could be fined £50, but it's the owners of the premises who carry the can if they fail to stop you, with a potential fine of £2500.

● **Time** During the winter, the whole of Britain is on Greenwich Meantime (GMT). The clocks move one hour forward on the last Sunday in March, remaining on British Summer Time (BST) until the last Sunday in October.

● **Telephone** From outside Britain the international country access code for Britain is ☎ 44 followed by the area code minus the first 0, and then the number you require. Within Britain, to call a landline number with the same code as the landline phone you are calling from, the code can be omitted: dial the number only. If you're using a mobile phone that is registered overseas, consider buying a local SIM card to keep costs down.

● **Emergency services** For police, ambulance, fire or coastguard dial ☎ 999 or ☎ 112.

PLANNING YOUR WALK

Baggage transfer
- **Footprints of Sussex** (☎ 01903-813381, 🖳 www.footprintsofsussex.co.uk, West Sussex) offer standalone baggage transfer service subject to availability.
- **Sherpa Van Project** (☎ 01748-826917, 🖳 www.sherpavan.com, North Yorkshire).
- **South Downs Discovery** (☎ 01403-275332, 🖳 www.southdownsdiscovery .com, Horsham). Their website has lots of SDW information on it.
- **South Downs Baggage Transfers** (☎ 0844-870 8648, 🖳 www.southdowns baggagetransfers.com, Petersfield).

MOUNTAIN BIKING

The South Downs Way is perfect for cyclists. It is Britain's first long-distance bridleway so it is specifically geared to horse-riders, cyclists and walkers. The entire route can be followed on two wheels on wide tracks which are, on the whole, well drained, with only a few very steep sections either side of the major river valleys. There are occasional sections where walkers and cyclists must follow different routes but these are well marked with blue chevrons indicating byeways (yellow for footpaths).

TAKING DOGS ALONG THE WAY

Dogs are allowed on the South Downs but should be kept on a lead whenever there are sheep around. Considering the Downs is a prime sheep-farming area this is most of the time and it is worth remembering that farmers are perfectly within their rights to shoot any dog they believe to be worrying their sheep. See Appendix B, p186 for detailed information on long-distance walking with dogs.

DISABLED ACCESS

Many of the councils are taking steps to improve access to the Sussex and Hampshire countryside but, unfortunately, some parts of the South Downs Way are still quite inaccessible to disabled people.

Nevertheless, there are stretches of the Way that can be followed quite easily, particularly where roads provide direct access to the top of the hills such as at **Ditchling Beacon** (see p143). Here there are gates designed for wheelchair users and there are also plenty of benches at intervals along the path to the west of Ditchling Beacon. **Devil's Dyke** (see p139) is another good spot where access is relatively easy and the path not too rough.

The **Seven Sisters Country Park** (see box p167) has good facilities for the disabled both in the park and at the visitor centre and access to the beach at Cuckmere Haven is quite straightforward. Disabled Ramblers (🖳 www.dis abledramblers.co.uk) occasionally organise rambles around Beachy Head.

Further west the easiest stretches of the Way can be found to the west of **Bignor Hill** (see p112), where there's a car park near the top, and on **Harting Down** (p101) which has a relatively long stretch of gentle, level pathways. **Queen Elizabeth Country Park** (p93) has wide, level tracks and easy access.

Budgeting

The amount of money you take with you depends on where you plan to stay and how you're going to eat. If you camp and cook your expenses can be low but most people prefer to have at least some of their meals cooked for them and even the hardiest camper may be tempted into a B&B when the rain is falling.

CAMPING

It is possible to survive on not much more than £10 per person per day by camping at the cheapest sites and cooking all your own food. However, it is always best to take more than you think necessary to cover those inevitable luxuries like a warm bed after a day walking in the pouring rain.

If you like to treat yourself to a pint at the end of the day remember that one costing less than £3 is a rare thing in the south of England. Bearing this in mind it is worth counting on £15 per day.

CAMPING BARNS AND HOSTELS

The **camping barn** called Gumber Bothy (see p114) will set you back just £10 per night and if you're a member you can pay as little as that at some **YHA hostels** in quieter times. Hostels along the route cost from £13 to £20 (less £3 if you're a YHA member), making this kind of accommodation a bargain. The YHA charges for beds in its hostels following the modern online model with lowest prices during quieter periods and rates increasing with popularity of location and date. Rooms are surprisingly good for such a budget price.

Hostels usually have a self-catering kitchen allowing you to survive on cheap food from the supermarket or local shop. However, if you want to make use of their meals expect to pay £4.95 for breakfast, around £5 for a packed lunch and £6.50-9 for an evening meal. Now and then, however, you may prefer to eat out which would add to your daily expenditure. To cover the cost of a night in a hostel, the occasional bar meal and drink count on at least £25 per person per day. If you are planning on eating out most nights this figure is likely to be nearer £30 per day.

B&Bs

B&B rates can be as little as £25 per person per night but are usually nearer £30-40 per person for two sharing a room (most places add a single occupancy supplement of £10 or more). Breakfast is, of course, almost always included in the total cost but if an evening meal is offered you will be charged an extra £10-15 for it. If you decide to treat yourself to pub meals, beer and other goodies you will probably need around £45-60 per person per day.

EXTRAS

Don't forget all those little things that secretly push up your daily bill – post-cards, stamps, beer, ice-cream, buses here, buses there, more beer and getting back to Winchester at the end of your walk. All these extras will probably add up to between £50 and £100.

Itineraries

This guidebook has not been divided up into rigid daily stages. Instead, it's structured to make it easy for you to plan your own itinerary. The South Downs Way can be tackled in any number of ways, the most challenging of which is to do it all in one go. This requires about one week. Others may prefer to walk it over a series of short breaks, coming back year after year to do a bit more. Some choose to walk only the best bits.

To help plan your walk the **plan maps** (see end of the book) and the **table of town and village facilities** (pp30-1) give a rundown on the essential information you will need regarding accommodation possibilities and services. Alternatively, you could follow one of the **suggested itineraries** (see below for B&Bs, opposite for hostels and p32 for camping) which are based on preferred type of accommodation and walking speed. There is also a list of recommended **day and weekend walks** (see pp33-4) which cover the best of the path, all of which are well served by public transport. The **public transport map** is on p45.

	STAYING IN B&BS					
	Relaxed pace		**Medium pace**		**Fast pace**	
Night	**Place**	**Approx distance** miles/km	**Place**	**Approx distance** miles/km	**Place**	**Approx distance** miles/km
0	Winchester		Winchester		Winchester	
1	Cheriton	8/13	Cheriton	8/13	Exton	12/19.5
2	Exton	7/11	East Meon	13/20	South Harting	16.5/26.5
3	East Meon	6/9.5	South Harting	12.5/20	Amberley	20/32
4	Buriton	8.5/13.5	Heyshott	10/16	Pyecombe	20.5/33
5	Cocking	11/18	Amberley	11/17.5	Kingston	11/17.5
6	Amberley	13.5/21.5	Steyning	13/21	Alfriston	13/21
7	Steyning	13/21	Kingston	20/32	Eastbourne	12.5/20
8	Pyecombe	9.5/15	Alfriston	13/21		
9	Kingston	11.5/18.5	Eastbourne	12.5/20		
10	Rodmell	5/8				
11	Alfriston	8/13				
12	Eastbourne	12.5/20				

Once you have an idea of your approach turn to **Part 4** for detailed information on accommodation, places to eat, and other services in each village and town on the route. Also in Part 4 you will find route descriptions to accompany the detailed trail maps.

WHICH DIRECTION?

There are many criteria that will determine in which direction to tackle the Way. It always seems a good idea to finish a walk with something that was worth walking towards. With this in mind Winchester is a far more attractive place to finish in than Eastbourne. Thus, east to west seems a good choice of direction. However, the scenery improves towards the eastern end and what finer place to conclude the walk than by the sea and on top of the white cliffs of the Seven Sisters and Beachy Head. Another factor is the prevailing wind which normally comes from the south-west. Having the wind at your back is a great help so this would also suggest starting at Winchester and finishing at Eastbourne.

Although the maps in Part 4 are arranged in a west to east direction, times for walking in both directions are always given so that the book can be used back to front.

SUGGESTED ITINERARIES

The itineraries below are based on different accommodation types – B&Bs, hostels/camping barns and campsites, with each one divided into three categories of walking speed. They really are only suggestions and all of them can be easily adapted by using the more detailed information on accommodation

STAYING IN HOSTELS/CAMPING BARNS

Night	Relaxed pace Place	Approx distance miles/km	Medium pace Place	Approx distance miles/km	Fast pace Place	Approx distance miles/km
0	Winchester*		Winchester*		Winchester*	
1	Cheriton*	8/13	Cheriton*	8/13	East Meon	18/29
2	East Meon	13/20	East Meon	13/20	Buriton*	9/14.5
3	Buriton*	9/14.5	Sth Harting*	12.5/20	Bignor	19.5/31.5
4	Cocking*	11.5/18.5	Bignor	16/25.5	Truleigh Hill	20/32
5	Bignor	9/14.5	Truleigh Hill	20/32	Rodmell	21/33.5
6	Washington*	12.5/20	Ditchling*	10.5/17	Eastbourne	20.5/33
7	Truleigh Hill	8.5/13.5	Rodmell	13.5/21.5		
8	Ditchling*	10.5/17	Alfriston	8/13		
9	Kingston*	10/16	Eastbourne	12.5/20		
10	Rodmell	5/8				
11	Alfriston	8/13				
12	Eastbourne	12.5/20				

* No hostels/camping barns at places marked; alternative accommodation available

PLANNING YOUR WALK

PLANNING YOUR WALK

			TOWN AND
Place name (Places in brackets are a short walk off the SDW)	**Distance from previous place** approx miles/km	**Cash machine** (**ATM**)/ **Bank**	**Post Office**	**Tourist Information Centre/Point** (**TIC**)/(**TIP**)
Winchester	0	✔	✔	TIC
Chilcomb	2/3.5			
(Cheriton)	4.5/7(+1.5)		✔	
Exton	5.5/9			
(East Meon)	5/8(+1)		✔	
(Buriton)	7.5/12(+0.5)			
(Petersfield)	(+2)	✔	✔	TIC
(South Harting)	3.5/5.5(+0.5)		✔	
(Cocking)	7/11(+0.5)		✔	
(Heyshott)	2/3(+0.5)			
(Graffham)	1.5/2.5(+1)		✔	
(Sutton & Bignor)	4/6.5(+1)			
(Bury & W Burton)	2.5/4(+1)		✔	
Houghton Bridge	1/1.5			
Amberley	1.5/2.5		✔	
(Arundel)	(+4)	✔	✔	TIP
(Storrington)	3/4.5(+1.5)	✔	✔	TIP
(Washington)	3/4.5(+0.5)			
(Steyning, Bramber & Upper Beeding)	4/6(+1)	✔	✔	TIP
(Fulking)	6.5/11(+0.5)			
(Poynings)	2/3(+0.5)			
Pyecombe	2/3			
(Clayton)	1/2(+0.5)			
(Ditchling)	1.5/2(+1.5)		✔	
(Plumpton)	2/3(+0.5)			
(Lewes)	1/1.5(+3)	✔	✔	TIC
(Kingston-nr-Lewes)	5/8(+1)			
Rodmell & Southease	4/6			
(West Firle)	3.5/5.5(+1)		✔	
(Alciston & Berwick)	2.5/4(+1)			
Alfriston	2/3		✔	
Litlington	1/2			
Exceat/Seven Sisters	1.5/2.5			TIC
Birling Gap	4/6			
Beachy Head	3/4.5			
Meads Village	1.5/2.5	✔	✔	
Alternative (inland) route from Alfriston				
(Milton Street)	1/2(+0.5)			
(Wilmington)	(+1)			
Jevington	2.5/4			
Eastbourne	4/6	✔	✔	TIC

Total distance 100 miles/162km (via Seven Sisters), 97.5miles/158km (via Jevington)

VILLAGE FACILITIES

Eating Place ✔ = one; ✔✔= two ✔✔✔= three+	Food Store	Campsite	Hostel YHA or H (Ind Hostel) camping barn (CB)	B&B-style accommodation ✔= one, ✔✔= two ✔✔✔= three+	Place name (Places in brackets are a short walk off the SDW
✔✔✔	✔			✔✔✔	**Winchester**
		✔¹			**Chilcomb**
✔	✔			✔✔	**(Cheriton)**
✔		✔²		✔²	**Exton**
✔✔	✔	✔	H³	✔✔	**(East Meon)**
✔				✔✔	**(Buriton)**
✔✔✔	✔			✔✔	**(Petersfield)**
✔✔	✔			✔✔✔	**(South Harting)**
✔	✔			✔✔✔	**(Cocking)**
✔				✔✔	**(Heyshott)**
✔✔	✔	✔		✔	**Graffham**
✔		✔⁴	CB⁴	✔	**(Sutton & Bignor)**
✔				✔	**(Bury & W Burton)**
✔✔✔				✔✔	**Houghton Bridge**
✔✔	✔			✔✔	**Amberley**
✔✔✔	✔		YHA	✔✔✔	**(Arundel)**
✔✔✔	✔			✔✔✔	**(Storrington)**
✔	✔	✔			**(Washington)**
✔✔✔	✔	✔	YHA⁵	✔✔✔	**(Steyning, Bramber & Upper Beeding)**
✔					**(Fulking)**
✔✔		✔		✔	**(Poynings)**
✔				✔✔	**Pyecombe**
✔				✔	**(Clayton)**
✔✔	✔			✔✔	**(Ditchling)**
✔		✔✔			**(Plumpton)**
✔✔✔	✔			✔✔✔	**(Lewes)**
✔				✔	**(Kingston-nr-Lewes)**
✔			YHA¹	✔✔	**Rodmell & Southease**
✔	✔			✔	**(West Firle)**
✔✔				✔	**(Alciston & Berwick)**
✔✔✔	✔	✔	YHA	✔✔✔	**Alfriston**
✔✔					**Litlington**
✔✔			(CB schools only)	✔	**Exceat/Seven Sisters**
✔				✔✔	**Birling Gap**
✔					**Beachy Head**
✔✔✔	✔			✔	**Meads Village**
					Alternative (inland) route from Alfriston
✔					**(Milton Street)**
				✔	**(Wilmington)**
✔✔				✔	**Jevington**
✔✔✔	✔		YHA	✔✔✔	**Eastbourne**

PLANNING YOUR WALK

¹ 30- to 45-minute walk from village; ² one mile from village; ³ two miles from village;
⁴ at Gumber Bothy 10-20 mins from SDW; ⁵ at Truleigh Hill on SDW

	CAMPING					
	Relaxed pace		**Medium pace**		**Fast pace**	
Night	**Place**	**Approx distance** miles/km	**Place**	**Approx distance** miles/km	**Place**	**Approx distance** miles/km
0	Winchester*		Winchester*		Winchester*	
1	Cheriton	8/13	Exton	12/19.5	East Meon	18/29
2	Exton	7/11	Sth Harting*	16.5/26.5	Cocking*	19.5/31.5
3	East Meon	6/9.5	Bignor	16/25.5	Washington	18.5/29.5
4	Sth Harting*	12.5/20	Washington	12.5/20	Plumpton	20/32
5	Cocking*	8/13	Pyecombe	15/24	Alfriston	18.5/29.5
6	Bignor	9/14.5	Rodmell*	14/22.5	Eastbourne*	12.5/20
7	Washington	12.5/20	Alfriston	8/13		
8	Steyning	7.5/12	Eastbourne*	12.5/20		
9	Pyecombe	9.5/15				
10	Plumpton	5/8				
11	Rodmell*	10.5/17				
12	Alfriston	8/13				
13	Eastbourne*	12.5/20				

* There are no campsites at places marked with an asterisk but alternative accommodation is available

found in Part 4. Don't forget to add your travelling time from/to your accommodation both before and after the walk.

SIDE TRIP TO MOUNT CABURN

The only part of the South Downs that is not covered by the South Downs Way is the isolated hill near Lewes known rather grandly as Mount Caburn. It is something of an anomaly, being the only part of the Downs separated from the main spine of chalk hills. The hill's unique position makes it an excellent vantage point for admiring the rest of the Downs stretched out to the south, as well as the Ouse Valley and the county town of Lewes. The top of the hill is a National Nature Reserve renowned for its butterflies as well as its paragliders.

The hill is best approached from the village of Glynde where there is a train station. From the train station Mount Caburn (152m/498ft) looms above. Head towards the hill by walking up the road for five minutes. Just past the old village smithy (blacksmith), which is still being used, is a junction that marks the centre of Glynde village. Turn left and look for the stile in the hedgerow opposite the village shop. The path to the top of Mount Caburn follows the obvious route through the fields from the stile and takes about 30-45 minutes. The return is by the same route or via a path further to the north which drops through a small copse to emerge on the lane north of Glynde village.

❏ HIGHLIGHTS – THE BEST DAY AND WEEKEND WALKS

There is nothing quite like taking on a long-distance path in one go but sometimes the time needed is just not available.

The following list suggests a number of day and weekend walks covering the best of the South Downs Way, most of which are easily accessible using public transport (see pp41-6). Many walkers come back weeks, months or even years later to walk sections of the path they have missed. Fitter walkers will find that many of the weekend walks suggested here can be completed in a day.

Wide views from Beacon Hill near Exton
© Jim Manthorpe

DAY WALKS

Exton to Buriton
12 miles/19.5km (see pp87-94)
The best of the East Hampshire downland, passing over Old Winchester Hill and its magnificent hill-fort remains and Butser Hill, the highest hill on the Downs, with magnificent views over the Meon Valley and Queen Elizabeth Country Park.

Amberley to Steyning
13 miles/21km (see pp116-130)
Starting in one of the prettiest villages on the Way and ending in one of the most beautiful towns, this

Thatched cottage in East Meon
© Henry Stedman

walk provides extensive views from the spine of the Downs, taking in the famous local landmark of Chanctonbury Ring.

Devil's Dyke to Ditchling Beacon   **5 miles/8km (see pp140-2)**
Possibly the most spectacular dry valley on the Downs, Devil's Dyke is the magnificent starting point of this short section that continues by climbing over the isolated Newtimber Hill before ending at the beauty spot of Ditchling Beacon.

Kingston-near-Lewes to Southease   **5 miles/8km (see pp150-6)**
One of the quieter stretches of the Downs with fine views of Mount Caburn on the other side of the Ouse Valley and a little bit of literary history to be had at Rodmell, once the home of Virginia Woolf.

DAY WALKS (cont'd from p33)

Exceat to Eastbourne via Cuckmere Haven   9 miles/14.5km (see pp163-71)

Arguably the finest day of walking anywhere between Winchester and Eastbourne,

following the rollercoaster tops of the Seven Sisters chalk cliffs to the high point of Beachy Head high above Eastbourne.

Alfriston to Eastbourne via Jevington
10 miles/16km (see pp172-8)

Not as spectacular as the coastal route to Eastbourne but equally enjoyable, encompassing the beautiful Cuckmere Valley, the ramshackle timber-framed houses of Alfriston and the curious Long Man of Wilmington chalk figure.

On the white cliffs near Beachy Head
© Bryn Thomas

WEEKEND WALKS

Buriton to Amberley   23½ miles/38km (see pp98-116)

Stopping off in either Cocking or Midhurst for the night, this section takes in the fine wooded sections close to Buriton and the airy Harting Down on the first day, followed by Bignor Hill with its Roman Road, Stane Street, on the second day.

Amberley to Pyecombe   20½ miles/33km (see pp122-38)

Extensive views and the curious, enchanted Chanctonbury Ring are the highlights of the first day with a wide choice of places to stay in historic Steyning or Bramber with its castle. The second day follows the open top of the Downs all the way to the impressive valley of Devil's Dyke.

Eastbourne circular walk via Alfriston and Cuckmere Haven
19 miles/30.5km (see pp163-78)

If there is one section of the Downs that should be seen more any other it is this wonderful circular walk. Beginning and ending in Eastbourne, the walk combines the coastal and inland routes of the SDW. You'll pass through the beautiful villages of Jevington, Alfriston, Litlington and Westdean as well as walking the entire coastal section from Cuckmere Haven to Eastbourne. This is possibly the most spectacular walking that can be found anywhere in South-East England.

❏ Flint

Flint is a mineral found in bands within chalk and has played a big part in the history of the Downs. When man first found the ability to make tools the folk who lived on the Downs used flakes of flint to make arrowheads and knives. It was also found to be a very useful stone for starting fires. Today flint can be seen in local village architecture, being a very versatile building brick. The traditional Sussex Downs house and barn would not be the same if it were not for flint.

What to take

Deciding how much to take with you can be difficult. Experienced walkers know that you really should take only the bare essentials but at the same time you need to ensure you have all the equipment necessary to make the trip safe and comfortable.

KEEP IT LIGHT – OR USE A LUGGAGE-CARRYING SERVICE!

Carrying a heavy rucksack really can ruin your enjoyment of a good walk and can also slow you down a great deal, turning an easy seven-mile day into an interminable slog. Be ruthless when you pack and leave behind all those little home comforts that you tell yourself don't weigh that much really. Always pack the essentials, of course, but try to leave behind anything that you think might 'come in handy' but probably won't. This advice is even more pertinent to campers who have the added weight of camping equipment to carry.

HOW TO CARRY IT

The size of the **rucksack** you should take depends on where you are planning to stay and how you are planning to eat. If you are camping and cooking for yourself you will probably need a 65- to 75-litre rucksack which can hold the tent, sleeping bag, cooking equipment and food. Make sure your rucksack has a stiffened back and can be adjusted to fit your own back comfortably. This will make carrying the weight much easier.

Rucksacks are decorated with seemingly pointless straps but if you adjust them correctly it can make a big difference to your personal comfort while walking. Make sure the hip belt and chest belt (if there is one) are fastened tightly as this helps distribute the weight: most of it should be carried on the hips.

When packing the rucksack make sure you have all the things you are likely to need during the day near the top or in the side pockets. This includes a map, water bottle, packed lunch, waterproofs and this guidebook (of course!).

Consider taking a small **bum bag** or **day pack** for your camera, guidebook and other essentials.

If you are staying in bunkhouses and hostels you probably won't need to carry a sleeping bag or camping stove. All the youth hostels provide bedding and have cooking facilities. Some of the independent hostels, however, may not have such facilities so check with them beforehand. A 40- to 60-litre rucksack should be sufficient.

If you have gone for the B&B option you will probably find a 30- to 40-litre daypack is more than enough to carry your lunch, warm- and wet-weather clothes, camera and guidebook. If you're using a luggage carrying service (see pp23-6) you can just take a suitcase although a backpack is still better for the times at the beginning and end of your trip where you may have to carry your own luggage.

A good habit to get into is always to put things in the same place in your rucksack and memorise where they are. There is nothing more annoying than pulling everything out of your pack to find that lost banana when you're starving or that camera when there is a butterfly basking briefly on a rock ten feet away from you. It's also a good idea to keep everything in **canoe bags**, **waterproof rucksack liners** or strong plastic bags (or binliners). If you don't it's bound to rain.

FOOTWEAR

Boots
Your boots are the single most important item of gear that can affect the enjoyment of your hike. In summer you could get by with a light pair of trail shoes if you're carrying only a small pack, although this is an invitation for wet, cold feet if there is any rain and they don't offer much support for your ankles. Some of the terrain can be quite rough and wet so a pair of good walking boots is a safer bet. They must fit well and be properly broken in: it is no good discovering that your boots are slowly murdering your feet two days into a one-week walk.

Socks
The traditional wearing of a thin liner sock under a thicker wool sock is no longer necessary if you choose a high-quality sock specially designed for walking. A high proportion of natural fibres makes them much more comfortable. Three pairs are ample.

Extra footwear
Some walkers like to have a second pair of shoes to wear when not on the trail. Trainers, sport sandals or flip flops are all suitable as long as they are light.

CLOTHES

Experienced walkers will know the importance of wearing the right clothes. Always expect the worst weather even if the forecast is good. Modern technology in outdoor attire can seem baffling but it basically comes down to the old multi-layer system: a base layer to transport sweat away from your skin; a mid-layer to keep you warm; and an outer layer or 'shell' to protect you from the rain.

Base layer
Cotton absorbs sweat, trapping it next to the skin which will chill you rapidly when you stop exercising. A thin lightweight **thermal top** made from a synthetic material is better as it draws moisture away, keeping you dry. It will be cool if worn on its own in hot weather and warm when worn under other clothes in cooler conditions. A spare would be sensible. You may also like to bring a **shirt** or top for wearing in the evening.

Mid-layers
In the summer a woollen jumper or mid-weight polyester **fleece** will suffice. For the rest of the year you will need an extra layer to keep you warm. Both wool and fleece, unlike cotton, have the ability to stay reasonably warm when wet.

Outer layer
A decent **waterproof jacket** is essential year-round and will be much more comfortable (but also more expensive) if it's also 'breathable' to prevent the build up of condensation on the inside. This layer can also be worn to keep the wind off.

Leg wear
Whatever you wear on your legs it should be light, quick-drying and not restricting. Many British walkers find **polyester tracksuit bottoms** comfortable. Poly-cotton or microfibre trousers are excellent. Denim jeans should never be worn; if they get wet they become heavy, cold and bind to your legs. A pair of **shorts** is nice to have on sunny days. Thermal **longjohns** or thick tights are cosy if you're camping but are probably unnecessary even in winter. **Waterproof trousers** are necessary most of the year. In summer a pair of windproof and quick-drying trousers is useful in showery weather. **Gaiters** are not really necessary but may come in useful in wet weather when the vegetation around your legs is dripping wet.

Underwear
One or two changes of what you normally wear is fine.

Other clothes
A **warm hat** and **gloves** should always be kept in your rucksack; you never know when you might need them. In summer you should also carry a **sun hat** with you, preferably one which covers the back of your neck. Another useful piece of summer equipment is a **swimsuit**.

TOILETRIES

Take only the minimum: a small bar of **soap** (unless staying in B&Bs) in a plastic container which can also be used instead of shaving cream and for washing clothes; a tiny tube of **toothpaste** and a **toothbrush**; and one roll of **loo paper** in a plastic bag. If you are planning to defecate outdoors you will also need a **lighter** for burning the paper and a lightweight **trowel** for burying the evidence (see p64 for further tips). A **towel** (if camping or staying in a hostel), **razor**, **deodorant**, **tampons/sanitary towels** and a high-factor **sunscreen** should cover most needs.

FIRST-AID KIT

Medical facilities in Britain are excellent so you need only take a small kit to cover common problems and emergencies.

A basic kit will contain a pack of **aspirin** or **paracetamol** for treating mild to moderate pain and fever; **plasters/Band Aids** for minor cuts; 'moleskin',

PLANNING YOUR WALK

'Compeed' or 'Second skin' for blisters; a **bandage** for holding dressings, splints or limbs in place and for supporting a sprained ankle; an **elastic knee support** for a weak knee; a small selection of different sized **sterile dressings** for wounds; **porous adhesive tape**; **antiseptic wipes**; **antiseptic cream**; **safety pins**; **tweezers** and a small pair of **scissors**. Pack the kit in a waterproof container.

GENERAL ITEMS

Essential
The following should be in everyone's rucksack: a **water bottle/pouch** (holding at least one litre); a **torch** (flashlight) with spare bulb and batteries in case you end up walking after dark; **emergency food** which your body can quickly convert into energy; a **penknife**; a **watch** with an alarm; and a **bag** for packing out any rubbish you accumulate. A **whistle** is also worth taking. It can fit in a pocket and although you are very unlikely to need it you may be grateful of it in the unlikely event of an emergency (see p70).

Useful
Many would list a **camera** as essential but it can be liberating to travel without one once in a while; a **notebook** can be a more accurate way of recording your impressions. Other items include a **book** to pass the time on train journeys; a pair of **sunglasses** in summer; **binoculars** for observing wildlife; a **walking stick** or pole to take the strain off your knees and a **vacuum flask** for carrying hot drinks. Although the path is easy to follow a 'Silva' type **compass** is a good idea.

   A **mobile phone** is useful, especially as reception is generally good. Even so, make sure you always have the wherewithal to call from a public phone box in case you have no signal at the crucial moment. Calls to the emergency services (☎ 999, or ☎ 112 from a mobile) are free of charge. Calls cost a minimum of 40p, but increasingly you will need a credit, debit, BT or prepaid card instead. (Insert the card then follow the instructions.)

SLEEPING BAG

A sleeping bag is necessary only if you are camping. Clearly you won't need one if you are staying in bed and breakfasts and the same is true if you are planning on using hostels. Campers should find that a two- to three-season bag will cope but obviously in winter a warmer bag is a good idea. On hot summer nights you could get away with a one-season bag.

CAMPING GEAR

Campers need a decent **tent** (or bivvy bag if you enjoy travelling light) that's able to withstand wet and windy weather; a **sleeping mat**; a **stove** and **fuel** (there is special mention in Part 4 of which shops stock fuel); a **mug**; a **spoon**; a wire/plastic **scrubber** for washing up; and a pan or pot. One pot is fine for two people; some pots come with a lid that can be used as a plate or frying pan.

MONEY

There are not many banks along the Way so you will have to carry most of your money as **cash**. A **debit/credit card** is the easiest way to withdraw money either from banks or cash machines and can be used to pay in most larger shops, restaurants and hotels. A **cheque book** is very useful for walkers with accounts in British banks as a cheque will often be accepted where a card is not.

MAPS

The **hand-drawn maps** in this book cover the trail at a scale of 1:20,000 – plenty of detail and information to keep you on the right track; the **colour maps** at the back of the book are at a smaller scale covering the surrounding area.

To explore even further afield you might be interested in Ordnance Survey maps (☎ 0845-605 0505, 🖳 www.ordnancesurvey.co.uk for map sales and digital downloads). Relevant sheets include OS Landranger maps (pink cover) at a scale of 1:50,000, Nos 185, 197, 198 and 199 (£6.99 each) or OS Explorer Maps (orange cover) at 1:25,000 Nos 119, 120, 121, 122, 123 and 132 (£7.99 each). Enthusiastic OS map users can reduce the often considerable expense of purchasing them: members of the Ramblers (see box p40) can borrow up to 10 maps for a period of six weeks at 50p per map from their library (or £1 for the weatherproof version).

There's also a single-sheet Harveys *South Downs Way Map* (Harvey Maps, £12.95, 🖳 www.harveymaps.co.uk) at a scale of 1:40,000.

RECOMMENDED READING

Many bookshops and most of the tourist information centres along the South Downs Way stock all or at least some of the following books.

An excellent read recounting **one person's experience** of his walk is *The South Downs Way* (£7.99) by Martin King.

The best guidebook specifically aimed at the **wildlife** of the region is *Downland Wildlife – A Naturalist's Year in the North & South Downs* by John S Burton, published by Phillips. However, it is out of print and only available from specialist/second-hand booksellers or online.

For a more general guide there are plenty of books to choose from including the *Collins Bird Guide* (£18.99) by Lars Svensson et al.

A good field guide is the *New Birdwatcher's Pocket Guide to Britain and Europe* (£9.99) by Peter Hayman and Rob Hume: it is packed with illustrations of 430 European bird species.

The RSPB's *Pocket Guide to British Birds* (£5.99, Simon Harrap and David Nurney) is also recommended. Birds are identified by their plumage and song.

One of the best field guides to **British flora** is *The Wildflowers of Britain and Ireland* (£18.99) by Marjorie Blamey et al.

The Field Studies Council (☎ 0845-345 4071, 🖳 www.field-studies-council .org) publishes a series of **identification guides** in the form of laminated sheets

(£2.75-3.75 each) showing commonly found birds, trees, flowers etc and including 'Features of the South Downs Way'.

There are also several field guide apps for smartphones, including those that can aid in identifying birds from their song as well as by their appearance.

❑ SOURCES OF FURTHER INFORMATION

Tourist Information Centres

Tourist Information Centres (TICs) are based in towns throughout Britain and provide all manner of locally specific information and an accommodation-booking service. As funding for TICs is reduced some are becoming TIPs (Tourist Information Points) staffed by volunteers and with limited opening hours.

The following TICs lie on or near the Way: **Winchester** (☎ 01962-840500, ☐ www .visitwinchester.co.uk); **Petersfield** (☎ 01730-268829); **Midhurst** (☎ 01730-812251, ☐ www.visitmidhurst.com or for further details on the wider area look at ☐ www .visitchichester.org); **Lewes** (☎ 01273-483448, ☐ lewes.tic@lewes.gov.uk); **Eastbourne** (☎ 0871-663 0031, ☐ www.visiteastbourne.com). **Arundel** (☐ www.sussex bythesea.com) is now a TIP.

In addition there are a number of visitor centres such as the ones at Queen Elizabeth Country Park (see p93) and Seven Sisters Country Park (see box p166).

● **Tourism South East** This regional tourist board (☐ www.visitsoutheasteng land.com) is responsible for the official tourist information centres. Their website has a wealth of information regarding accommodation, things to see and do, and they can keep you informed about upcoming festivals and events.

● **South Downs Society** Supported entirely by donations and subscriptions, this society (☐ www.SouthDownsSociety.org.uk) has been around since 1923, helping to protect and conserve the Downs which they have divided into 12 distinct areas, each of which is under the care of a volunteer district officer. Their main responsibility is to peruse all planning applications that may affect the Downs. They also arrange a programme of strolls and walks, on and around the Downs, throughout the year.

Organisations for walkers

● **Backpackers' Club** (☐ www.backpackersclub.co.uk) A club for people who are involved or interested in lightweight camping through walking, cycling, skiing and canoeing. They produce a quarterly magazine, provide members with a comprehensive advisory and information service on all aspects of backpacking, organise weekend trips and also publish a farm-pitch directory. Membership is £12 per year.

● **Long Distance Walkers' Association** (☐ www.ldwa.org.uk) An association of people with the common interest of long-distance walking. Membership includes a journal three times per year giving details of challenge events and local group walks as well as articles on the subject. Information on over 500 Long Distance Paths is presented in the LDWA's Long Distance Walkers' Handbook. Membership is currently £13 per year, £19.50 for a family.

● **Ramblers** (formerly Ramblers' Association; ☐ www.ramblers.org.uk) Looks after the interests of walkers throughout Britain. They publish a large amount of useful information including their quarterly *Walk* magazine (£5.99 to non members). The website also has a discussion forum. Membership costs £31/41/19.50 individual/joint/concessionary; £10 discount for individual/joint membership if paid by direct debit.

Getting to and from the South Downs Way

It could not be easier to reach the South Downs from London as there are numerous road and rail links not just to Winchester and Eastbourne, the start and finish of the walk, but to many other points along the Way. Most parts of the South Downs Way are no more than 1^1/$_2$-2 hours from the capital. Access from other parts of Britain often involves going via London but there are rail services to the south coast via Reading.

From the continent there are air links to London and Southampton, rail links to Ashford International and London as well as ferry routes between various ports in France and Southampton, Portsmouth and Newhaven. The rail line running across the south coast goes from Dover to Ashford International, then to Hastings and along the coast to Eastbourne and Brighton.

NATIONAL TRANSPORT

By rail
The two main rail operators for services to locations along the South Downs are Southern Railway and SouthWest Trains. First Capital Connect provide services from St Pancras International/London Bridge to Brighton, and Winchester is

❏ **Getting to Britain**
● **By air** The nearest international airport to Winchester is Southampton Airport (🖳 www.southamptonairport.com) on the south coast. The alternative would be to fly to London's Gatwick (🖳 www.gatwickairport.com) or Heathrow airports (🖳 www.heathrowairport.com), both of which serve destinations worldwide.
● **From Europe by train** Eurostar (🖳 www.eurostar.com) operates a high-speed passenger service via the Channel Tunnel between Paris/Brussels and London. The Eurostar terminal in London is at St Pancras International station: some services also stop at Ashford International. For information about the various rail services to Britain from the continent contact your national rail service provider or visit 🖳 www.railteam.eu.
● **From Europe by coach** Eurolines (🖳 www.eurolines.com) have a huge network of long-distance coach services connecting over 500 cities in 25 European countries to London. However, these tickets often don't work out that much cheaper than flying the same route with a budget airline which is also far quicker.
● **From Europe by car** Eurotunnel (🖳 www.eurotunnel.com) operates a shuttle **train** service for vehicles via the Channel Tunnel between Calais and Folkestone, taking an hour between the motorway in France and the motorway in England.

There are many **ferry** routes between France (Caen, Calais, Cherbourg, Dieppe, Dunkerque, Le Havre and St Malo) and the south coast ports of England such as Dover, Newhaven, Poole and Portsmouth. There are also services from Spain (Bilbao and Santander) to Portsmouth. Look at 🖳 www.ferrysavers.com or 🖳 www.direct ferries.com for a full list of companies and services.

PLANNING YOUR WALK

a stop on some Cross Country routes. See box below and map p45 for contact and service details. Timetables, ticket and fare information can be found on their websites; it is also possible to buy tickets online. Alternatively, timetable and fare information can be found at **National Rail Enquiries** (☎ 08457-484950; 🖥 www.nationalrail.co.uk). Another useful site is 🖥 www.thetrainline.com with timetables, fares and an online ticket-purchasing facility. Trains from London Waterloo stop at Winchester and Petersfield and from London Victoria there are regular services to Amberley, Arundel, Hassocks, Brighton, Lewes, Newhaven, Seaford, Falmer, Southease and Eastbourne. Services from St Pancras International/London Bridge call at Hassocks and Brighton.

❏ USEFUL RAIL SERVICES   [see map p45]

Southern Trains (☎ 0845-127 2920, 🖥 www.southernrailway.com)
(Note: all services to/from London Victoria stop at Clapham Junction, East Croydon & Gatwick Airport; also note that not all stops are listed below)
- London Victoria to Bognor Regis via Horsham, Christ's Hospital, Billingshurst, Pulborough, Amberley, Arundel, Ford, & Barnham, Mon-Sat 2/hr, Sun 1/hr
- London Victoria to Brighton, daily 2-3/hr
- London Victoria to Eastbourne via Haywards Heath, Wivelsfield, Plumpton, Lewes, Polegate & Hampden Park, daily 1-2/hr
- Ashford International to Brighton via Eastbourne, Hampden Park, Polegate, Berwick, Glynde, Lewes & Falmer, daily 1/hr
- Ore to Brighton via Hastings, Hampden Park, Eastbourne, Polegate, Berwick, Glynde, Lewes & Falmer, Mon-Sat 1/hr
- Portsmouth to Littlehampton via Havant & Chichester, Mon-Sat 2/hr
- Chichester to Brighton via Worthing, Mon-Sat 2/hr, Sun 1/hr
- Arundel to Chichester (change at Barnham), Mon-Sat 2/hr, Sun 1/hr
- Brighton to Seaford via Falmer, Lewes & Newhaven, daily 2/hr (stops at Southease 1/hr)
- Eastbourne to Lewes, Mon-Sat 2-3/hr, Sun 2/hr

First Capital Connect (☎ 0845-700 0125, 🖥 www.firstcapitalconnect.co.uk)
- St Pancras International to Brighton via London Bridge, East Croydon, Gatwick Airport, Three Bridges, Haywards Heath, Burgess Hill & Hassocks, Mon-Fri 1-2/hr, Sat & Sun London Bridge to Brighton 1-2/hr (1/hr stops at Hassocks)

SouthWest Trains (☎ 0845-600 0650, 🖥 www.southwesttrains.co.uk)
- London Waterloo to Southampton/Bournemouth/Weymouth via Clapham Junction & Winchester, Mon-Sat 4/hr, Sun 3/hr
- London Waterloo to Portsmouth via Woking, Guildford, Haslemere, Petersfield & Havant, daily 2/hr
- London Waterloo to Portsmouth via Woking, Basingstoke & Winchester, daily 1/hr
- Weymouth/Poole/Bournemouth to Winchester, daily 1-3/hr
- Southampton to Reading via Winchester, Mon-Sat 2/hr, Sun 1/hr

Cross Country Trains (☎ 0844 811 0124, 🖥 www.crosscountrytrains.co.uk)
- Bournemouth to Manchester Piccadilly via Winchester, Reading & Birmingham daily 1/hr
- Southampton to Newcastle via Winchester, Reading, Birmingham & York, Mon-Sat 1/hr

PLANNING YOUR WALK

If you think you may want to book a taxi for when you arrive details of companies are given in Part 4. Alternatively, visit 🖳 www.traintaxi.co.uk for details of taxi companies operating at rail stations throughout England. It is also often possible to book train tickets that include bus travel to your ultimate destination: enquire when you book your train ticket or look at Plus Bus's website (🖳 www.plusbus.info).

By coach

Coach travel is generally cheaper but takes longer than the train. **National Express** is the principal coach (long-distance bus) operator in Britain and has services to a number of destinations on or near the Way.

Megabus (🖳 www.megabus.com/uk) is part of the Stagecoach group and it operates low-cost coach/rail services; destinations served include Winchester. Visit their website for details of their services.

❏ **USEFUL COACH SERVICES**   **[see map p45]**

National Express (☎ 0871-781 8181, 🖳 www.nationalexpress.com)
Note: not all stops are listed – contact National Express for full details.

024	London Victoria Coach Station (VCS) to Hastings via East Grinstead, Uckfield, Polegate, **Eastbourne**, Pevensey Bay, Bexhill & St Leonards, 1/day
025	London VCS to **Eastbourne** via Rottingdean, Saltdean, Peacehaven, Newhaven & Seaford, 1/day
031	London Victoria Coach Station (VCS) to **Petersfield** via Farnborough, Aldershot & Farnham, 1/day
032	London (VCS) to Southampton via **Winchester**, 5/day
203	Heathrow Airport to Portsmouth via **Winchester** & Southampton, 8/day
310	Oxford to Poole via Newbury, **Winchester**, Portsmouth, Bournemouth & Poole, 1/day
315	Helston to **Eastbourne** via Falmouth, Truro, Plymouth, Exeter, Bridport, Dorchester, Weymouth, Poole, Bournemouth, Southampton, Portsmouth, Chichester, **Arundel**, Worthing, Brighton, Newhaven & Seaford, 1/day
539	Birmingham to Bournemouth via Oxford, Newbury & **Winchester,** 1/day

PLANNING YOUR WALK

By car

The south of England is overrun with dual carriageways and bypasses so there is no shortage of 'A' roads to follow down to the Downs. On holiday weekends, however, be prepared for long tailbacks as everyone heads for the coast. There are main roads from London passing through Winchester, Petersfield, Cocking, Amberley and Arundel, Washington, Pyecombe, Lewes, Brighton and Eastbourne.

By air

Although there are local airports, such as the one at Shoreham, the easiest way to fly to the South-East from other corners of England is to get a flight to Gatwick or Southampton. See 🖳 www.chooseclimate.org for the true costs of flying.

LOCAL TRANSPORT

Hampshire, West Sussex and East Sussex all have excellent local transport networks which make planning linear day and weekend walks easy. The public transport map opposite summarises all the useful routes; see box below for the contact details for the relevant operators, the route numbers and routes as well as an indication of the frequency of service in both directions. For more information contact traveline (☎ 0871 200 2233, 🖳 www.travelinesoutheast.org.uk.

The tourist information centres along the Downs can provide, free of charge, a comprehensive local transport timetable for their particular region.

PLANNING YOUR WALK

❏ **LOCAL BUS SERVICES**   **[see map opposite]**

bluestar (☎ 023-8023 1950, 🖳 www.bluestarbus.co.uk)
1   Southampton to Winchester, Mon-Sat 3/hr, Sun 2/hr

Brighton & Hove Buses (☎ 01273-886200, 🖳 www.buses.co.uk)
2   Rottingdean to Shoreham via Woodingdean, Brighton & Hove, Mon-Sat 2/hr, Sun 1/hr
2a   Rottingdean to Steyning via Woodingdean, Brighton, Hove, Shoreham, Upper Beeding & Bramber, daily 1/hr
12   Brighton to Eastbourne via Rottingdean, Saltdean, Peacehaven, Newhaven, Seaford, Exceat (Seven Sisters CP) & East Dean, Mon-Sat 4/hr, Sun 2/hr
12a   Brighton to Eastbourne via Rottingdean, Newhaven, Seaford, Exceat (Seven Sisters CP), East Dean, Birling Gap & Beachy Head, Mon-Sat 2/hr (same route as No 12 but with some additional stops)
13X   Brighton to Eastbourne via Rottingdean, Saltdean, Peacehaven, Seaford, Birling Gap & Beachy Head, Apr to late June Sat, Sun & bank holidays 1/hr, late June to mid Sep daily 1/hr
20X   Brighton to Steyning via Hove, Shoreham, Bramber & Upper Beeding, Mon-Fri 2/day Shoreham to Steyning and 2-3/day Brighton to Steyning in afternoon
28   Brighton to Lewes, Mon-Sat 2/hr plus 2/hr to Ringmer, Sun 1/hr and continues to Uckfield, Crowborough & Tunbridge Wells
29/29a   Brighton to Tunbridge Wells via Lewes, Uckfield & Crowborough, Mon-Sat 3/hr, Sun 1/hr
77   Brighton to Devil's Dyke, Apr-Jul Sat, Sun & bank holidays plus Jul & Aug daily 1-2/hr
79   Brighton to Ditchling Beacon, Apr-Sep, Sat, Sun & bank holidays 1/hr, Oct-Mar Sun & bank holidays 1/hr

Compass Travel (☎ 01903-690025, 🖳 www.compass-travel.co.uk) (see also p118)
23   Worthing to Horsham via Washington, Sun & bank hols 6/day (see also Metrobus)
73   Storrington to Pulborough via Amberley, Tue & Fri 2/day
74   Storrington to Horsham, Mon-Sat 4/day
84   Worthing to Chichester via Arundel, Mon-Sat 4/day
99   Chichester to Petworth via Goodwood, East Dean, Charlton, Singleton Graffham, Sutton & Bignor, Mon-Sat 4/day but only stops if prebooked (☎ 01903-264776)
100   Burgess Hill to Pulborough via Henfield, Upper Beeding, Bramber, Steyning Washington & Storrington, Mon-Sat 1/hr   *(cont'd overleaf)*

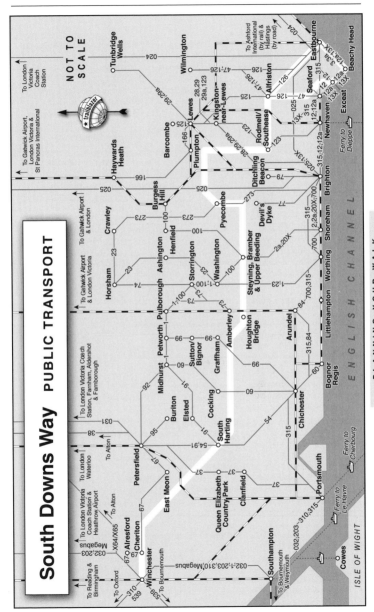

South Downs Way PUBLIC TRANSPORT

PLANNING YOUR WALK

❏ LOCAL BUS SERVICES (cont'd from p44)

Countryliner (☎ 0844 477 1623 for timetables, 🖥 www.countryliner-coaches.co.uk)

54	Petersfield to Chichester via S Harting, Uppark & Compton, Mon-Sat 5/day
91	Midhurst to Petersfield via Elsted & South Harting, Mon-Sat 5-6/day
92	Midhurst to Petersfield, Mon-Fri 4-5/day, Sat 2/day
95	Buriton to Buriton circular route via Petersfield & Steep, Mon-Sat 8/day
125	Barcombe to Alfriston via Cooksbridge, Offham, Lewes, Glynde, Firle, Selmeston & Berwick (Drusillas), Mon-Fri 3/day plus 1/day Lewes to Alfriston, Sat Barcombe to Lewes 4-5/day
166	Lewes to Haywards Heath via Plumpton & Wivelsfield, Mon-Fri 6/day, Sat 3/day and starts/ends in Malling

Cuckmere Community Bus (☎ 01323-870920, 🖥 www.cuckmerebus.freeuk.com)

125	Lewes to Alfriston via Glynde, Firle, Charleston Farmhouse (3/day when open), Selmeston & Berwick, Sat 5/day (operated by Countryliner Mon-Fri)
126	Seaford to Eastbourne via Alfriston, Drusillas, Wilmington, Polegate & Willingdon, Sun & Bank hols 4-5/day
47	Cuckmere Valley Rambler: Berwick Station circular route via Drusillas Zoo Park, Alfriston, Seaford, Seven Sisters Country Park, Litlington, Lullington & Wilmington, late Mar to late Oct Sat, Sun & public hols 1/hr
Note:	They also operate some limited-frequency services, driven by volunteers. These include: 40 (Berwick to Seaford via Drusillas, Wilmington, Lullington, Litlington, Charleston, Westdean & Exceat, Tue & Fri 1/day); 42 (Berwick to Hailsham circular route via Alciston & Alfriston, Wed 2/day, Fri 1-2/day); 44 (Berwick to Eastbourne via Polegate & Langney, Mon 1/day, Tue 1/day, Thur 2-3/day); services will stop wherever it is safe

Metrobus (☎ 01293-449191, 🖥 www.metrobus.co.uk)

23	Crawley to Worthing via Horsham, Ashington & Washington, Mon-Sat approx 1/hr, Sunday service operated by Compass (see box p44)
273	Brighton to Crawley via Pyecombe, Mon-Fri 6/day, Sat 3-4/day

Renown Coaches (☎ 01424-210744, 🖥 www.renowncoaches.co.uk)

123	Lewes to Newhaven via Kingston, Rodmell & Southease, Mon-Fri 8/day, Sat 4/day
126	Eastbourne to Seaford via Wilmington, Drusillas & Alfriston, Mon-Fri 8/day, Sat 4/day, in winter Mon-Sat 2-4/day

Stagecoach (🖥 www.stagecoachbus.com)

1	Midhurst to Worthing via Petworth, Pulborough, Storrington, Washington & Findon, Mon-Sat 1/hr, Sun 7/day
3/3A	Foot of Beachy Head to Eastbourne via Meads Village, Mon-Sat 3/hr, Sun 1/hr
37	Havant to Petersfield via Waterlooville, Clanfield, Queen Elizabeth Country Park, Mon-Sat approx 1/hr (connects with No 38)
38	Alton to Petersfield, Mon-Sat 5/day (connects with No 37)
60	Bognor Regis to Midhurst via Chichester, West Dean, Singleton & Cocking, Mon-Sat 2/hr, Sun 1/hr
X64/X65	Alton to Winchester, Mon-Sat 2/hr, Sun 6/day
67	Winchester to Petersfield via Alresford, Cheriton, Bramdean, West Meon & East Meon, Mon-Sat approx 1/hr
700	(Coastliner) Arundel to Brighton via Littlehampton, Goring, Worthing, Shoreham & Hove, Mon-Sat 2/hr, Sun 1/hr (plus Southsea to Brighton via Portsmouth, Havant, Chichester, Bognor Regis, Littlehampton, Goring, Worthing, Shoreham & Hove, Mon-Sat 2/hr, Sun 1/hr, as well as Chichester to Brighton via stops as above, Mon-Sat 2/hr)

PLANNING YOUR WALK

THE ENVIRONMENT AND NATURE

2

Flora and fauna

The South Downs region is essentially a man-made landscape. Centuries of farming have shaped these rolling hills and left a unique habitat for a variety of common and not-so-common species. Left alone the South Downs would revert to scrub and woodland. This may not appear to be a great tragedy. However, the habitat that would be lost is a much scarcer one that provides sanctuary to a variety of endangered species which rely on the unique chalk grassland environment. The Downs are not free of trees either. The plough never reached the steep scarp slope that runs along the northern edge of the Downs. Indeed there is a healthy balance between the open grassland of the high ground and the deciduous beech woodland which can claim to be some of the oldest and most undisturbed woodland in Britain.

Any walker on the Way, however, will notice the precarious relationship between man and the Downs. This corner of England is one of the most populated parts of Europe and the demands on the land have been great. In recent times large chunks of the Downs have been eaten away to be replaced by major roads such as the A3 and M3 (see box p60) and to make way for the expanding south-coast towns such as Brighton. Nevertheless, some good has come out of the race to build homes and roads. More and more people are noticing the value of the South Downs as the area comes under increasing pressure and this has culminated in the award of National Park status. Whether the protection afforded by this status outweighs the increased pressure from ever-greater numbers of tourists is something of a hot debate.

Tourists who are walkers are lucky enough to be travelling at a speed that allows them to appreciate the wildlife around them. Anyone who lives and works in a high-pressure environment – and particularly cities – will find a walk along the top of the Downs to be something of a therapeutic exercise. However, too many people bring the stress of work with them to the countryside, walking as if they have a train to catch. To gain more from a walk on the Downs it is worth allowing yourself the chance to wind down. Look around, not at your feet, walk slowly and take breaks. Quiet and observant walkers are far more likely to notice the plants and maybe the animals of the Downs.

BUTTERFLIES

The Downs are famous for their butterflies. Many of the National Nature Reserves in the area have been set up specifically because of the variety and number of butterflies. One of the most prevalent is the **meadow brown** (*Maniola jurtina*), a very common species, dusty brown in colour with a rusty orange streak and dark, false eyes. They can be seen in meadows all across the Downs. The small **gatekeeper** (*Pyronia tithonus*) likes similar habitat and is also widespread throughout the Downs. They are identified by their deep orange and chocolate-brown markings.

The **peacock** (*Inachis io*) is surely Britain's most beautiful butterfly; it's quite common in this area. The markings on the wings are said to mimic the eyes of an animal to frighten off predators. Also common is the impressive **red admiral** (*Vanessa atalanta*). Owing to climate change it is now starting to overwinter in Britain and appears to be thriving. The **brimstone** (*Gonepteryx rhamni*) is also widespread, though well camouflaged as its wings look very like leaves; the **white admiral** (*Limenitis camilla*), however, is declining in numbers but may still be seen in some woodland sites. Although it has also recently been in decline in other parts of the country, the **small tortoiseshell** (*Aglais urticae*) is still widespread here and also in towns and villages. Other very common butterflies include the **small white** (*Pieris/Artogeia rapae*) and the **large white** (*Pieris brassicae*). Both can travel large distances, some migrating from continental Europe each year.

Along many of the country lanes and tracks the **speckled wood** (*Pararge aegeria*) can be seen basking on hedgerows. It is a small dark butterfly with a few white spots and six small false eyes at the rear.

There are a number of butterflies that are synonymous with chalk downland, notably the butterflies known as blues. The **holly blue** (*Celastrina argiolus*) and **Chalkhill blue** (*Polyommatus/Lysandra coridon*) are both similar in appearance, being very small and pale blue in colour, although the Chalkhill blue has a dark strip on the edge of each wing. The **common blue** (*Polyommatus icarus*) is even smaller and as the name suggests is the most common of the blues. The underside of its wings is a dusty brown colour with small orange and white spots.

A rare downland butterfly is the **Duke of Burgundy fritillary** (*Hamearis lucina*) which you may be lucky enough to see on Beacon Hill. It has pale orange spots on small dark wings. Another rarity that relies on chalk grassland is the **silver spotted skipper** (*Hesperia comma*), a diminutive yellow butterfly with small white flashes on the undersides of the wings.

Finally, the **brown argus** (*Aricia agestis*), a small dark butterfly with distinctive orange spots along the edges of each wing, is another that is restricted to chalk grassland; it can sometimes be seen flying close to the ground.

FLOWERS

Many of the flowering meadows that once covered large stretches of downland farmland have been destroyed by modern farming techniques. However, in

Peacock
Inachis io

Small Tortoiseshell
Aglais urticae

Common Blue
Polyommatus icarus

Brimstone
Gonepteryx rhamni

Chalkhill Blue
Polyommatus/Lysandra coridon

Painted Lady
Cynthia cadui

Small Garden/Cabbage White
Pieris/Artogeia rapae

Red Admiral
Vanessa atalanta

Meadow brown
Maniola jurtina

Large Garden/
Cabbage White
Pieris brassicae

White Admiral
Limenitis camilla

Common Dog Violet
Viola riviniana

Common Centaury
Centaurium erythraea

Honeysuckle
Lonicera periclymemum

Wild marjoram
Origanum vulgare

Germander Speedwell
Veronica chamaedrys

Herb-Robert
Geranium robertianum

Lousewort
Pedicularis sylvatica

Self-heal
Prunella vulgaris

Scarlet Pimpernel
Anagallis arvensis

Viper's Bugloss
Echium vulgare

Ramsons (Wild Garlic)
Allium ursinum

Bluebell
Hyacinthoides non-scripta

Dog Rose
Rosa canina

Meadow Buttercup
Ranunculis acris

Gorse
Ulex europaeus

Tormentil
Potentilla erecta

Birdsfoot-trefoil
Lotus corniculatus

Ox-eye Daisy
Leucanthemum vulgare

St John's Wort
Hypericum perforatum

Primrose
Primula vulgaris

Cowslip
Primula veris

Common Ragwort
Senecio jacobaea

Red Admiral butterfly (*Vanessa atalanta*) on
Hemp Agrimony (*Eupatorium cannabinum*)

Foxglove
Digitalis purpurea

Early Purple Orchid
Orchis mascula

Pyramidal Orchid
Anacamptis pyramidalis

Bell Heather
Erica cinerea

Heather (Ling)
Calluna vulgaris

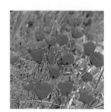

Common Poppy
Papaver rhoeas

Rosebay Willowherb
Epilobium angustifolium

Common Vetch
Vicia sativa

Forget-me-not
Myosotis arvensis

Rowan (tree)
Sorbus aucuparia

Old Man's Beard
Clematis vitalba

Red Campion
Silene dioica

places, efforts are being made to revive these by encouraging farmers to employ more flower-friendly methods.

Meadows

The dominant grass found in fields all over the Downs is the appropriately named **sheep's fescue** (*Festuca ovina*) which was cultivated specifically for pastureland and is the grass of choice for downland sheep.

Of far greater interest are the likes of the **common poppy** (*Papaver rhoeas*) with its spectacular deep red petals. They often colonise arable fields and path edges, preferring well-disturbed soil. Entire fields turn red in the flowering season in late summer.

Earlier in the season walkers are likely to come across the **cowslip** (*Primula veris*) and its head of pale yellow flowers. The flowers flop down in small bunches earning the plant the old nickname 'bunch of keys'.

Perhaps one of the most beautiful of the downland flowers is the **round headed rampion** (*Phyteuma orbiculare*). Its striking dark blue flowers have earned it the local name 'The Pride of Sussex'.

The tiny yellow flower of **tormentil** (*Potentilla tormentilla*) can be seen hugging the ground in short grassland. It gets its name from an age when it was used as a medicinal remedy for diarrhoea and haemorrhoids: the taste is so foul that it tormented whoever took it.

Another tiny flower that can also be found close to the ground is the **scarlet pimpernel** (*Anagallis avensis*), a member of the primrose family. The flowers are just 5mm in diameter but stand out from their grassy background thanks to their light red colour.

Many people assume orchids to be so rare as to be nearly impossible to find. In truth there are a number of fairly common species that may readily be seen flowering on the Downs, usually around mid-summer. These include the **early purple orchid** (*Orchis mascula*) which can be seen in rough grassland. It stands about 10-15cm tall and has an elongated head of pinky-purple flowers.

There are of course some species that do fit the rare orchid label including the **fly orchid** (*Ophrys insectifera*) with flowers resembling small insects. These cleverly designed flowers attract wasps which pick up the pollen and take it on to the next insect-shaped flower they see. Another orchid with the same tactic is the **bee orchid** (*Ophrys apifera*) whose flowers are shaped like, well, bees.

Apart from the orchids, one of the most endangered and also one of the most striking flowering plants that may be seen, particularly on the Downs above Eastbourne, is **pheasant's-eye** (*Adonis annua*) with its blood red petals and large seed head.

In overgrown areas thorny **gorse** (*Ulex europeous*) bushes brighten up the summer with their small yellow flowers that burst open from February until June, filling the air with a coconut-like scent.

Woodland and hedgerows

There are several flowering plants associated with open woods and woodland edges. In May the pink flowers of the slightly inaccurately named **red campi-**

on (*Silene dioica*) come into view along woodland edges and at the foot of hedgerows while deeper into the woods the floor becomes covered with **bluebells** (*Hyacinthoides non-scripta*) in the early spring. Other common woodland flowering plants include the **wood anemone** (*Anemone nemorosa*) with its round white flowers which cover forest floors in a similar way to bluebells. A more isolated flower, although sometimes seen growing in small groups, is the cheerful yellow **primrose** (*Primula vulgaris*).

Bramble (*Rubus fruticosus*) is a common woodland and hedgerow species with small sharp thorns. It spreads rapidly, engulfing everything in its path. In its favour, blackberries appear on the branches in the autumn to provide sustenance for hungry birds and greedy walkers.

In hedgerows and along woodland edges you'll see the distinctive feathery climber, **old man's beard** (*Clematis vitalba*), also known as traveller's joy. The feathery part of the plant is actually the fruit.

The **foxglove** (*Digitalis purpurea*) is a very tall and graceful plant with white or purple trumpet-like flowers. It is commonly spotted along hedgerows, roadside verges and in shady woodland. Other fairly common woodland species that are just as comfortable on hedgebanks include the **forget-me-not** (*Myosotis arvensis*) which has very small blue flowers and **cow parsley** (*Anthriscus sylvestris*), a tall plant with a head of white flowers.

Perhaps the most unusual and to some eyes the ugliest of plants, found in dark corners of beech woodland, is the **bird's nest orchid** (*Neottia nidus-avis*), so-called because of its nest-like root system that intertwines across the ground.

TREES

Over the last few hundred years the once-extensive forest cover in southern England has been fragmented into a patchwork of copses and coppiced woodland. Trees were felled for fuel and for shipbuilding and, in the case of the South Downs, to clear land for agricultural needs. In more recent times many of the hedgerows that helped create the familiar patchwork landscape have been grubbed up to create much larger fields.

Nevertheless, there are parts of the Downs that have survived the threat from axe and chainsaw. The north-facing scarp slope was, and still is, too steep for clearing and too inaccessible for ploughing. Consequently, this is where most of the trees are found. Although there are still areas of semi-natural or ancient mixed woodland, much of the remaining woodland has been coppiced, an old method of promoting growth of more numerous and narrower trunks by cutting a tree at its base. Coppicing was common in hazel stands and the resulting product used in constructing fences and making furniture.

Although coppicing is no longer widespread it is still practised in some parts today by enthusiasts of old woodland crafts and also by conservationists who recognise that coppiced woodland can be beneficial to certain species.

Most of the woodland the walker will encounter on the Downs is mixed deciduous, made up largely of beech and ash but there are many other species to look out for.

Tree species

The **beech** (*Fagus sylvatica*) with its thick, silvery trunk is one of the most attractive native trees. It can grow to a height of 40 metres with the high canopies blocking out much of the light. As a result the floors of beech woodlands tend to be fairly bare of vegetation. They favour well-drained soil, hence their liking for the steep scarp slope. In autumn the colours of the turning leaves can be quite spectacular.

One species that does survive the shady floor of beech woodland is the distinctive **common holly** (*Ilex aquifolium*) with its dark waxy leaves which have sharp points. Holly varies in size, usually growing as a sprawling bush on the woodland floor or in hedgerows but also as a tree when established in more isolated locations.

Famous for its longevity, lasting for well over a thousand years in some cases, the **common yew** (*Taxus baccata*) is abundant in churchyards but there are also natural stands on the scarp slope and among beech woodland. The dark glossy needles are quite distinctive as is the flaky red bark of the often gnarled and twisted old trunks and branches. Do not be tempted to eat the bright red berries; they're poisonous. Another tree with red berries is the **hawthorn** (*Crataegus monogyna*). It has small leaves and is usually found in hedgerows but can also grow as a small tree. In early autumn the berries provide food for woodland birds and are particularly popular with blackbirds.

MAMMALS

The well-drained soil of chalk downland is ideal habitat for the **badger** (*Meles meles*), a sociable animal with a distinctive black-and-white-striped muzzle. Badgers live in family groups in large underground 'setts'. They are rarely spotted since they tend to emerge after dark to hunt for worms in the fields. Sadly, they are more commonly seen dead on the road: after hedgehogs they are the most inept at crossing roads.

The **fox** (*Vulpes vulpes*) is another common mammal on the Downs. Although they prefer to come out at night they are not exclusively nocturnal; particularly in summer they may be out in broad daylight in some of the quieter corners of the hills though the best time to spot a fox is at dusk when you might see one trotting along a field or woodland edge.

The **rabbit** (*Oryctolagus cuniculus*) is seemingly everywhere on the Downs. The well-drained, steep grassland is ideal for their warrens.

The **grey squirrel** (*Sciurus carolinensis*) was introduced from North America at the end of the 19th century. Its outstanding success in colonising Britain is very much to the detriment of other native species including the red squirrel. Greys are bigger and stockier than reds and to many people the reds, with their tufted ears, bushy tails and small beady eyes, are the far more attractive of the two. Sadly there are no red squirrels anywhere on the Downs.

The **roe deer** (*Capreolus capreolus*) is a small, native species of deer that tends to hide in woodland. They can sometimes be seen, alone or in pairs, on field edges or clearings in the forest but you are more likely to hear the sharp dog-like bark made when they smell you coming.

At dusk **bats** can be seen hunting for moths and flying insects along hedgerows, over rivers and around street lamps. All seventeen species in Britain are protected by law. The commonest, and smallest, species is the **pipistrelle** (*Pipistrellus pipistrellus*). Although it is only about 4cm long it can eat up to 3000 insects in one night. You may also be lucky enough to see the slighter larger **Daubenton's** bat (*Myotis daubentonii*) hunting for mosquitoes over rivers and ponds.

If the Downs were made for any one species it is probably the **brown hare** (*Lepus europaeus*) which, if you are observant, can be seen racing across the fields on the hilltops. Hares are bigger than rabbits, with longer hind legs and ears, and are arguably far more graceful than their prolific little cousins. Some other small but fairly common species to keep an eye out for include the carnivorous **stoat** (*Mustela erminea*), its smaller cousin the **weasel** (*Mustela nivalis*), the **hedgehog** (*Erinaceus europaeus*) and a number of species of **voles**, **mice** and **shrews**.

REPTILES

The **adder** (*Vipera berus*) is the only poisonous snake in Britain. It is easily recognised by the distinctive zig-zag markings down its back and a diamond shape on the back of its head. On summer days adders bask in sunny spots such as on a warm rock or in the middle of a path so watch your step. Adders tend to move out of the way quickly but should you be unlucky enough to inadvertently step on one and get bitten sit still and send someone else for help. Their venom is designed to kill small mammals, not humans. A bite is unlikely to be fatal to an adult but *is* serious enough to warrant immediate medical attention, especially in the case of children. Nevertheless, the likelihood of being bitten is minuscule. Walkers are far more likely to frighten the adder away once it senses your footsteps.

The **grass snake** (*Natrix natrix*), an adept swimmer, is a much longer, slimmer snake with a yellow collar around the neck. It's non-venomous but does emit a foul stench should you attempt to pick one up. It's much better for you and the snake to leave it in peace.

The **common lizard** (*Lacerta/Zootoca vivipara*) is a harmless creature which can often be seen basking in the sun on rocks and stone walls. About 15cm long, it is generally brown with patterns of spots or stripes. However, you are far more likely to hear them scuttling away through the undergrowth as you approach.

A curious beast, looking like a slippery eel or small snake, is the **slow worm** (*Anguis fragilis*) which despite the name is neither a worm nor indeed an eel or snake but a legless lizard. Usually a glossy grey or copper colour, they can be seen on woodland floors and in grassland. They are completely harmless and usually slip away into the leaf litter when they hear footsteps.

THE ENVIRONMENT AND NATURE

BIRDS

The chalk grassland of the Downs is ideal for a variety of bird species but the grassy hillsides are not the only habitat on the Downs. There are many woodland species in the beech forests on the steep scarp slope, freshwater species on the rivers and sea birds by Cuckmere Haven and the Seven Sisters cliffs. The following list gives just a few of the birds that may be seen while walking on the Downs.

LAPWING/PEEWIT
L: 320MM/12.5"

Scrubland and chalk grassland

One of the most attractive birds the Downs walker might spot, usually seen feeding on open arable farmland, is the **lapwing** (*Vanellus vanellus*), also known as the peewit. It has long legs, a short bill and a distinctive long head crest. Sadly, this attractive bird is declining in numbers. The name comes from its lilting flight, frequently changing direction with its large rounded wings. It is also identified by a white belly, black and white head, black throat patch and distinctive dark green wings.

Towards dusk **barn owls** (*Tyto alba*) hunt for voles along field and woodland edges. To see a barn owl, with its ghostly white plumage, is a real treat but their dwindling numbers make such a sighting increasingly rare.

The colourful little **stonechat** (*Saxicola rubicola*) with its deep orange breast and black head is among the more commonly sighted of Downland birds. They are easily identified by their habit of flitting from the top of one bush to another, only pausing to call out across the fields. The stonechat's call much like two stones being struck together, hence the name stonechat.

STONECHAT
L: 135MM/5.25"

The **yellowhammer** (*Emberiza citrinella*), also known as the yellow bunting, can sometimes be seen perched on the top of gorse bushes. Most field guides to birds along with most old romantic country folk claim that the distinctive song of the yellowhammer sounds like 'a little bit of bread and no cheese'. At a push they are right but the yellowhammer is certainly no talking parrot.

The call of the **skylark** (*Alauda arvensis*) can probably be considered the sound of the Downs. This small, buff-coloured, ground-nesting lark is usually heard but not often seen. The characteristic flight pattern, rising steadily upwards on rapid wingbeats whilst twittering

YELLOWHAMMER
L: 160MM/6.25"

THE ENVIRONMENT AND NATURE

SKYLARK
L: 185MM/7.25"

relentlessly, is what makes the skylark such a distinctive little bird. However, the skylark is virtually impossible to see it against the blue sky but if you look carefully you might just spot it way up high.

Woodland

A common raptor that is often heard before it's seen is the **buzzard** (*Buteo buteo*), a large broad-winged bird of prey which looks much like a small eagle. It is dark brown in appearance but slightly paler on the underside of the wings. It has a distinctive mewing call and can be spotted soaring ever higher on the air thermals or sometimes perched on the top of fenceposts. Buzzards are less common towards the eastern end of the Downs where the woodland cover is not so great. They are far easier to spot above the dense woodland on the West Sussex Downs and around the Meon Valley in Hampshire.

The **kestrel** (*Falco tinnunculus*), a small falcon, is much smaller than the buzzard and is far more prevalent. It hovers expertly in a fixed spot above grassland and roadside verges, even in the strongest of winds, hunting for mice and voles. Similar in size and appearance but rarely seen is the **hobby** *(Falco subbuteo)* which appears in the summer months, often on the margins of woodlands.

The **green woodpecker** *(Picus viridis)* is not all green, sporting a bright red and black head. They are sometimes spotted clinging to a vertical tree trunk or feeding on the ground in open fields. The most common view, however, is as the bird flies away when disturbed. The undulating flight pattern is characterised by rapid wing beats as the bird rises followed by a pause when the bird slowly drops. This is accompanied by a loud laughing call that has earned the bird its old English name of yaffle.

GREEN WOODPECKER
L: 330MM/13"

WOODCOCK
L: 330MM/13"

The **woodcock** *(Scolopax rusticola)*, with its long straight beak and plump body, is common in damp woodland where it can lie hidden thanks to its leafy brown plumage. It is most easily sighted in spring at dusk and dawn. This is when the males perform their courtship flight, known as 'roding', which involves two distinct calls, one a low grunting noise, the other a sharp 'k-wik k-wik' call.

Conservation of the South Downs

Ever since the Industrial Revolution and the rapid development over the last 200 years the English countryside has been put under a great deal of strain. The South Downs were once wooded hills, home to wolves, wild boar and other species that have long since departed. The need to feed an increasing population led to much of the countryside being cleared and ploughed. The result of this is the landscape we see today, although the traditional patchwork pattern of fields and hedgerows has been replaced in some parts of the Downs by much larger fields, the hedgerows having been torn out.

The South Downs is, then, a man-made landscape: even the woodland has been coppiced and the meadows ploughed at one time or another. This is not necessarily a bad thing, however. The resulting habitat is a rare one that provides an essential niche for endangered species, most notably the butterflies for which the Downs are famous.

Although the Downs, positioned in a populous corner of England, continue to be put under pressure from road and housing projects, the increasing awareness of the value of our natural (or perhaps semi-natural) heritage has resulted in greater efforts in the conservation of the Downs. There are a number of groups, on both a local and national scale and on both a voluntary and government basis, who help protect the species, habitats and buildings of the Downs. They also help visitors to get the most out of their trip to the countryside whilst at the same time trying to ease the pressure brought by the increase in tourist numbers.

Now that the South Downs have finally been granted National Park status (see p56) the effort to conserve the area should become less of a struggle owing to the increased environmental protection and financial benefits that the National Park designation brings.

❑ **Dew ponds**
The chalk soil of the Downs is highly permeable so there is rarely any standing or free-flowing water available for livestock. To combat the problem farmers have, since prehistoric times, constructed dew ponds. These small, circular ponds are designed to collect and retain water for the sheep and cattle that graze the dry hilltops. Despite their name, dew accounts for very little of the moisture that collects in these man-made bowls; most of it is rainwater. The water is prevented from filtering through the chalk thanks to a base layer of straw and clay, although modern-day dew ponds usually have a layer of concrete instead.

Many dew ponds are hundreds of years old and in a state of disrepair, being overgrown and barely recognisable as ponds. However, in recent years many have been restored, either because of their historic interest or simply to be used again for their original purpose. Good examples of dew ponds can be seen near Chanctonbury Ring and also between Southease and Alfriston.

THE ENVIRONMENT AND NATURE

GOVERNMENT AGENCIES AND SCHEMES

Natural England

Natural England is the single government body responsible for identifying, establishing and managing National Parks, Areas of Outstanding Natural Beauty, National Nature Reserves, Sites of Special Scientific Interest, and Special Areas of Conservation.

The highest level of landscape protection is the designation of land as a **National Park** which recognises the national importance of an area in terms of landscape, biodiversity and as a recreational resource. This designation does not signify national ownership and they are not uninhabited wildernesses, making conservation a knife-edged balance between protecting the environment and the rights and livelihoods of those living in the park.

In April 2011 the South Downs became England's ninth National Park, and its most densely populated (see box below). Some 85 per cent of the land within the South Downs National Park is agricultural, so this balancing act is particularly critical here.

The **National Trail Officer** (see box p58) works closely with Natural England and councils to keep the South Downs Way in good condition although the work on the ground is often undertaken by the local highway authorities.

The next level of protection within the National Park includes National Nature Reserves and Sites of Special Scientific Interest. There are over 200

❏ **How the South Downs became a National Park**

The South Downs almost became one of the first designated national parks back in the 1950s but the proposal was rejected on the grounds that the area did not offer sufficient recreational possibilities for the public. This seems rather surprising today when you consider the number of walkers, cyclists, horse-riders and paragliders who use the hills. National Park status is not just about providing an area of fun for outdoor enthusiasts, however. It is about protecting the area from harmful development such as road building, a real problem in the South-East, and preserving the natural and cultural heritage of the area.

In 1999 the Department for the Environment proposed that the Countryside Agency, now part of Natural England, designate the South Downs a National Park. A Designation Order was published in late 2002 and in November 2003 a public inquiry began, to hear the views of those likely to be affected by the change. In 2006 a report was passed to the Secretary of State. After several more delays and legal wrangles, in 2009 it finally was announced that the South Downs would receive National Park status, and the newly appointed South Downs National Park Authority (🖥 www.south downs.gov.uk) officially assumed responsibility for it on 1st April 2011.

Although at 1648 sq km it is not the largest in area (that distinction going to the Lake District National Park at 2292 sq km), being only an hour from London it encompasses several large towns including Petersfield and Lewes, and is by far the most densely populated of all the National Parks, with around 108,000 residents.

❏ **National Trails**
The South Downs Way is one of 15 National Trails (🖳 www.nationaltrails.co.uk) in England and Wales. These are Britain's flagship long-distance paths which grew out of the post-war desire to protect the country's special places, a movement which also gave birth to National Parks and AONBs. The Pennine Way was the first to be created.

National Trails in England are designated and largely funded by Natural England and are managed on the ground by a National Trail Officer. They co-ordinate the maintenance work undertaken by the local highway authority and landowners to ensure that the trail is kept to nationally agreed standards.

National Nature Reserves (NNRs) in England. Those along the course of the South Downs Way include: Beacon Hill (see p85), just before the village of Exton; Old Winchester Hill (see p86), just after Exton; Butser Hill (see p91) several miles further along the path and Lullington Heath (p175).

There are about 4100 **Sites of Special Scientific Interest (SSSIs)** in England ranging in size from little pockets protecting wild flower meadows, important nesting sites or special geological features, to vast swathes of upland, moorland and wetland. SSSIs are a particularly important designation as they have some legal standing. They are managed in partnership with the owners and occupiers of the land who must give written notice before initiating any operations likely to damage the site and who cannot proceed without consent from Natural England. SSSIs along the South Downs Way include: Cheesefoot Head (see p81), Butser Hill (see p91), Heyshott Down (see p106), Chanctonbury Hill (see p128) and Seaford to Beachy Head (see p170).

Special Areas of Conservation (SACs) are designated by the European Union's Habitats Directive and provide an extra tier of protection to the areas that they cover. Along the South Downs Way Butser Hill NNR and SSSI is also a SAC. See Natural England's website (see box p59) for further information about all of these.

The South Downs Way is included in the **Environmental Stewardship Scheme (ESS)**, which provides financial incentives to farmers and landowners to employ agricultural methods that will conserve the landscape and wildlife.

Together, all these sites make up a vital network of wildlife habitats across the South Downs. It is essential that good wildlife sites are buffered and linked by wildlife corridors, such as hedgerows, enabling species to move freely across the landscape.

There is no doubt that National Park status and the NNR, SSSI, SAC and ESS designations play a vital role in safeguarding the land they cover for future generations. However, the very fact that we rely on these labels for protecting limited areas begs the question: what are we doing to the vast majority of land that remains relatively unprotected? Surely we should be aiming to conserve the natural environment outside protected areas just as much as within them.

THE ENVIRONMENT AND NATURE

CAMPAIGNING AND CONSERVATION ORGANISATIONS

The **National Trust** (NT; ☎ 0844-800 1895, 🖳 www.nationaltrust.org.uk) is a charity with 3.8 million members which aims to protect, through ownership, threatened coastline, countryside, historic houses, castles, gardens and archaeological remains for everyone to enjoy. In particular the NT cares for over 600 miles of British coastline, 248,000 hectares of countryside and 300 historic buildings and monuments. It manages large sections of the Downs including an area of chalk grassland on the Seven Sisters between the hamlet of Crowlink and Birling Gap (see p168), Devil's Dyke (see p139), Harting Down (see p101), and Newtimber Hill (see p139). It also owns various properties on the Way, such as Monk's House (see p154) in Rodmell and the Alfriston Clergy House (see box p160), its first ever property, bought in 1896 for the sum of £10; both of these properties are open to the public.

The **Wildfowl & Wetlands Trust** (WWT; ☎ 01453-891900, 🖳 www.wwt.org.uk) is the biggest conservation organisation for wetlands in the UK with over 4000 acres of land under their management. Their centre at Arundel (☎ 01903-883355, 🖳 www.wwt.org.uk/visit/arundel; see p119) is well-known and very popular with visitors year-round.

The **Wildlife Trust** (🖳 www.wildlifetrusts.org) has regional branches covering the area along the South Downs Way. They undertake projects to improve conditions for wildlife and promote public awareness of it as well as acquiring land for nature reserves to protect particular species and habitats. The Sussex Wildlife Trust (🖳 www.sussexwildlifetrust.org.uk) manages the Amberley Wild Brooks network of ponds and marshland along with Ditchling Beacon and Malling Down, Lewes. The Hampshire and Isle of Wight Wildlife Trust (🖳 www.hwt.org.uk) manages St Catherine's Hill, Winchester.

❏ **Statutory bodies**
- **Department for Environment, Food and Rural Affairs** (🖳 www.defra.gov.uk) Government ministry responsible for sustainable development in the countryside.
- **Natural England** (☎ 0845-600 3078; 🖳 www.naturalengland.org.uk) Their relevant regional offices for the South East Region are Winchester (☎ 0300-060 2514) and Worthing (☎ 0300-060 0300).
- **English Heritage** (☎ 0870-333 1181, 🖳 www.english-heritage.org.uk) Organisation whose central aim is to make sure that the historic environment of England is properly maintained. It is officially known as the Historic Buildings and Monuments Commission for England. Bramber Castle (see p132) is one of the properties it manages.
- **South Downs National Park Authority** (☎ 0300-303 1053, 🖳 www.southdowns.gov.uk).
- **Hampshire County Council** (☎ 0845-603 5636, 🖳 www.hants.gov.uk).
- **East Sussex County Council** (☎ 0345-608 0190, 🖳 www.eastsussex.gov.uk).
- **West Sussex County Council** (☎ 01243-777100, 🖳 www.westsussex.gov.uk).

The **Royal Society for the Protection of Birds** (RSPB; 🖥 www.rspb .org.uk) was the pioneer of voluntary conservation bodies and although it does-n't have any reserves directly on the South Downs Way, there is one near Pulborough, a couple of miles north of Storrington. The wet grassy meadows here attract ducks, geese, swans and wading birds.

Butterfly Conservation (🖥 www.butterfly-conservation.org) was formed in 1968 by some naturalists who were alarmed at the decline in the number of butterflies, and moths, and who aim to reverse the situation. They now have 31 branches throughout the British Isles and operate 33 nature reserves and also sites where butterflies are likely to be found: these include Beachy Head and Malling Down. The two branches relevant to the South Downs Way are Hampshire and the Isle of Wight (🖥 www.hantsiow-butterflies.org.uk) and Sussex (🖥 www.sussex-butterflies.org.uk).

There are also smaller conservation groups such as the **Murray Downland Trust** (🖥 www.murraydownlandtrust.org.uk) which manages five reserves (Heyshott Escarpment, Heyshott Down, Buriton, Under Beacon, and The Devil's Jumps) in West Sussex and East Hampshire. The Trust's main objective is to 'rescue and enhance neglected areas of unimproved chalk downland' but it also looks after some ancient monuments in the area such as the Bronze Age archaeological site (see p108). Access to the Trust's sites is permitted except when the area should be left undisturbed for conservation reasons. The trust relies on human volunteers to help clear the land in its care but sheep are often brought in during the winter months to eat the scrub that threatens the grassland.

The South Downs Society (🖥 www.southdownssociety.org.uk) campaigns specifically for the conservation and enhancement of the landscape of the national park. The Society describes itself as operating as a 'critical friend' of the South Downs National Park Authority. They have divided the Downs from Winchester to Eastbourne into areas, each looked after by a volunteer District Officer whose main task is to look at planning applications in the area and respond accordingly. In 2012 they were in discussion with a commercial ener-gy provider to minimise the impact of a huge offshore wind farm that is pro-posed for a site within view of the South Downs National Park. These discus-sions included the plans not only to place all power cables underground but to bury existing overhead power lines as well, by way of compensation for the dis-ruption resulting from the cabling work .

BEYOND CONSERVATION

The ideas embodied in nature conservation have served us well over the last century. Without the multitude of designations which protect wildlife and land-scape there is no doubt that the countryside of England would be far more impoverished than it is today. However, in some respects the creation of nature reserves and other protected areas is an admission that we are not looking after the rest of our environment properly.

THE ENVIRONMENT AND NATURE

If we can't keep the soil, air and water free from contamination or prevent man's activities from affecting the world's climate nature reserves will have little lasting value. Similarly, if decisions made by national government, the European Union (EU) or the World Trade Organisation (WTO) continue to fragment communities and force farmers, foresters and fishermen to adopt unsustainable practices, those who are best placed to protect the land and wildlife will end up destroying it.

Those who care about the wildlife and countryside of England now need to step beyond the narrow focus of conservation. We need to find ways to reconnect with the natural world and re-learn how to live in balance with it. This not only demands action on a personal level, for which walking in the wild is surely an ideal tutor, but also a wholesale rethink of the basic assumptions underlying the political and economic policies.

❏ Roads, roads, roads

Over the years the Downs have been subjected to a great deal of road building. The most notable blots on the landscape are the A3 dual carriageway through Queen Elizabeth Country Park, the A27 Brighton bypass which guides traffic across a large swathe of downland just south of Ditchling Beacon, and the highly controversial M3 link through Twyford Down.

It is the latter, however, that caught the media attention thanks largely to the unprecedented protests between 1992 and 1994 by people from all walks of life, many of whom chained themselves to the highest branches of the trees on the Down for weeks on end. Sadly for Twyford Down it was all in vain and the scheme went ahead.

The result is a desecrated chalk hill and a saving of 12 minutes on the average journey time between Southampton and London. The government tried to appease the protesters by closing the old Winchester bypass that the M3 extension replaced and returning it to its natural state. It is now almost impossible to trace the old route of the road when looking down from the top of St Catherine's Hill but in the opposite direction is the new stretch of motorway, bigger, noisier and uglier than its predecessor.

MINIMUM IMPACT & OUTDOOR SAFETY

Minimum impact walking

Walk as if you are kissing the Earth with your feet
Thich Nhat Hanh *Peace is every step*

The popularity of the 'Great Outdoors' as an escape route from the chaos of modern living has experienced something of a boom over the last decade or so. It is therefore important to be aware of the pressures that each of us as visitors to the countryside exert upon the land. The South Downs are particularly vulnerable, situated as they are in the most populous corner of the British Isles. Thousands of people explore the network of trails that criss-cross these historic chalk hills.

Minimum impact walking is all about a common-sense approach to exploring the countryside, being mindful and respectful of the wildlife and those who live and work on the land. Those who appreciate the countryside will already be aware of the importance of safeguarding it. Simple measures such as not dropping litter, keeping dogs on leads to avoid scaring sheep and leaving gates as you find them will already be second nature to anyone who regularly visits the countryside. However, there are a number of other measures that are not quite so well known and are worth repeating here.

ECONOMIC IMPACT

Rural businesses and communities in Britain have been hit hard in recent years by a seemingly endless series of crises. In addition, they have to compete with the omnipresence of chain supermarkets that are now so common in towns across Britain. Faced with such competition local businesses struggle to survive. Visitors to the countryside can help these local businesses by 'buying locally'. It benefits the local economy as well as the consumer.

Buy local
Look and ask for local produce to buy and eat. Not only does this cut down on the amount of pollution and congestion that the transportation of food creates, so-called 'food miles', but also ensures that you are supporting local farmers and producers – the very people who have moulded the countryside you have come to see and who are in

the best position to protect it. If you can find local food which is also organic so much the better.

Support local businesses

It's a fact of life that money spent at local level – perhaps in a market, or at the greengrocer, or in an independent pub – has a far greater impact for good on that community than the equivalent spent in a branch of a national chain store or restaurant. While no-one would advocate that walkers should boycott the larger supermarkets, which after all do provide local employment, it's worth remembering that businesses in rural communities rely heavily on visitors for their very existence. If we want to keep these shops and post offices, we need to use them. The more money that circulates locally and is spent on local labour and materials, the greater the impact on the local economy and the more power the community has to effect the changes it wants to see.

Encourage local cultural traditions and skills

No two parts of the countryside look the same. Buildings, food, skills and language evolve out of the landscape and are moulded over hundreds of years to suit the locality. Discovering these cultural differences is part of the pleasure of walking in new places. Visitors' enthusiasm for local traditions and skills brings awareness and pride, nurturing a sense of place; an increasingly important role in a world where economic globalisation continues to undermine the very things that provide security and a feeling of belonging.

ENVIRONMENTAL IMPACT

By choosing a walking holiday you are already minimising your impact on the environment. Your interaction with the countryside and its inhabitants, whether they be plant, animal or human, can bring benefits to all. The following are some ideas on how you can go a few steps further in helping to minimise your impact on the natural environment while walking the South Downs Way.

Use public transport whenever possible

Both Sussex and Hampshire are blessed with an excellent public transport system (see pp44-6). There are various bus routes which drop off and pick up passengers at convenient start and finish points for day walks along the Downs and there are many buses linking the Way with nearby towns and villages. There are also plenty of bus and train links to get the walker to the Downs in the first place, making a car quite unnecessary.

Never leave litter

Leaving litter shows a total disrespect for the natural world and others coming after you. As well as being unsightly, litter kills wildlife, pollutes the environment and can be dangerous to farm animals. Please take your rubbish with you so you can dispose of it in a bin in the next village. It would be very helpful if you could pick up litter left by other people, too.

● **Is it OK if it's biodegradable?** No. Apple cores, banana skins, orange peel and the like are an eyesore, encourage flies, ants and wasps and ruin a picnic spot for others. They also promote a higher population of scavengers such as carrion crows and magpies, an explosion of which can have a detrimental effect on rarer bird species.

Those who use the excuse that orange peel is natural and biodegradable are simply fishing for an excuse to clear their conscience. Biodegradable? Yes, but surprisingly slowly. Natural? The South Downs have never been known for banana plantations and orange groves.

● **The lasting impact of litter** A piece of orange peel left on the ground takes six months to decompose; silver foil 18 months; a plastic bag 10 years; clothes 15 years; and an aluminium can 85 years.

Erosion

● **Stay on the main trail** The effect of your footsteps may seem minuscule but when they are multiplied by several thousand walkers each year they become rather more significant. Avoid taking shortcuts, widening the trail or taking more than one path; your boots will be followed by many others. This is particularly pertinent on the South Downs where there is such a huge volume of visitors.

● **Consider walking out of season** Unfortunately, most people prefer to walk in the spring and summer which is exactly the time of year when the vegetation is trying to grow. Walking on the South Downs in the autumn and winter can be just as enjoyable as in the high season and eases the burden on the land during the busy summer months. The quieter season also gives the walker a greater chance of a peaceful walk away from the crowds and there are fewer people competing for accommodation.

Respect all wildlife, plants and trees

If you come across wildlife keep your distance and don't watch for too long. Your presence can cause considerable stress, particularly if the adults are with young or in winter when the weather is harsh and food is scarce.

Young animals are rarely abandoned. If you come across young birds keep away so that their mother can return. Never pick flowers, leave them for others to enjoy too and try to avoid breaking branches off or damaging trees in any way.

The code of the outdoor loo

As more and more people discover the joys of the outdoors, issues like toilet business rapidly gain importance. How many of us have shaken our heads at the sight of toilet paper strewn beside the path or, even worse, someone's dump left in full view? In some parts of the world where visitor pressure is higher than in Britain walkers and climbers are required to pack out their excrement. This could soon be necessary here. Human excrement is not only offensive to our senses but, more importantly, can infect water sources.

MINIMUM IMPACT & OUTDOOR SAFETY

● **Where to go** Wherever possible **use a toilet**. Public toilets are marked on the trail maps in this guide and you will also find facilities in pubs, cafés and camp-sites along the Way.

If you do have to go outdoors choose a site at least **30 metres away from running water** and 200 metres from any high-use areas such as hostels and beaches, or from any sites of historic or archaeological interest. Carry a small trowel and dig a small hole about 15cm (6") deep in which to bury your excrement. It decomposes quicker when in contact with the top layer of soil or leaf mould. Use a stick to stir loose soil into your deposit as well, as this speeds up decomposition even more. Do not squash it under rocks as this slows down the composting process. If you have to use rocks to cover it make sure they are not in contact with your faeces.

● **Toilet paper and tampons** Toilet paper takes a long time to decompose whether buried or not. It is easily dug up by animals and may then blow into water sources or onto the path. The best method for dealing with it is to **pack it out**. Put the used paper inside a paper bag which you then place inside a biodegradable bag. Then simply empty the contents of the paper bag at the next toilet you come across and throw the bag away. You should also pack out **tampons** and **sanitary towels** in a similar way; they take years to decompose and will be dug up and scattered about by animals.

Wild camping

There is very little opportunity for wild camping along the length of the Downs. Most of the land is private farmland and much of this is arable cropland. If the urge to camp away from an organised site is too much to resist always ask the landowner first. If the opportunity for wild camping is there take it. Camping in such an independent way is an altogether more fulfilling experience than camping on a designated site.

Living in the outdoors without any facilities allows the walker to briefly live in a simple and sustainable way in which everyday activities from cooking and eating to personal hygiene suddenly take on greater importance. Remember that by camping off the beaten track you accept added responsibilities. By taking on board the following suggestions for minimising your impact the whole experience of wild camping will be a far more satisfying one.

● **Be discreet** Camp alone or in small groups and spend only one night in each place. Pitch your tent late in the day and move off as early in the morning as you can.

● **Never light a fire** The deep burn caused by camp fires, no matter how small, seriously damages the turf and can take years to recover. Cook on a camp stove instead.

● **Don't use soap or detergent** There is no need to use soap; even biodegradable soaps and detergents pollute streams. You won't be away from a shower for more than a couple of days. Wash up without detergent; use a plastic or metal scourer, or failing that some bracken or grass.

● **Leave no trace** Enjoy the skill of moving on without leaving any sign of having been there. Make a final check of your campsite before heading off; pick up any litter that you or anyone else has left, so leaving the place in a better state than you found it.

ACCESS

The south-east corner of England is the most populated area of the British Isles and is criss-crossed by some of the busiest roads in the country. Thankfully, there are also countless public footpaths and rights of way for the large local population and visitors alike. But what happens if you want to explore some of the local woodland or tramp across a meadow? Most of the land on the South Downs is agricultural land and, unless you are on a right of way, it's off limits. However, the 'Right to Roam' legislation (see below) has opened up some previously restricted land to walkers.

Rights of way
As a designated National Trail (see box p58) the South Downs Way is a public right of way – this is either a footpath, a bridleway or a byway; the South Downs Way is made up of all three.

Rights of way are theoretically established because the owner has dedicated them to public use. However, very few rights of way are formally dedicated in this way. If the public has been using a path without interference for 20 years or more the law assumes the owner has intended to dedicate it as a right of way. If a path has been unused for 20 years it does not cease to exist; the guiding principle is 'once a highway, always a highway'.

On a public right of way you have the right to 'pass and repass along the way' which includes stopping to rest or admire the view or to consume refreshments. You can also take with you a 'natural accompaniment' which includes a dog but obviously could also be a horse on bridleways and byways. All 'natural accompaniments' must be kept under close control.

Farmers and land managers must ensure that paths are not blocked by crops or other vegetation, or otherwise obstructed, and the route is identifiable and the surface is restored soon after cultivation. If crops are growing over the path you have every right to walk or ride through them, following the line of the right of way as closely as possible. If you find a path blocked or impassable you should report it to the appropriate highway authority. Highway authorities are responsible for maintaining public rights of way. Along the South Downs Way the highway authorities are Hampshire County Council, East Sussex County Council and West Sussex County Council (see box p59). The councils are also the surveying authority with responsibility for maintaining the official definitive map of public rights of way.

Right to roam
For many years groups such as the **Ramblers** (see box p40) and the **British Mountaineering Council** (⌨ www.thebmc.co.uk) campaigned for new and

wider access legislation. This finally bore fruit in the form of the Countryside & Rights of Way Act of November 2000, colloquially known as the CRoW Act or 'Right to Roam'. It came into full effect on 31 October 2005 and gave access for 'recreation on foot' to mountain, moor, heath, down and registered common land in England and Wales. In essence it allows walkers the freedom to roam responsibly away from footpaths, without being accused of trespass, on about four million acres of open, uncultivated land. The areas of access land open to walkers are shown on new edition OS Explorer maps.

'Right to Roam' does not mean free access to wander over farmland, woodland or private gardens and much of the true chalk grassland of the South Downs has long since been ploughed up. Along with this, most of that which remains is already annexed as national and local nature reserves where access is relatively unrestricted anyway, so the results of the CRoW Act on the South Downs Way might not be quite as liberating as expected.

For those who wish to get off the beaten track and away from the crowds there are plenty of lesser-known rights of way. Follow any of these and you are likely to spend the whole day alone, which is not an easy thing to do in this part of England. However, if you want to leave the path entirely and beat your own trail through the woods and fields always check with local landowners.

Those who do exercise their 'right to roam' should remember that this added freedom comes with the responsibility to respect the immediate environment. This is particularly pertinent on the South Downs where most of the land is worked by farmers and is the home to a variety of wildlife. Always keep this in mind and try to avoid disturbing domestic and wild animals.

The Countryside Code

❏ **The Countryside Code**
● Be safe – plan ahead and follow any signs
● Leave gates and property as you find them
● Protect plants and animals, and take your litter home
● Keep dogs under close control
● Consider other people

The countryside is a fragile place which every visitor should respect. The countryside code seems like common sense but sadly some people still seem to have no understanding of how to treat the land they walk on. Everyone visiting the countryside has a responsibility to minimise the impact of their visit so that other people can enjoy the same peaceful landscapes. It does not take much effort. It really is common sense. Below is an expanded version of the revised Countryside Code, launched in July 2004 under the new logo 'Respect, Protect and Enjoy':

● **Be safe** Walking on the South Downs Way is pretty much hazard free but you're responsible for your own safety so follow the simple guidelines outlined on pp68-70.

● **Leave all gates as you found them** Normally a farmer leaves gates closed to keep livestock in but may sometimes leave them open to allow livestock access to food or water. Leave them as you find them and if there is a sign, follow the instructions.

❏ **Lambing**
Most of the South Downs Way passes through private farmland, some of which is pasture for sheep. Lambing takes place from mid-March to mid-May when dogs should not be taken along the path. Even a dog secured on a lead is liable to disturb a pregnant ewe. If you should see a lamb or ewe that appears to be in distress contact the nearest farmer.

● **Leave livestock, crops and machinery alone** Help farmers by not interfering with their means of livelihood.

● **Take your litter home** 'Pack it in, pack it out'. Litter is not only ugly but can be harmful to wildlife. Small mammals often become trapped in discarded cans and bottles. Many walkers think that orange peel and banana skins do not count as litter. Even biodegradable foodstuffs attract common scavenging species such as crows and gulls to the detriment of less dominant species.

● **Keep your dog under control** Across farmland dogs should be kept on a lead. During lambing time they should not be taken with you at all (see box above).

● **Enjoy the countryside and respect its life and work** Access to the countryside depends on being sensitive to the needs and wishes of those who live and work there. Being courteous and friendly to those you meet will ensure a healthy future for all based on partnership and cooperation.

● **Guard against all risk of fire** Accidental fire is a great fear of farmers and foresters. Never make a campfire and take matches and cigarette butts out with you to dispose of safely.

● **Keep to paths across farmland** Stick to the official path across arable or pasture land. Minimise erosion by not cutting corners or widening the path.

● **Use gates and stiles to cross fences, hedges and walls** The South Downs Way is well supplied with stiles where it crosses field boundaries. On some of the side trips you may find the path less accommodating. If you have to climb over a gate because you can't open it always do so at the hinged end.

● **Help keep all water clean** Leaving litter and going to the toilet near a water source can pollute people's water supplies. See p62 and p63 for more advice.

● **Take special care on country roads** Drivers often go dangerously fast on narrow winding lanes. To be safe, walk facing the oncoming traffic and carry a torch or wear highly visible clothing when it's getting dark.

● **Protect wildlife, plants and trees** Care for and respect all wildlife you come across along the South Downs Way. Don't pick plants, break trees or scare wild animals. If you come across young birds that appear to have been abandoned leave them alone.

● **Make no unnecessary noise** Enjoy the peace and solitude of the outdoors by staying in small groups and acting unobtrusively.

Outdoor safety and health

AVOIDANCE OF HAZARDS

Walking does not come much more hazard-free than on the South Downs; however, these low southern hills should be given as much respect as their loftier counterparts. Good preparation is just as important here as it is on the northern mountains.

The following common-sense advice should ensure that those out for a day walk as well as those embarking on the whole route enjoy a safe walk. Always make sure you have **suitable clothes** to keep you warm and dry, whatever the conditions, as well as a spare change of inner clothes. Every rucksack should have inside it a compass, torch and simple first-aid kit (see p37). A whistle is unlikely to be necessary due to the close proximity of people and villages but it does not hurt to take one anyway. The **emergency signal** is six blasts on the whistle or six flashes with a torch.

Take more **food** than you expect to eat. High-energy snacks such as chocolate, fruit, biscuits and nuts are useful for those last few gruelling miles each day. With the Downs being made of permeable chalk there is a distinct lack of running water so make sure you have at least a one-litre **water bottle** or **pouch** that can be refilled when the opportunity arises.

You need to drink plenty of water when walking; 3-4 litres per day depending on the weather. There are a few drinking water taps placed conveniently along the path. These are marked on the maps in Part 4. If you start to feel tired, lethargic or get a headache it may be that you are not drinking enough. Thirst is not a good indicator of when to drink; stop and have a drink every hour or two. A good indicator of whether you are drinking enough is the colour of your urine – the lighter the better. If you are not needing to urinate much and your urine is dark yellow you may need to increase your fluid intake.

It is a good idea to be aware of where you are throughout the day. **Check your location** on the map regularly. Getting lost on the Downs is unlikely to be a major cause for concern but it can turn a pleasant day's walk into a stressful trudge back in the dark, praying that the pub chef has not gone home. If you do get lost it is unlikely to be long before someone passes by who does know their Bottoms from their Downs.

If you are walking alone you must appreciate and be prepared for the increased risk. It is always a good idea to leave word with somebody about where you are going; you can always ring ahead to book accommodation and let them know you are walking alone and what time you expect to arrive. Don't forget to contact whoever you have left word with to let them know you've arrived safely. Carrying a mobile phone can be useful though you cannot rely on getting good reception.

Be aware that as much of the South Downs Way is on a chalk ridge high above the surrounding countryside, there may be a steep climb down to, and back up from, the adjacent towns and villages.

To ensure you have a safe trip it is well worth following this advice:

● Keep to the path – avoid steep sections of the escarpment and old quarries
● Be aware of the increased possibility of slipping over in wet or icy weather, especially where the chalk is exposed
● Wear strong sturdy boots with good ankle supports and a good grip. In very dry stable weather trainers or sandals are fine
● Be extra vigilant with children
● In an emergency dial ☎ 999.

FOOTCARE

Caring for your feet is vital; you're not going to get far if they are out of action. Wash and dry them properly at the end of the day, change your socks every few days and if it is warm enough take your boots and socks off when you stop for lunch to allow your feet to dry out in the sun.

It is important to 'break in' new boots before embarking on a long walk. Make sure the boots are comfortable and try to avoid getting them wet on the inside. If you feel any 'hot spots' stop immediately and apply a few strips of zinc oxide tape and leave them on until the area is pain free or the tape starts to come off. If you have left it too late and a blister has developed you should surround it with 'moleskin' or any other blister treatment to protect it from abrasion. Popping it can lead to infection. If the skin is broken keep the area clean with antiseptic and cover with a non-adhesive dressing material held in place with tape.

SUNBURN

It can happen, even in England and even on overcast days. The only surefire way to avoid it is to stay wrapped up but that's not really an option. What you must do, therefore, is to smother yourself in sunscreen (with a minimum factor of 15) and apply it regularly throughout the day. Don't forget your lips, nose, the back of your neck and even under the chin to protect you against rays reflected from the ground.

HYPOTHERMIA

Also known as exposure, this occurs when the body can't generate enough heat to maintain its normal temperature, usually as a result of being wet, cold, unprotected from the wind, tired and hungry. The risk of hypothermia while walking on the Downs is extremely small. However, it is worth being aware of the dangers. Hypothermia is easily avoided by wearing suitable clothing, carrying and eating enough food and drink, being aware of the weather conditions and checking the morale of your companions.

Early signs to watch for are feeling cold and tired with involuntary shivering. Find some shelter as soon as possible and warm the victim up with a hot drink and some chocolate or other high-energy food. If possible give them another warm layer of clothing and allow them to rest until feeling better.

If allowed to worsen, strange behaviour, slurring of speech and poor co-ordination will become apparent and the victim can quickly progress into unconsciousness, followed by coma and death. In the unlikely event of a severe case of hypothermia, quickly get the victim out of wind and rain, improvising a shelter if necessary. Rapid restoration of bodily warmth is essential and best achieved by bare-skin contact: someone should get into the same sleeping bag as the patient, both having stripped to their underwear with any spare clothing under or over them to build up heat. Send urgently for help.

HYPERTHERMIA

Hyperthermia occurs when the body generates too much heat, eg heat exhaustion and heatstroke. Not an ailment that you would normally associate with the south of England, heatstroke is a serious problem nonetheless. Symptoms of **heat exhaustion** include thirst, fatigue, giddiness, a rapid pulse, raised body temperature, low urine output and, if not treated, delirium and finally a coma. The best cure is to drink plenty of water.

Heatstroke is another matter altogether, and even more serious. A high body temperature and an absence of sweating are early indications, followed by symptoms similar to hypothermia (see p69) such as a lack of co-ordination and convulsions. Coma and death will follow if treatment is not given instantly. Sponge the victim down, wrap them in wet towels, fan them, and get help immediately.

WEATHER FORECASTS

The South Downs is one of the driest parts of what is a notoriously wet island. However, the weather can still change from blazing sunshine to a stormy wet gale in the space of a day. The wind, in particular, can be surprisingly severe along the top of the Downs. Couple this with rain and a nice walk can turn into a damp battle against the elements. For detailed local weather outlooks online log on to ⌨ www.bbc.co.uk/weather or ⌨ www.metoffice.gov.uk.

DEALING WITH AN ACCIDENT

● Use basic first aid to treat the injury to the best of your ability.
● Try to attract the attention of anybody else who may be in the area. The emergency signal is six blasts on a whistle, or six flashes with a torch.
● If possible leave someone with the casualty while others go to get help. If there are only two people, you have a dilemma. If you decide to get help leave all spare clothing and food with the casualty.
● Telephone ☎ 999 and ask for the emergency services. They will assist in both offshore and onshore incidents. Be sure you know exactly where you are before you call. Report the exact position of the casualty and their condition.

ROUTE GUIDE & MAPS 4

Using this guide

This route guide has been divided according to logical start and stop points. However, these are not intended to be strict daily stages since people walk at different speeds and have different interests. The maps can be used to plan how far to walk each day but note that these are walking times only (see box below).

The **route summaries** describe the trail between significant places and are written as if walking the path from west to east. To enable you to plan your own itinerary **practical information** is presented clearly on the trail maps. This includes walking times for both directions, places to stay, camp and eat, as well as shops where you can buy supplies. Further service **details** are given in the text under the entry for each place.

For **map profiles** see the colour pages at the end of the book. For an overview of this information see itineraries on pp28-34 and the village and town facilities table on pp30-1.

TRAIL MAPS

Scale and walking times   [see map key, p191]
The trail maps are to a scale of 1:20,000 (1cm = 200m; $3^1/8$ inches = one mile). Walking times are given along the side of each map and the arrow shows the direction to which the time refers. Black triangles indicate the points between which the times have been taken. **See note below on walking times**.

The time-bars are a tool and are not there to judge your walking ability. There are so many variables that affect walking speed, from the weather conditions to how many beers you drank the previous evening. After the first hour or two of walking you will see how your speed relates to the timings on the maps.

❏ **Important note – walking times**
Unless otherwise specified, **all times in this book refer only to the time spent walking**. You will need to add 20-30% to allow for rests, photography, checking the map, drinking water etc. When planning the day's hike count on 5-7 hours' actual walking.

Up or down?

The trail is shown as a dashed line. An arrow across the trail indicates the gradient; two arrows show that it's steep. Note that the *arrow points uphill*, the
opposite of what OS maps use on steep roads. A good way to remember our
style is: '**front-pointing** on crampons **up** a steep slope' and 'open arms – Julie
Andrews-style – **spreading out** to unfold the view **down** below'. If, for example, you are walking from A (at 80m) to B (at 200m) and the trail between the
two is short and steep it would be shown thus: A— — — >> — — – B.
Reversed arrow heads indicate downward gradient.

Accommodation

Apart from in large towns where some selection of places has been necessary,
almost every place to stay that is within easy reach of the trail is marked. Details
of each place are given in the accompanying text.

For **B&B-style accommodation** the number and type of rooms is given
after each entry: **S** = single room (one single bed), **T** = twin room (two single
beds), **D** = double room (one double bed), **Tr** = triple room (three single beds
or one double and one single), **F** = family room (usually a double and bunk
beds, or a double and two singles). Thus family rooms can usually also be used
as a double or twin.

Unless otherwise stated rates quoted are **per room** based on two people
sharing a room for a one-night stay; rates are usually discounted for longer
stays. Where a single room (sgl) is available the rate for that is quoted if different from the rate per person. The rate for single occupancy (sgl occ) of a
double/twin may be higher, and the rate for three or more sharing a family
room may be lower. Single room and where relevant single occupancy rates are
also provided. At some places the only option is a room rate; this will be based
on two people sharing. Many places either do not accept single-night bookings
at peak times or they charge extra for them. Most B&Bs don't accept
credit/debit cards but some guesthouses and hotels do.

The text also mentions whether the premises have **wi-fi** (WI-FI); if a **bath** is
available (✍) for at least one room; and whether **dogs** (🐾) are welcome. Most
places will not take more than one dog in a room and also accept them subject
to prior arrangement. Some make an additional charge (usually per night but
occasionally per stay) while others may require a deposit which is refundable if
the dog doesn't make a mess.

GPS waypoints

The numbered GPS waypoints refer to the list on pp183-6.

Other features

Features are marked on the map when pertinent to navigation. In order to avoid
cluttering the maps and making them unusable not all features have been
marked each time they occur.

WINCHESTER   MAP 1, p77

Winchester is a city steeped in history. The area was settled as long ago as 450BC when the nearby **St Catherine's Hill** was inhabited by a Celtic tribe. After the Roman occupation came the Dark Ages of 400-600AD during which time it is believed that **King Arthur** reigned from here. Many romantics today believe the city to be the site of legendary Camelot.

Things brightened up after the Dark Ages when in 871 **King Alfred the Great** (849-899) made the city the capital of Saxon England. He has probably had the greatest influence on the city so it is not

This gravestone beside Winchester Cathedral recommends that you should drink strong beer when hot and so avoid the fate of Thomas Thetcher. 'Small' beer was weak beer.

surprising that a **bronze statue** of him, constructed in 1901, stands in the Broadway. **St Swithun** (see box below) is also inextricably linked with Winchester.

In 1066 **William the Conqueror** arrived in Hastings and made his way to Winchester where he duly took charge and ordered the building of the castle. Soon after, in 1079, work began on the cathedral.

Other famous people who have links with the city include **Winston Churchill** and **Eisenhower** who reviewed their troops at Peninsula Barracks the day before D-Day. Those with more tenuous associations include **John Keats** who was inspired to pen *Ode to Autumn* while wandering around the water meadows here in 1819.

The city has had a long and sometimes turbulent history but it is well worth spending an afternoon or the whole day exploring the compact city's many sights.

What to see and do

Winchester Cathedral (☎ 01962-857200, 🖳 www.winchester-cathedral.org.uk; Mon-Sat 9.30am-5pm, Sun 12.30am-3pm, £6.50) stands elegantly in parkland in the city centre. The spectacular nave is said to be the longest Gothic cathedral nave in the world. The best time to visit the cathedral is during the Sunday morning service when the choir can be heard.

The cathedral has witnessed many a historic event: **Henry III** was baptised here in 1207 and it was also the scene of the marriage of **Mary Tudor** to **Philip of Spain** in 1554. In more recent history it became the final resting place in 1817 of **Jane Austen** (see box p74). Her grave and memorial is in the north aisle of the cathedral.

ROUTE GUIDE AND MAPS

❏ The Legend of St Swithun

St Swithun, once bishop of Winchester, died in 862AD. Before his death he asked to be buried outside the Old Minster and was duly interred in accordance with his wishes. St Swithun, however, had not counted upon the wishes of Bishop Aethelwold who on 15 July 971 decided to extend the Minster. The expansion plans required the temporary opening of St Swithun's grave before he was carefully re-interred within the new Minster's walls. On the day of the re-interment it began to rain and did not stop for forty days. To this day the legend says that if it rains on St Swithun's Day it will rain for the next forty days. Some would say this is not unusual for England in July.

Tours include Cathedral Tours (Mon-Sat hourly between 10am and 3pm), which includes a look at the twelfth-century Winchester Bible; Tower Tours (Jun-Aug Mon-Sat 2.15pm plus Sat 11.30am, Sep-May Sat 11.30am & 2.15pm, Wed 2.15pm; £6) and Crypt Tours (Mon-Sat 10.30am, 12.30pm & 2.30pm).

Even though the cathedral is the centrepiece of the city there are other equally fascinating places such as the remains of **Wolvesey Castle** (Apr-Sep daily 10am-5pm; free), the palace (residence) for the bishops of Winchester until about the 1680s.

On College St, not far from Wolvesey Castle, is the house where **Jane Austen** died. (It's the yellow building next to the college although be aware that this is a private residence so don't peer through the windows).

Also near the cathedral is the **City of Winchester Museum** (☎ 01962-863064, 🖥 www.winchester.gov.uk/museums; Apr-Oct Mon-Sat 10am-5pm, Sun noon-5pm, Nov-Mar Tue-Sat 10am-4pm, Sun noon-4pm, admission free). The museum traces the history of the city from the Romans to the Victorians and most things in between.

Some of the exhibits in Winchester's museums can be viewed online at 🖥 www.winchestermuseumcollections.org.uk.

Next to **Westgate**, one of two city gates, is the **Great Hall** (☎ 01962-846476, 🖥 www3.hants.gov.uk/greathall, Castle Ave; daily 10am-5pm, free but donations of £2 are welcome; tours are available on request), the only surviving part of Winchester Castle. Here, on the west wall, hangs, so legend has it, *the* table around which King Arthur and his Knights of the Round Table sat. Carbon dating has quashed that particular story, however, and

The Round Table in the Great Hall

the table is actually a few hundred years too young to have been used by Arthur, having been constructed around the end of the thirteenth century; but it's still a mightily impressive disc of oak, weighing over a ton and elaborately painted during the time of Henry VIII with a beautiful Tudor rose. The Great Hall is also famous for the trial of **Sir Walter Raleigh** for treason in 1603.

In the heart of the city is **City Mill** (☎ 01962-870057, 🖥 www.nationaltrust.org.uk/winchestercitymill; Feb half term to end of Nov, daily 10am-5pm; Dec 10.30am-4pm, other times Fri-Mon 11am-4pm, closed 23-31 Dec; admission £3.70/£4.10 with gift aid; NT and Wildlife Trust members free), a working water mill

---

❏ Jane Austen
Jane Austen, born near Basingstoke in Hampshire in 1775, is one of the most important English novelists, having written such classics as *Pride and Prejudice*, *Persuasion* and *Northanger Abbey*. In 1816 she began writing *Sanditon* but in the same year she contracted Addison's disease and the novel was never completed. As her condition worsened she moved to a house in Winchester where she spent the last few weeks of her life, dying at the age of 41 on 18 July 1817.

sitting astride the River Itchen. Although there has been a mill on this site for centuries the present building dates from 1743. On most Saturdays and Sundays (11am-4pm) visitors can watch demonstrations of flour milling. Call to check the details if you are interested in seeing this.

It is possible to visit **Winchester College** (☎ 01962-621209, 🖳 www.win chestercollege.co.uk; one-hour tours, Mon, Wed, Fri & Sat 10.45am, noon, 2.15pm & 3.30pm, Tue & Thur 10.45am & noon, Sun 2.15pm & 3.30pm, year-round except Christmas and New Year; admission £6) which was founded in 1382 by William of Wykeham, then Bishop of Winchester, and is said to be the oldest continuously running school in the country. Originally it was home to 70 pupils but it now has more than 700. Amongst the buildings included in the tour are the 14th-century chapel, the College Hall, the 17th-century schoolroom and the medieval cloister.

Services

The **tourist information centre** (TIC; ☎ 01962-840500, 🖳 www.visitwinchester .co.uk; May-Sep Mon-Sat 10am-5pm, Sun & bank holiday Mon 11am-4pm, Oct-Apr Mon-Sat 10am-5pm) is on the ground floor of the Guildhall on High St; they now boast two free internet access terminals for visitors.

Those arriving or leaving by coach will find the main **bus station** opposite the TIC. The **train station** is about five minutes' walk from the city centre on Station Rd (see pp41-6 for details of public transport to and from Winchester).

On the pedestrianised High St there are countless **banks** and **cash machines** while the main **post office** (Mon-Sat 9am-5.30pm) is now housed in the local branch of WH Smith at the top of the High St.

There are several **supermarkets**; the biggest, Sainsbury's, adjoins **Brooks Shopping Centre** on Middle Brook St.

Last-minute hiking equipment (including blister kits) can be found in any of the **outdoor shops**, including Millets and Blacks, which are situated on the High St. **Lloyds Pharmacy** (Mon, Wed-Fri 8.45am-

5.30pm, Tues & Sat 9am-5pm) is near the TIC at 155 High St.

Free **internet access** can be found at the TIC and also inside the Discovery Centre (Mon-Fri 9am-7pm, Sat 9am-5pm, Sun 10am-4pm) on Jewry St.

Where to stay

Being a popular tourist destination, Winchester is blessed with plenty of affordable and not-so-affordable guesthouses and hotels. However, the demand on accommodation throughout the year is such that booking well in advance is strongly recommended to avoid a night on the park bench by the cathedral.

Close to the city centre and offering the chance to stay in a traditional old inn is *Westgate Hotel* (☎ 01962-820222; 6D en suite, 1D/1T shared bathroom; ➡; WI-FI; 🐾) at 2 Romsey Rd. B&B here is from £70 to £85; there is no single occupancy rate.

Slightly further out is *5 Clifton Terrace* (☎ 01962-890053; 1D, T or F/1D, both with private bathroom; ➡; WI-FI) with B&B for £69-79, or £59 if you're on your own.

Cathedral Cottage (☎ 01962-878975, www.cathedralcottagebandb.co.uk; 1D en suite, WI-FI, shower only) at 19 Colebrook St is just a stone's throw from the cathedral with a cosy room from £85 (from £55 for single occupancy) overlooking a pretty cottage garden, in which you can have your English or continental breakfast served if you wish. Occasionally during term time they also have a single room available for £45 – phone for more details.

Nearby at 10 Colebrook Place is the delightful *Wolvesey View* (☎ 01962-852082, www.wintonian.co.uk; 1S/1D/1F; ➡ shared bathroom; WI-FI) where welcoming host John offers B&B from £48-58 for the single, £74-82 for the double and from £88-96 for the family room. The house used to belong to Sir Alec Guinness.

Another good bet is *53a Parchment Street* (☎ 01962-849962; 1D en suite; from £75, or £65 single occupancy), a terraced townhouse on a quiet street yet close to the hubbub of the centre.

Winchester Royal (☎ 01962-840840, 🖳 www.forestdale.com; 10S/33D/28T/3

ROUTE GUIDE AND MAPS

suites, all en suite, ● all but 4-5 rooms have baths; ✂ £7.50; WI-FI £6 for 90 minutes; rates vary but expect to pay £85-160 for a standard double, less if booking more than a week in advance: check website) on St Peter St. This 16th-century townhouse was once a bishop's residence then a convent but now offers luxurious hotel accommodation with four-poster beds in some of the rooms and a walled garden.

Further from the bustling centre are several affordable guesthouses in a Victorian part of town: *5 Compton Road* (☎ 01962-869199, ☐ www.winchesterbed andbreakfast.net; 2D or T, both rooms share a bathroom; ●; WI-FI) with B&B from £60, £45 single occupancy. They serve cereals, fruit and toast for breakfast, will prepare packed lunches (with advance notice) and have drying facilities. Subject to a £15 charge, and a two-night booking, they will pick walkers up from Exton and take them back the next day. There is also long-stay parking available for SDW walkers for around £60 per week.

St Margaret's (☎ 01962-861450, ☐ www.stmargaretsbandb.com; 2S/1D/1T; 2 shared bathrooms, ● both with baths; WI-FI), 3 St Michael's Rd, offering B&B from £65 for two sharing, the singles costing £40 per night.

A few minutes' walk south of here, at 50 Christchurch Rd, is comfortable and popular *Giffard House* (☎ 01962-852628, ☐ www.giffardhotel.co.uk; 4S/2T/7D; all en suite; ● baths in some rooms; WI-FI) with singles from £75, doubles from £95 and twins from £105.

At 75 Kingsgate St is *The Wykeham Arms* (☎ 01962-853834, ☐ wykehamarm swinchester.co.uk/; 2S/10D/2T, all en suite; ● baths in most rooms but not the singles; ✂ £7.50; WI-FI), a cosy inn with quality rooms priced from £115 (£99 single occupancy). It's named after William of Wykeham who founded Winchester College.

Where to eat and drink

There are plenty of places to eat in Winchester from little street cafés to traditional old timber-framed pubs.

There are several cafés on the High St including the upmarket French chain *Maison Blanc* with seating outside.

For quick eats, *Greggs Bakery* (☎ 01962-813580; Mon-Sat 8am-6pm, Sun 9.30am-4.30pm), on the High St, is a good place to go for ideas for packed lunches as is the wonderful **Winchester street market** (☎ 01962-848325) held Wed (9am-3pm), Fri & Sat (9am-5pm) on Middle Brook St; the exact location is dependent on the weather. The farmers' market is also held here on the second and last Sundays of the month.

There's also *West Cornwall Pasty Company* (Mon-Sat 8.10am-6pm, Sun 9.15am-5pm), with pasties starting at just £2.65. On St George's St there are several good places for simple yet filling fare including *Yummy Thai* (☎ 01962-870088) and *Fish & Chips* next door; both are open 11am-10pm daily.

For teas and light lunches the *Forte Tea Rooms & Brasserie* (Mon-Fri 9am-5pm, Sat 9am-5.30pm, plus Sun when the farmers' market is on), 78 Parchment St, is popular, traditional and recommended. They claim that their food is locally sourced and freshly prepared and it certainly tastes as if it is. Another highly-recommended place for teas and light lunches is *Ginger Two for Tea* (☎ 01962-877733; Mon-Fri 7.30am-4pm, Sat 8.30am-6pm & Sun 8.30am-5pm) at 28 St Thomas St. Has a great selection of teas, coffees, tempting cakes, salads, sandwiches and paninis. Smoked salmon with salad is £6.25. It can get very busy, though.

For something Italian you could try *Ask* (☎ 01962-849464; Sun-Thur 11am-10pm, Fri & Sat 11am-11pm) on the High St; they have a large range of pizzas and pasta dishes from £7.45. There's also the *Gourmet Pizza Company* (☎ 01962-842553; Mon-Sat 11am-11pm, Sun 11am-10.30pm) which is consistently recommended.

There are numerous places to eat lining Jewry St. *Buddy's Diner* (5 Jewry St; Mon noon-9pm, Tue-Wed 8.30am-9pm, Thur & Fri 8.30am-10pm, Sat 9am-10pm, Sun 9am-9pm) is an American-themed burger place (burgers from £7.20) that

Winchester MAP 1

Where to stay
- 4 5 Clifton Terrace
- 5 The Westgate Hotel
- 7 Winchester Royal
- 8 53a Parchment Street
- 22 Cathedral Cottage
- 23 Wolvesey View
- 24 5 Compton Rd
- 25 St Margaret's
- 26 The Wykeham Arms

Where to eat and drink
- 1 Gurkha Chef
- 2 Porterhouse Steakhouse
- 3 Brasserie Blanc
- 6 Buddy's Diner
- 9 Forte Tea Rooms & Brasserie
- 10 Yummy Thai
- 11 Fish & Chips
- 12 Ask
- 13 Ginger Two for Tea
- 14 The Old Vine
- 15 West Cornwall Pasty Co
- 16 Gourmet Pizza Company
- 17 The Eclipse Inn
- 18 Greggs Bakery
- 19 Maison Blanc
- 20 Gandhi Indian Restaurant
- 21 The Crown and Anchor
- 26 The Wykeham Arms
- 27 Black Rat

35 – 45 MINS

M3

CATHEDRAL

¼ mile

500 metres

River Itchen

M3 Motorway

Turn left after crossing bridge

Chalk Ridge

Fivefields Rd

East Hill

30 – 40 MINS

CATHEDRAL

Train Station

Clifton Terrace

Great Hall

Westgate

Hyde St

Discovery Centre (Internet)

Jewry St

St George's St

Brooks Shopping Centre

Sainsbury's

Middle Brook St

Lloyds Pharmacy

Bus station

City Mill

High St

WHSmith

The Square

Broadway

Guildhall & TIC

Alfred statue

Wolvesey Castle

City of Winchester Museum

Cathedral

Winchester College

Jane Austen's House

Kingsgate St

Kingsgate

Canon St

Southgate St

St James La

Compton Rd

To Giffard House, 3 mins

ROUTE GUIDE AND MAPS

offers pancake breakfasts as well as cock-tails (£4.75), beers and shakes. Further up Jewry St at No 24 is **Porterhouse Steakhouse** (☎ 01962-810532; Sun-Thur noon-10.30pm, Fri & Sat noon-11pm) with high quality steaks from £19.95.

Spicier food can be found at the **Gandhi Indian Restaurant** (☎ 01962-863940; daily noon-2.30pm & 6pm-mid-night) near the roundabout at the bottom of Broadway; typical tandoori dishes start at £6.95. For more subcontinental fare though with a Himalayan twist there's **Gurkha Chef** (☎ 01962-842843; Mon-Sat noon-2.30pm & 6-11pm, Sun 6-10.30pm), a Nepalese restaurant and takeaway at 17 City Rd.

There are numerous pubs to choose from. Near the TIC is **The Crown and Anchor** (☎ 01962-620849; food Tue-Sat noon-8pm, Sun & Mon noon-4pm), which has no-nonsense dishes such as chicken & chips in a basket for £4.95.

One of the most attractive and historic pubs in the city is at 25 The Square: **The Eclipse Inn** (☎ 01962-865676; food Mon-Fri noon-2.30pm, Sat & Sun noon-3pm) is a tiny whitewashed, timber-framed house which once served as a 16th-century recto-ry and is rumoured to be haunted. They are now just as famous for their Sunday roasts (£9.25) which boast over a dozen different vegetables on the plate!

The Wykeham Arms (see Where to stay: Mon-Sat noon-3pm, Sun noon-3.30pm; daily 6-9.30pm) serves top-class gastro-pub fare (main dishes around £16) using local produce.

In the other direction, on Minster St, **The Old Vine** (☎ 01962-854616; food Mon-Fri noon-2.30pm & 6.30-9.30pm, Sat noon-3pm & 6.30-9.30pm, Sun noon-3pm & 6.30-9pm), another refurbished old pub that offers a traditional ploughman's lunch for £5.95 and more substantial dishes from £11.50.

For some top-notch food that's great value there's a branch of the famous French chef Raymond Blanc's **Brasserie Blanc** (☎ 01962-810870, 🖳 www.brasserieblanc .com; Mon-Fri noon-2.45pm & 5.30-10pm, Sat noon-10.30pm, Sun noon-9pm). The menu changes seasonally and they use local produce; there are set lunches from £10.95 and dinners from £14.

Perhaps the best restaurant in Winchester is the **Black Rat** (☎ 01962 844465, 🖳 www.theblackrat.co.uk; dinner daily 7-9.30pm and lunch 12-2.30pm at weekends) at 88 Chesil St. They were awarded a Michelin star in 2011. Expect to spend around £50 per person for a really memorable dinner.

Moving on

There are regular **trains** to London Waterloo, Southampton and Portsmouth as well as to Reading and along the coast to Brighton. Cross Country run services between Bournemouth and Manchester via Winchester.

From the **bus station** there is a regular National Express **coach** service to Heathrow Airport and London; Megabus's London to Bournemouth and Leeds to Portsmouth (via Birmingham) services also stop in Winchester (see box p43). For Southampton you should take bluestar's No 1 bus while for Petersfield and the villages in between take Stagecoach's No 67; see the public transport map and table, pp44-6.

The route guide

WINCHESTER TO EXTON   MAPS 1-7

These **12 miles (19.5km, 4¼-5¾ hrs)** begin at the cathedral in the centre of Winchester. The route takes you from the cathedral grounds, along the main shopping street, past the statue of King Alfred then down beside the River Itchen. It does not take long for the South Downs Way to leave the city and enter the rolling East Hampshire countryside but first you must cross the M3.

On crossing the bridge spanning the noisy motorway spare a thought for the remains of **Twyford Down**. This once beautiful hill a few miles to the south was, despite vociferous and well-publicised demonstrations, ruthlessly sliced in two as part of a highly controversial road improvement scheme (see box p60).

Once away from the noise of the road the path crosses a field before arriving at **Chilcomb** (see below). The church aside, there's little in the way of shops or services to keep you in Chilcomb so once you have admired the thatched cottages head on up the lane for the gradual but steady ascent to **Cheesefoot Head** (Map 3) where there are great views to the north over the Itchen Valley.

Where the trail crosses the busy A272 you'll need to follow this main road if you're going down to **Cheriton** (40-50 mins, see below).

CHILCOMB   MAP 2, p80
Chilcomb is the first of several beautiful Hampshire villages passed through on the way to Sussex. In fact Chilcomb is one of the older settlements, with a **church** (off the path to the south) that pre-dates Winchester Cathedral.

For accommodation, campers will find pitches from around £12 for a two-person tent at *Morn Hill Camping and Caravan Site* (☎ 01962-869877; mid Mar to end Sep). To get there turn left where the path

hits the junction of lanes just before Chilcomb. Follow the lane up to the busy A31 then follow this road as far as the big roundabout a mile further east.

There's also a B&B, *Complyns* (☎ 01962-861600, 🖳 www.complyns.co.uk; 1D/1T, 🛁 shared bathroom), a seventeenth-century former farmhouse with rooms for £65 or £35-40 single occupancy. They have a boiler house where you can dry clothes and packed lunches are available on request.

CHERITON   MAP 4a, p82
On hot sunny days the locals can be seen paddling in the clear waters of the tiny River Itchen, which bubbles out of the chalk about a mile south of Cheriton and runs straight through the village passing beautiful thatched houses and the village green. The village is some 40 to 50 minutes from the official route of the South Downs

Way so unfortunately, unless you are planning on staying the night here, you are likely to miss Cheriton's quaint charms.

Those who do make the visit should bear in mind that it was not always such a peaceful and charming spot. In 1644, during the English Civil War, the Battle of Cheriton took place just to the east of the village, off Lamborough Lane.   (cont'd on p82)

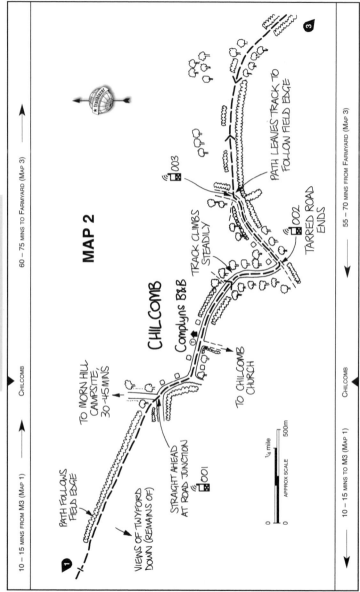

MAP 2

CHILCOMB

Complyns B&B

10 – 15 MINS FROM M3 (MAP 1)   CHILCOMB   60 – 75 MINS TO FARMYARD (MAP 3)

55 – 70 MINS FROM FARMYARD (MAP 3)

10 – 15 MINS TO M3 (MAP 1)   CHILCOMB

PATH FOLLOWS FIELD EDGE

VIEWS OF TWYFORD DOWN (REMAINS OF)

STRAIGHT AHEAD AT ROAD JUNCTION

001

TO MORN HILL CAMPSITE, 30-45 MINS

TO CHILCOMB CHURCH

002
TARRED ROAD ENDS

TRACK CLIMBS STEADILY

003

PATH LEAVES TRACK TO FOLLOW FIELD EDGE

¼ mile
APPROX SCALE
500m

0

0

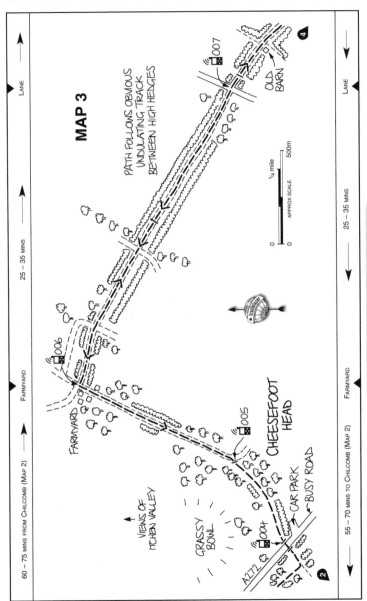

MAP 3

PATH FOLLOWS OBVIOUS UNDULATING TRACK BETWEEN HIGH HEDGES

007

OLD BARN

LANE

25 – 35 MINS

¼ mile

500m

0

0

APPROX SCALE

25 – 35 MINS

LANE

006

FARMYARD

005

CHEESEFOOT HEAD

CAR PARK

BUSY ROAD

004

GRASSY BOWL

A272

VIEWS OF ITCHEN VALLEY

60 – 75 MINS FROM CHILCOMB (MAP 2)

FARMYARD

55 – 70 MINS TO CHILCOMB (MAP 2)

(*cont'd from p79*) The clash between the Parliamentarians and the Royalists resulted in the deaths of 2000 men with the Parliamentarians coming out on top. To this day it is claimed that 'Lamborough Lane ran with the blood of the slain'.

In the centre of the village is a very useful combined **post office**, **shop**, **newsagent** and **off-licence** (☎ 01962-771251; Mon-Sat 7.30am-6pm, Sun 7.30am-1pm) that is open long hours but note that the post office part opens only on Monday (9am-1pm) and Thursday (1.30-4.30pm).

Accommodation-wise, the 14th-century, thatched *Old Kennetts Cottage* (☎ 01962-771863, ✉ dc3pegasus@gmail.com; 1D with private shower; 🐾; WI-FI) has a self-contained part of the house for guests costing £65 for the double.

The charming *Flowerpots Inn* (☎ 01962-771318; 1D/2T all en suite with showers; 🐾; food daily noon-1.45pm & 6-8.45pm, except Sun & Bank hol eves, though these hours can vary depending on demand) on the outskirts of the village has a range of excellent beers; the Flowerpots Bitter is definitely worth a taste though the pub is closed 3-6pm (3-7pm on Sundays). As well as the beer they have a decent bar menu and B&B from £85, or £49 for single occupancy.

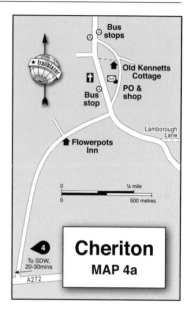

Cheriton
MAP 4a

Stagecoach **bus** No 67 passes through Cheriton on its way between Winchester and Petersfield and stops in the centre of the village, next to the church; see the public transport map and table, pp44-6.

The route continues along leafy country lanes and tracks through a typically English landscape of patchwork fields, hedgerows and pockets of woodland. Along this section is *The Milbury's* (Map 5, p84; ☎ 01962-771248; food daily noon-2pm, Mon-Fri 6.30-9pm, Sat 6-9pm) which makes an ideal lunch stop. A filled baguette and chips is £5.95; steak and kidney pudding costs £12.95. Even if you do not plan on eating here it is still worth dropping in for a drink, though the pub is closed 3-6pm. While you're here you should take a few minutes to admire the 250-year-old **indoor treadmill** and 300ft-deep (92m) well which is lit all the way to the bottom. The pub's name refers to the Mill Barrow, a Bronze Age burial ground just a short distance to the south-east.

The highlight of the day appears rather unexpectedly at the top of **Beacon Hill** (Map 6, p85), a National Nature Reserve and the first real taste of steep downland scenery. The view over the Meon Valley to Old Winchester Hill is a fine reward for the day's effort.

(*cont'd on p87*)

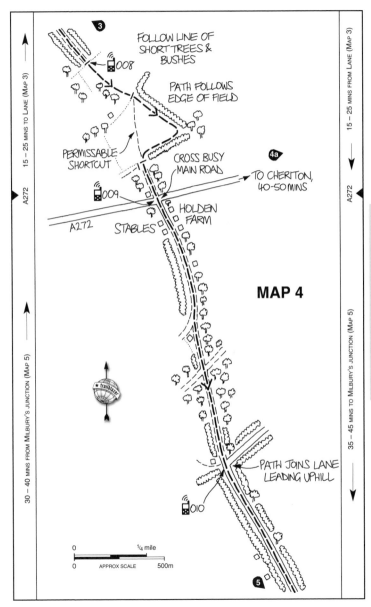

3

FOLLOW LINE OF SHORT TREES & BUSHES

008

PATH FOLLOWS EDGE OF FIELD

PERMISSABLE SHORTCUT

4a

CROSS BUSY MAIN ROAD

TO CHERITON, 40-50 MINS

009

HOLDEN FARM

A272

STABLES

MAP 4

PATH JOINS LANE LEADING UPHILL

010

15 – 25 MINS TO LANE (MAP 3)

A272

30 – 40 MINS FROM MILBURY'S JUNCTION (MAP 5)

15 – 25 MINS FROM LANE (MAP 3)

A272

35 – 45 MINS TO MILBURY'S JUNCTION (MAP 5)

ROUTE GUIDE AND MAPS

trailblazer

0   ¼ mile
0   APPROX SCALE   500m

5

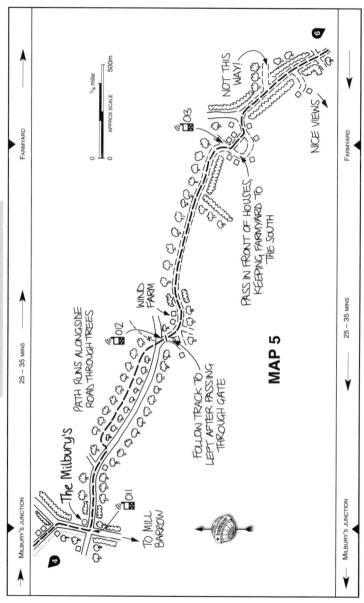

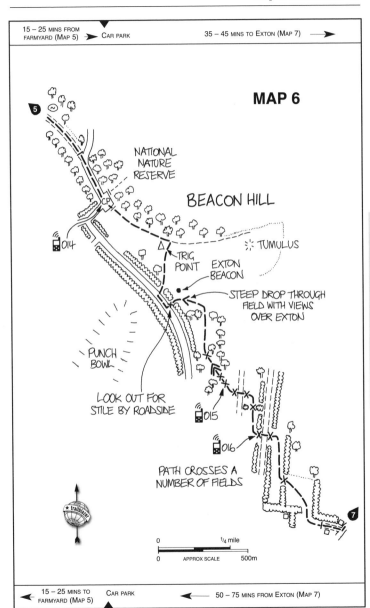

MAP 6

NATIONAL
NATURE
RESERVE

BEACON HILL

CP

☎ 014

△ TRIG
POINT

☀ TUMULUS

EXTON
BEACON

STEEP DROP THROUGH
FIELD WITH VIEWS
OVER EXTON

PUNCH
BOWL

LOOK OUT FOR
STILE BY ROADSIDE

☎ 015

☎ 016

PATH CROSSES A
NUMBER OF FIELDS

5

7

ROUTE GUIDE AND MAPS

★ trailblazer

0   ¼ mile

0   500m
APPROX SCALE

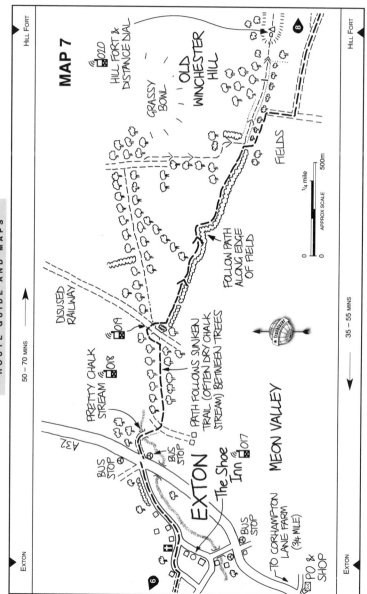

MAP 7

HILL FORT

HILL FORT

EXTON

EXTON

HILL FORT & DISTANCE DIAL

◻020

OLD WINCHESTER HILL

GRASSY BOWL

FIELDS

⑧

FOLLOW PATH ALONG EDGE OF FIELD

DISUSED RAILWAY

◻019

PRETTY CHALK STREAM

◻018

PATH FOLLOWS SUNKEN TRAIL (OFTEN DRY CHALK STREAM) BETWEEN TREES

50 – 70 MINS

35 – 55 MINS

¼ mile

500m

APPROX SCALE

BUS STOP

BUS STOP

A32

EXTON

The Shoe Inn   ◻017

MEON VALLEY

BUS STOP

TO CORHAMPTON LANE FARM (¾ MILE)

PO & SHOP

⑥

(*cont'd from p82*) **Beacon Hill** is one of a number of hills in southern England where beacons or bonfires were lit to warn of invasions, most notably in the 16th century because of the Spanish Armada and more recently in June 2012 as part of the celebrations for the Queen's Diamond Jubilee.

There have been plans to change the course of the South Downs Way across the Meon Valley ongoing for many years; they're unable to go ahead unless rights across some land are granted which is unlikely over the next few years. For now the trail goes through the pretty village of **Exton** – and all the better for it.

EXTON — MAP 7

The Meon valley is known for its natural beauty and also for the Meon villages, all of which claim to be the prettiest in the area. Exton is the smallest of them, if you discount the adjoining hamlets of Meonstoke and Corhampton, and dates back to at least 940AD when it was first mentioned in official documents. It also merited an entry in the Domesday Book of 1086 in which it is described as a hamlet of one church and two mills. Today it's a charming hamlet of attractive old cottages and one rather good public house.

The **Village Store** (Mon-Sat 5.30am-7pm, Sun 7am-4pm) incorporates the **Post Office** (Mon-Fri 9am-5.30pm, Sat 9am-12.30pm) and is 500m along the road towards Corhampton Lane Farmhouse.

Where to stay and eat

A little way from the village, about a mile down Corhampton Lane (off Map 7), is ***Corhampton Lane Farm*** (☎ 01489-878755; 1D/1T, ☛) with **camping** pitches for £5 per camper and B&B for £70, or £45 for single occupancy. The rooms both have private facilities, one with a bath. Campers can use the toilet, simple kitchen and wash basin in the barn. Lifts to and from the village are available by arrangement.

There is only one choice in terms of food but it is a good one: ***The Shoe Inn*** (☎ 01489-877526, 🖳 www.theshoeinn.moonfruit.com/; food Mon-Fri noon-2.15pm & 6-9pm, Sat & Sun noon-3pm & 6-9pm) is a friendly village pub with real ales and real food though it's closed every afternoon (3-6pm) during the week. South Downs lamb's liver and New Forest Bacon with onions is £10.50. The pub's name derives from the building next door which used to be the village cobbler's. There's a nice garden across the road and on hot days they now even open an ice cream parlour here.

EXTON TO BURITON — MAPS 7-12

This fine stretch of the Way covering **12½ miles (20km, 4½-6 hrs)** takes the walker beside **Old Winchester Hill** (Map 7, opposite), a typical downland hill of chalk grassland and steep ancient woodland and a National Nature Reserve. The top of the hill boasts one of the finest Iron Age hill-fort sites in the south. The old earthworks clearly mark the outline of the fort and a display board has an artist's impression of how it once would have looked when the earthy banks were lined with the wooden stakes that formed the walls of the fort.

It is clear why it was positioned here since the views in all directions are spectacular, stretching as far as the Isle of Wight on a clear day. However, presumably the soldiers of the time appreciated the views for the strategic advantage it gave them and not just because they were so magnificent. After descending off Old Winchester Hill there is the option of a short and highly recommended detour into **East Meon**.

However, right on the SDW, shortly before the turn-off to East Meon, is *Meon Springs* (Map 8; ☎ 01730-823134, 🖥 www.meonsprings.com), a fly-fishing base where you can pick up refreshments (they have a licensed bar) and bike spares, fill up your water bottles and **camp** (£6.50 per person) if you have a tent. The site has a toilet and washing facilities.

EAST MEON   MAP 8a

East Meon is only a half-hour detour from the official path and is well worth the effort for a lunch stop or overnight stay. There are records of a settlement at East Meon stretching as far back as 400AD and the whole area was once a royal estate belonging to King Alfred. Anyone visiting the village should take a look at the 900-year-old **church** at the foot of the hill where you can also admire the 14th-century **courthouse** which was once part of a monastery.

The **post office** (Mon-Fri 9am-5pm, Sat 9am-noon) and **East Meon Stores** (Mon-Fri 7am-6pm, Sat 7am-5pm, Sun 8am-1pm) are on the High St. The Stores are surprisingly well stocked and also sell a good range of postcards of the surrounding area.

Stagecoach **bus** No 67 wends its way through the village on its way between Winchester and Petersfield; see the public transport map and table, pp44-6.

Where to stay and eat

In the centre of the village, *Ye Olde George Inn* (☎ 01730-823481, 🖥 www.yeoldegeorgeinn.net; 3D/2T, all en suite; 🐾; �; WI-FI; food Mon-Sat noon-2.30pm & 6.30-9.30pm, Sun noon-3pm: book ahead at weekends) has B&B from £90, or £55 for single occupancy. This is the posher of the two pubs; it also has an à la carte restaurant.

Long House (☎ 01730-823239; 1D/1T; 🐾; �; WI-FI) lies just round the corner from the end of Frogmore Lane, about a mile from the village on the road to Ramsdean. B&B in this friendly establishment with the world's most powerful shower is from £75, or £40 for single occupancy. Booking is essential and packed lunches are available by prior arrangement.

The Izaak Walton (☎ 01730-823252; food Tue-Sat noon-2pm & 6.30-9pm, Sun roast noon-7.15pm), a freehouse pub named after the famous local angler, serves good local cuisine in its restaurant section.

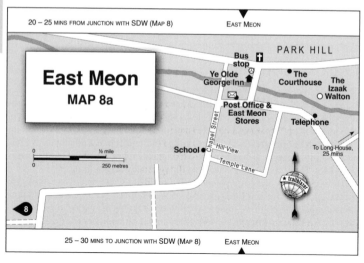

ROUTE GUIDE AND MAPS

20 – 25 MINS FROM JUNCTION WITH SDW (MAP 8)   EAST MEON

East Meon
MAP 8a

PARK HILL

Bus stop
Ye Olde George Inn
☒ Post Office & East Meon Stores
Chapel Street
Hill-View
School ●
Temple Lane

The Courthouse ●
The Izaak O Walton
Telephone

To Long House, 25 mins

★ trailblazer

0   ½ mile
0   250 metres

8

25 – 30 MINS TO JUNCTION WITH SDW (MAP 8)   EAST MEON

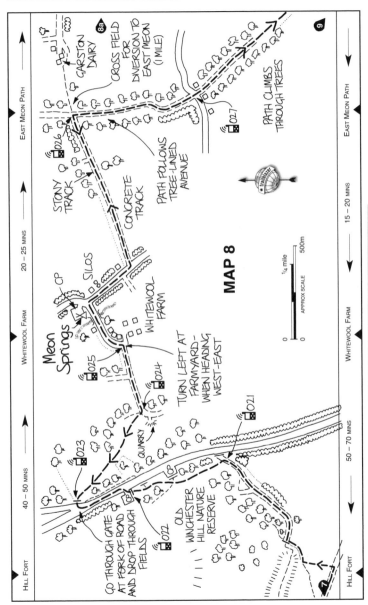

GARSTON DAIRY

CROSS FIELD FOR DIVERSION TO EAST MEON (1 MILE)

8a

9

EAST MEON PATH

026

PATH FOLLOWS TREE-LINED AVENUE

STONY TRACK

CONCRETE TRACK

027

PATH CLIMBS THROUGH TREES

EAST MEON PATH

20 – 25 MINS

CP

SILOS

WHITEWOOL FARM

MAP 8

¼ mile

500m

0

0

APPROX SCALE

15 – 20 MINS

WHITEWOOL FARM

Meon Springs

025

024

TURN LEFT AT FARMYARD – WHEN HEADING WEST–EAST

021

023

QUARRY

50 – 70 MINS

40 – 50 MINS

GO THROUGH GATE AT FORK OF ROAD AND DROP THROUGH FIELDS

022

OLD WINCHESTER HILL NATURE RESERVE

7

HILL FORT

HILL FORT

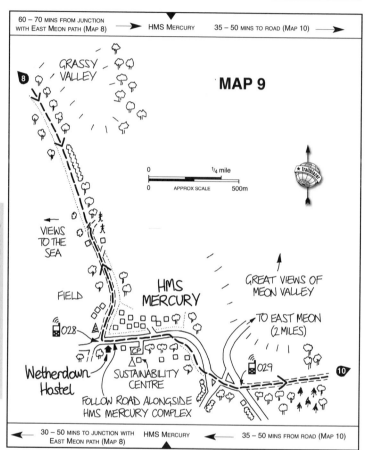

MAP 9

GRASSY VALLEY

8

VIEWS TO THE SEA

GREAT VIEWS OF MEON VALLEY

FIELD

HMS MERCURY

TO EAST MEON (2 MILES)

028

029

10

Wetherdown Hostel

SUSTAINABILITY CENTRE

FOLLOW ROAD ALONGSIDE HMS MERCURY COMPLEX

0 ——— ¼ mile
0 ——— APPROX SCALE ——— 500m

★ trailblazer

❏ **Butser Hill**
Butser Hill (Map 10), on the western side of the A3, is another National Nature Reserve and is managed by Natural England (see p56). It is also the highest point on the South Downs at 270m and is home to over thirty species of butterfly including the tiny, difficult-to-spot but exquisite Chalkhill blue (see opposite p48). As a consequence it is considered one of the most important areas of chalk grassland on the Downs. It was also the original starting point for the South Downs Way before it was decided to extend the path all the way to Winchester.

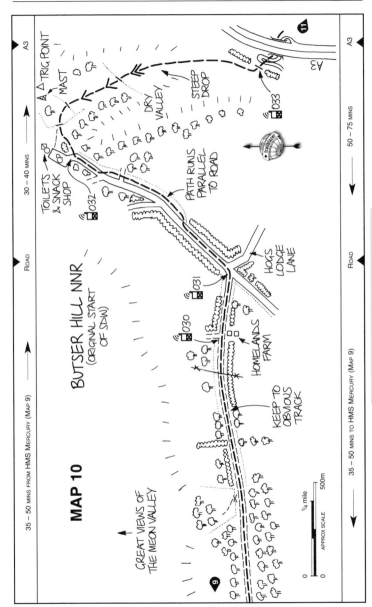

After the turn off to East Meon there is a tough pull up the slope towards **HMS Mercury** (Map 9, p90), a Naval Signal School, situated about two miles past the village. Right on the South Downs Way on the edge of the HMS Mercury complex is a hostel called ***Wetherdown Lodge*** (☎ 01730-823549, 🖥 www.sustainability-centre.org; 39 beds; ☞; 🐾; WI-FI), which is part of the Sustainability Centre. As you'd expect, everything is environmentally friendly and they use renewable energy. They offer B&B for £21.50 per person in shared twin or triple rooms (£28.50 single occupancy) for walkers and anyone else who doesn't arrive by car; and **camping** (£10 per night or £8 for walkers). They also have two tipis (tepees) and three yurts available from £15-25 per person depending on the spec of the yurt. The campsite has showers, running water and compost toilets. Campers may appreciate the fact that they allow camp fires (£8 for firewood and kindling). There's also an on-site *café* (Wed-Sun 10am-4pm) that can provide packed lunches if booked in advance and even evening meals for groups.

It is at the HMS Mercury complex that the true line of the Downs begins, stretching east as a high-level ridge, interrupted only by a few river valleys, all the way to Beachy Head near Eastbourne.

The Way continues along the broad ridge with fine views over the Meon valley to the north culminating in the highest point of the South Downs at Butser Hill (270m). **Butser Hill** (see Map 10, p91) is another National Nature Reserve, earning its status for its fine chalk grassland. The only blot on the landscape here is the car park at the top of the hill and the less-than-attractive A3 dual carriageway that slices through the lower flanks.

Once past the din of racing traffic the path climbs steadily back to the top of the downland escarpment above Buriton, passing through the **Queen Elizabeth Country Park** (Map 11 opposite), a magnificent natural mixed

---

❏ Queen Elizabeth Country Park

The South Downs Way cuts right through the heart of this vast protected area which includes the chalk downland of Butser Hill. To the east of the hill the park is dominated by one of the largest expanses of unbroken woodland cover in the South-East, comprising both ancient broadleaved wood and beech and conifer plantations.

The park (🖥 www3.hants.gov.uk/qecp; open all the time) is popular with daytrippers and picnickers largely thanks to its proximity to the main A3 road. If you prefer to escape the crowds it is worth exploring some of the smaller trails that crisscross the park. The **Visitor Centre** (Map 11; ☎ 023-9259 5040, 🖥 www.hants.gov.uk/countryside/qecp; Mar-Oct daily 10am-5.30pm, Nov-mid Dec & early Jan-Feb daily 10am-4.30pm) can provide maps and guides to the park. The centre houses a **shop** and café offering a selection of cakes and snacks.

Stagecoach's No 37 (Liss to Havant) **bus** stops on the A3. The northbound stop lies just beyond the slip road under the A3 (the slip road needs to be used with care). Access to the park from the stop on the south side is no problem. Either way make sure you let the driver you know you want to stop here and also if you are waiting at the bus stop make sure you can be seen. See the public transport map and table pp44-6 for further details.

woodland that covers the rolling Downs for miles around, just as it has done through the centuries. If the accommodation in **Buriton** (see p94) is booked up you could head into the old market town of **Petersfield** (see p94), where there are several places offering B&B.

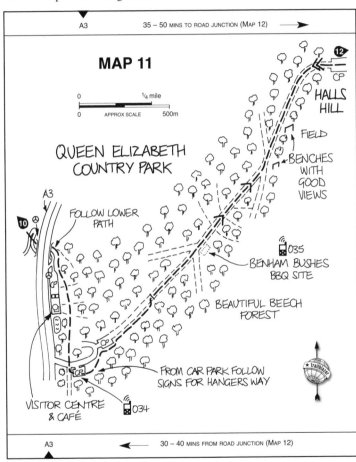

A3   35 – 50 MINS TO ROAD JUNCTION (MAP 12) →

MAP 11

0 ——— ¼ mile
0 ——— APPROX SCALE ——— 500m

QUEEN ELIZABETH
COUNTRY PARK

A3

12

CP

HALLS HILL

FIELD

BENCHES WITH GOOD VIEWS

FOLLOW LOWER PATH

10

035

BENHAM BUSHES BBQ SITE

BEAUTIFUL BEECH FOREST

CP

FROM CAR PARK FOLLOW SIGNS FOR HANGERS WAY

VISITOR CENTRE & CAFÉ

034

A3   ← 30 – 40 MINS FROM ROAD JUNCTION (MAP 12)

ROUTE GUIDE AND MAPS

❏ **Important note – walking times**
Unless otherwise specified, **all times in this book refer only to the time spent walking**. You will need to add 20-30% to allow for rests, photography, checking the map, drinking water etc.

BURITON   MAP 12

Buriton is yet another pretty village commanding an enviable position at the foot of the wooded downland escarpment.

The **Church of St Mary** by the duck pond is of particular interest as the interior dates back to the 12th century.

Countryliner Coaches **bus** No 95 runs between Buriton and Petersfield (see public transport map and table, pp44-6).

Where to stay and eat

In the village there's *The Maple Inn* (formerly the Master Robert Inn; ☎ 01730-267275; 4D/2T all en suite; ✒; 🐾 except in rooms) with B&B from £35 per person (£50 for single occupancy). It also serves traditional pub grub (Mon-Sat noon-2pm & 6.30-8.30pm, Sun roast open approx noon-2.30pm) and the bar is open all day at weekends. However, a better accommodation choice if you can bear the walk is *Nursted Farm* (☎ 01730-264278; 🖳 www.nurstedfarm.co.uk; 1D or F/2T, 2 ensuite and the other with private facilities, ✒), a magnificent old farmhouse about a mile and a half up the lane with B&B from £30 per person. There is plenty of wildlife to spot in the garden and the owner has lived there all his life so he knows a thing or two about the area.

The Five Bells (☎ 01730-263584, 🖳 www.fivebells-buriton.co.uk; food Mon-Sat noon-2pm & 7-9pm, Sun noon-4pm) is a great pub with friendly staff and good food. Opening hours have been extended so it's now open all through the afternoons, too.

PETERSFIELD   MAP 12a, p97

This market town still retains charm, despite attempts to turn it into something bland and modern with supermarkets and a small shopping arcade.

Petersfield Museum (☎ 01730-262601, 🖳 www.petersfieldmuseum.co.uk; Mar-Dec Tue-Sat 10am-4pm; admission free), behind The Square, has old newspaper cuttings, photos and antique maps of the local area.

Tucked down an alley to the right of St Peter's Church in The Square is the **Flora Twort Gallery** (☎ 01730 260756; Mar-Dec Tue-Sat 10am-4pm) which exhibits paintings by Flora Twort as well as historic costumes from the Bedales collection.

An oasis of calm amongst the bustle is afforded by **Petersfield Physic Garden** (open daily, admission free), reached via an alley off the High St. It features many of the characteristics and plant varieties of a 17th century town garden with herbs, topiary and an orchard and plenty of benches to relax on with your takeaway lunch.

Services

The **library** (☎ 0845 6035631; Mon, Tue & Thur 9am-5pm, Wed 9am-7pm, Fri 9.30am-7pm, Sat 9am-1pm), 27 The Square, offers wi-fi and free **internet access** for one hour.

The **Tourist Information Centre** (☎ 01730-268829; Mon-Thur 9am-5pm, Fri 9.30am-5pm, Sat 9am-1pm) is also in the library. The **post office** (Mon-Fri 9am-5.30pm, Sat 9am-12.30pm) is located on the edge of The Square.

On the High St there are various banks with ATMs, as well as a branch of the **camping shop** Millets (Mon-Sat 9am-5.30pm, Sun 10am-4pm), while round the corner is Day-Lewis **Pharmacy** (Mon-Fri 9am-5.30pm, Sat 9am-5pm).

On the High St is a Boots and a small **supermarket**, while just off it is a larger one. There is also a **farmers' market** in The Square on the first Sunday of every month (10am-2pm).

There are regular **trains** from here to both London Waterloo and Portsmouth. National Express's London to Portsmouth No 31 **coach** service terminates here and **buses** leave from the town centre with Countryliner's No 54 (to Chichester) and Nos 91 & 92 (to Midhurst), and Stagecoach's No 67 (to Winchester) being the most useful; see the public transport map and table, pp44-6.

Where to stay

Tucked away behind a high hedge at 4 Heath Rd, pretty little 16th century *Border*

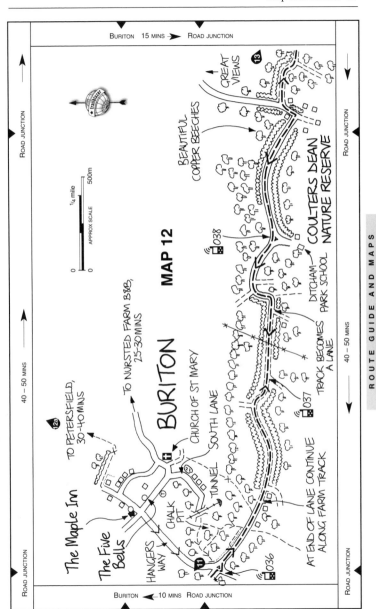

Cottage (☎ 01730-263179, 🖳 www.border cottage.co.uk; 1D or T with en suite shower; WI-FI) offers B&B from £65-75 depending on the breakfast option chosen. Single occupancy is from £50. Just up from there on the left is *15 High Street* (☎ 01730-263925, 🖳 www.number15.net; 1S/1D/1T, all with en suite showers) which offers B&B for £65 (£35 for the single).

At the end of Sheep St, *1 The Spain* (☎ 01730-263261, 🖳 www.1thespain.com; 2D/1T; 🐾; WI-FI; 🐕 by prior arrangement for a small additional charge) is a well-kept 18th-century townhouse with B&B from £70, or £46-50 for single occupancy. One double and the twin have en suite showers, the other double has a private bathroom with bath and shower.

Where to eat and drink

Petersfield is replete with eating places. On The Square, *The George* (☎ 01730-233343, 🖳 www.thegeorgepetersfield.co.uk; food daily 9am-3pm & 6-9pm) has undergone something of a conversion and is now a rather swish bistro and coffee house. Food is served throughout the day and they are stockists for the delicious Pieminister pies (£8.95).

Just off The Square on St Peter's Rd looking onto the church is trendy *Fusionbar-one* (☎ 01730-300870, 🖳 www.fusionbar-one.com; food daily noon-10pm). Relax on a squashy leather sofa while contemplating your personalised Pan-Asian fusion – choose your meat, then select from a range of noodles, curries or stir-fry options to have it cooked with. Mains from £6.

More traditional pub food can be found at *The Square Brewery* (☎ 01730-264291, 🖳 www.thesquarebrewery.com; food Mon, Tue, Thur-Sat 10am-4pm, Wed 6-9pm) serving food during the daytime only except for Wednesday's 2-for-1 steak night.

For cheap eats there's *Nicky's Fish & Chips* (☎ 01730 262188, Mon-Thur 11.30am-2pm & 5-10pm, Fri & Sat 11.30am-2pm & 4.30-10pm) at 15 Sheep St just off The Square. Alternatively head to Lavant St for several other options, including *Seafare Fish and Chip Shop* (☎ 01730-265702; Tue-Sat 11.30am-2pm, Mon-Thur 5-10pm, Fri & Sat 4.30-10pm), the Chinese rivals *Peking* (☎ 01730-233323; Mon-Thur 5-10.30pm, Fri & Sat 5-11.15pm, Sun 5.30-10pm) and the superior *Hong Kong House* (☎ 01730-265256; Tue-Thur & Sun 5-11pm, Fri & Sat noon-2pm & 5pm-midnight).

Going more upmarket, at 23 Lavant St, *Paradise Balti* (☎ 01730-262748 for takeaway, 01730-265162 to book a table, 🖳 www.paradise-restaurant.com; Sun-Thur noon-2.30pm & 5.30-11.30pm, Fri 5.30pm-midnight, Sat noon-2.30pm & 5.30pm-midnight) is a smart Indian restaurant with a takeaway service too.

Heading back towards The Square you'll find the *Spice Lounge* (☎ 01730-303303, 🖳 www.spiceloungepetersfield .co.uk; daily noon-2.30pm & 5.30-11.30pm) which serves a delicious chicken chilli masala for £8.95. Sharing the same building is the local-award-winning *La Piazzetta* (☎ 01730-260006, 🖳 http://lapi-azzetta.moonfruit.com; daily noon-2pm, 5.30-10pm), with pizzas from £6.60.

Other options for Italian food include the chains *Pizza Express* (☎ 01730-710357; Mon-Tue 11.30am-10.30pm, Wed-Sun 11.30am-11pm) on Chapel St or, along the High St, there's *Ask Pizza & Pasta* (☎ 01730-231113; Mon-Thur noon-11pm, Fri & Sat noon-11.30pm, Sun noon-10pm) with a large range of dishes including the vegetarian linguine alla genovese at £8.85.

On Chapel St is *Tai Tong Chinese Restaurant* (☎ 01730-263216; open lunchtimes noon-2pm daily except Mon, eves daily 5.30-11.30pm, Fri & Sat to midnight) with typical Chinese fare to eat-in or take away.

For a more upmarket dining experience, book a table at Michelin-starred chef Jake Watkins' small, swish and exclusive *JSW* (☎ 01730-262030; 🖳 www.jswrestaurant.com; Tue-Sat noon-1.30pm & 7-9.30pm). A two-course set menu which could include sea bass, ox cheek, lamb or guinea fowl costs £22.50 at lunch, £27.50 for dinner (Tue-Thur only), though there is an á la carte menu too. If you really want to

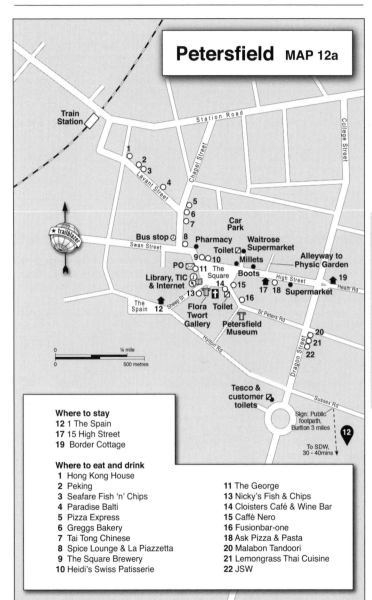

Petersfield MAP 12a

Train Station

Station Road

College Street

Chapel Street

Lavant Street

1
2
3
4

5
6
7

Car Park

Bus stop
Swan Street

Pharmacy
Toilet
8
9
10

Waitrose Supermarket
Millets

Alleyway to Physic Garden

PO
11
The Square

Boots

High Street

19

Library, TIC & Internet

14
15

17 18 Supermarket

Heath Rd

13
16

The Spain
12

Sheep St

Flora Twort Gallery

Toilet

Petersfield Museum

St Peters Rd

Hylton Rd

Dragon Street

20
21
22

0   ¼ mile
0   500 metres

Tesco & customer toilets

Sussex Rd

Sign: Public footpath, Buriton 3 miles

12

To SDW, 30 - 40mins

★ trailblazer

ROUTE GUIDE AND MAPS

Where to stay
12 1 The Spain
17 15 High Street
19 Border Cottage

Where to eat and drink
1 Hong Kong House
2 Peking
3 Seafare Fish 'n' Chips
4 Paradise Balti
5 Pizza Express
6 Greggs Bakery
7 Tai Tong Chinese
8 Spice Lounge & La Piazzetta
9 The Square Brewery
10 Heidi's Swiss Patisserie

11 The George
13 Nicky's Fish & Chips
14 Cloisters Café & Wine Bar
15 Caffè Nero
16 Fusionbar-one
18 Ask Pizza & Pasta
20 Malabon Tandoori
21 Lemongrass Thai Cuisine
22 JSW

splash out their five-course tasting menu is £45 at lunch and £55 in the evening.

In the same vicinity at 16-18 Dragon St is the restaurant-cum-takeaway *Lemongrass Thai Cuisine* (☎ 01730-267077, 🖳 www.lmpetersfield.co.uk; daily noon-2.30pm & 5.30-11pm with dishes such as *ped pad khing* (duck with ginger; £8.95), while next door at No 14 *Malabon Tandoori* (☎ 01730 268352, 🖳 www.mal abonrestaurant.co.uk; daily noon-2.30pm & 6-11.30pm) serves Indian & Bangladeshi meals to eat-in or take away and a vast menu with mains starting from £6.60.

For a relaxing coffee on the town square the Italian-style *Caffè Nero* (☎ 01730-261783; Mon-Sat 7.30am-6pm, Sun 8.30am-5pm) is just the place. They also serve a variety of light lunches. Also on The Square, nestled at the foot of the church, is *Cloisters Café and Wine Bar* (☎ 01730 233006, 🖳 www.cloisterswinebar.co.uk; Mon-Sat 7.30am-6pm, Sun 8am-5pm). Hearty appetites will enjoy fish and chips for £5.95, or for something lighter try their frittata for £4.95.

If you are looking for takeaway lunch ingredients try the popular *Heidi's Swiss Patisserie* (☎ 01730-231889; shop Mon-Sat 8.30am-5pm, coffee lounge to 4pm) next door to The Square Brewery, or for a tasty pasty head for *Gregg's Bakery* (☎ 01730-263450; Mon-Sat 7am-5pm) on Chapel St.

BURITON TO COCKING   MAPS 12-16

The route from Buriton follows tracks and lanes along the top of the South Downs escarpment for **10½ miles (17km, 3¾-4¾ hrs)**. It is very wooded before reaching South Harting (Map 13) so although the views are limited there is plenty of beautiful shady woodland to enjoy.

About ten minutes south of the Way where it crosses the B2146 is **Uppark House**.

❏ **Uppark House**
Uppark House (off Map 13, opposite; ☎ 01730-825857, 🖳 www.nationaltrust.org.uk/uppark; late Mar to late Oct Sun-Thur, gardens open 11.30am-5pm, house 12.30-4.30pm) is a magnificent 17th-century country home perched high on a hill with extensive views across the Downs and beyond. The Georgian interior and gardens can be toured for just £8.80; visiting the garden costs only £4.40.

One of the most remarkable things about Uppark is the near-perfect restoration of the building after it was all but gutted by a rampant fire in 1989.

SOUTH HARTING   MAP 13
From the top of Harting Down the village of South Harting with its distinctive church steeple is clearly visible and looks very inviting.

It's not a long walk to the village from the Way but you do have to climb back up the hill through the woods on the return. This can be a bit of a strain especially if you have been sampling the very fine ales in either of the village's two pubs.

The **Church of St Mary & St Gabriel** is interesting and contains an impressive statue of the Archangel Gabriel, by sculptor Philip Jackson, suspended from the ceiling. The village stocks are still by the path outside the church.

Services
The **post office** (Mon, Tue, Thur & Fri 9am-1pm & 2-5.30pm, Wed 9am-1pm only, Sat 9am-12.30pm) is on The Square and

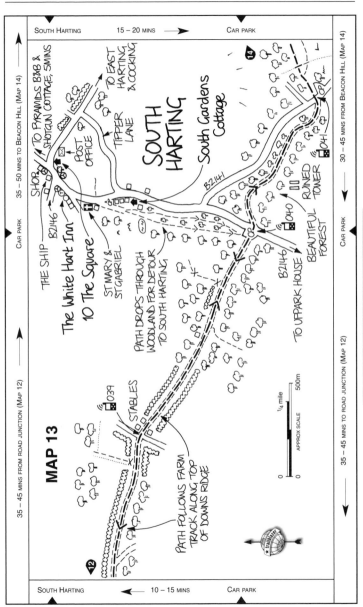

there is an excellent village **shop** (☎ 01730-825219; Mon-Fri 7am-7pm, Sat 7.30am-1pm, Sun 8am-1pm) on North Lane which sells a wide variety of provisions as well as hot pies and pasties, wine and beer. It's owned and run by the villagers.

Countryliner has a couple of useful **bus** services passing through: the No 91 will take you to either Petersfield or Midhurst and their No 54 service runs between Petersfield and Chichester; see the public transport map and table, pp44-6.

Where to stay
The most beautiful B&B in the village is the spectacular old timber-framed, thatched sixteenth-century *South Gardens Cottage* (☎ 01730-825040, 🖳 julia@randjhomes.plus.com; 2D, one en suite and one with a private bathroom; ❤), with a garden that's ablaze with flowers in the summer. B&B is from £40 per person in the en-suite, from £36 per person in the room with private facilities. There's also B&B at *10 The Square* (☎ 01730-825178; 1D en suite ❤ / 1T private bathroom), a small whitewashed cottage in the centre of the village, run by a friendly owner. A bed here costs from £35 per person.

At the other end of South Harting is a very good and architecturally unusual B&B: *Pyramids* (☎ 01730-825398; 1S/1T, both en suite; 🐾; WI-FI). On the right-hand side as you walk up North Lane, it's a modern house that's probably unique in that the ceiling of each room goes up into a pyramid. The tiles on the 'pyramids' are cedar-wood shingle and the views of the Downs from the house, particularly from the single room, are magnificent; the garden is also full of interest. The rate is from £35 per person.

A few minutes further up North Lane, *Shotgun Cottage* (☎ 01730-826878, 🖳 qejoy@hotmail.com; 3D or T/2F; ❤; 🐾; WI-FI) charges from £35 per person; £40

© JANE THOMAS

Visit South Harting church to see Philip Jackson's statue of the Archangel Gabriel

single occupancy. One of the doubles/twins and the family rooms are in a self-contained building so are ideal for groups of up to five people. One of the rooms in the house is en suite, the other has a private bathroom. To reach the cottage turn right into Pays Farm, which, like Pyramids, is on the right.

Further north up North Lane, just over a mile from South Harting, is *The Severals B&B* (☎ 01730-821720, 🖳 www.theseverals.co.uk; 1D or F en suite; WI-FI). The hospitable owners charge £88 (£55 sgl occ) and will collect/return walkers to the SDW.

Where to eat and drink
Unfortunately The Ship has now closed, leaving just the more upmarket *White Hart Inn* (☎ 01730-826708, food Mon-Sat noon-2.30pm & 6.30-9.30pm, Sun noon-8pm).

After South Harting the trees begin to thin out as the Way passes over **Harting Down**. The views open up over the patchwork fields below and the path climbs even higher onto **Beacon Hill** (Map 14).

There then follows another wooded section, the **Monkton Estate**, where it's worth listening out for peacocks before the path continues through the pastureland of **Cocking Down** down to the main road leading to Cocking. There is an interpretation board (see Map 16, p105) in the car park there.

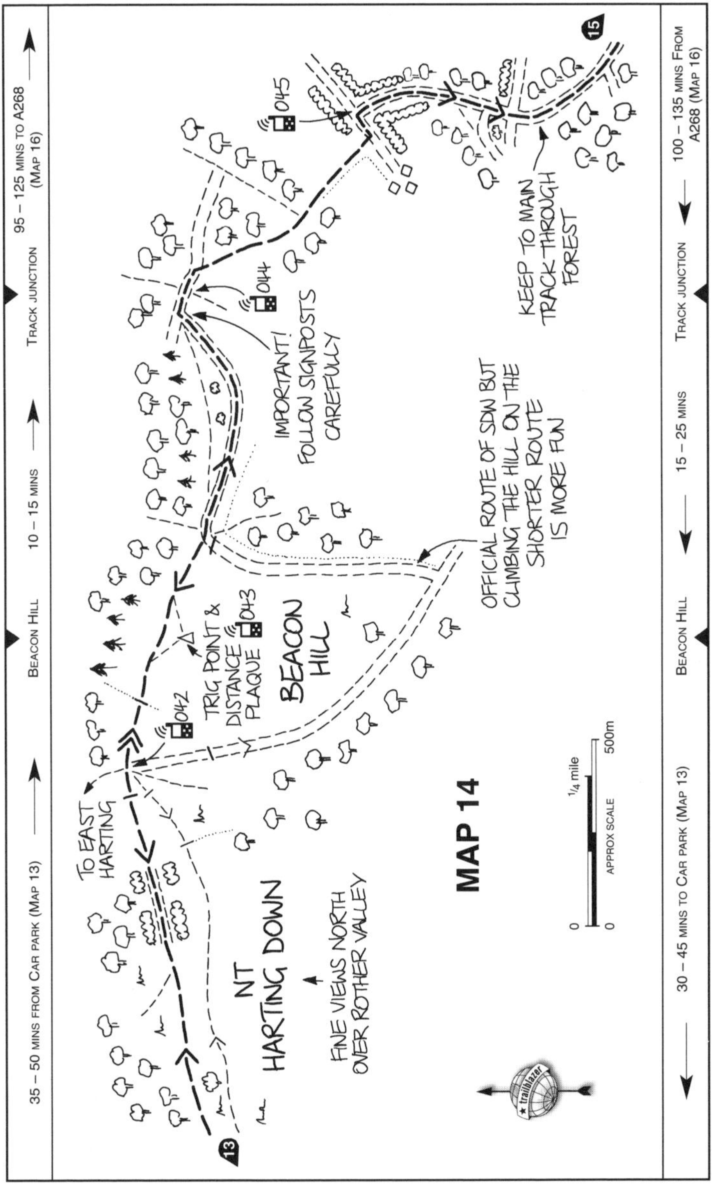

95 – 125 MINS TO A268
(MAP 16)

TRACK JUNCTION

10 – 15 MINS

BEACON HILL

35 – 50 MINS FROM CAR PARK (MAP 13)

☐045

☐044

IMPORTANT!
FOLLOW SIGNPOSTS
CAREFULLY

KEEP TO MAIN
TRACK THROUGH
FOREST

100 – 135 MINS FROM
A268 (MAP 16)

TRACK JUNCTION

15 – 25 MINS

BEACON HILL

30 – 45 MINS TO CAR PARK (MAP 13)

TRIG POINT &
DISTANCE
PLAQUE

△

☐042

☐043

BEACON
HILL

OFFICIAL ROUTE OF SDW BUT
CLIMBING THE HILL ON THE
SHORTER ROUTE IS MORE FUN

TO EAST
HARTING

NT
HARTING DOWN

FINE VIEWS NORTH
OVER ROTHER VALLEY

MAP 14

APPROX SCALE

0   ¼ mile

0   500m

15

13

MIDHURST off MAP 16, p105

If everywhere in Cocking (below) is booked up you can take the bus (see public transport map and table pp44-6) to Midhurst about two to three miles to the north where there is a wider choice of accommodation including the friendly *Pear Tree Cottage* (☎ 01730-817216; 1T/1D/1F, WI-FI) on Lamberts Lane. B&B is from £35-40 per person or from £50 for single occupancy. All the rooms are en suite and self contained and they contain a fridge, microwave and kettle. The owner

leaves the ingredients for a continental breakfast in the room the night before so guests are free to do what they want for their meals.

Failing that try the **tourist information centre** (☎ 01730-812251, 🖳 www. visitmidhurst.com; Mon-Fri 9am-12.30pm, 1.30-5pm) which has moved offices but is still in the same building. Midhurst also has a range of eating places, a Tesco Express, Barclays Bank and other services should you find yourself here.

❏ **Glorious Goodwood – not so glorious for walkers**
Goodwood (🖳 www.goodwood.co.uk), near Singleton, has long been associated with country pursuits such as horse-racing and shooting but is also host to sports such as flying and motor racing. The Festival of Speed, held every July, celebrates the history of motor sport and is one of many events held here around the year. Whilst these are probably not of interest to walkers of the South Downs Way, the relevance is that accommodation in the area is often booked up months in advance so it is probably worth checking the dates for events (see the Goodwood website) before you set off.

COCKING MAP 16, p105

Cocking is pleasant enough but the busy main road that slices the village in two has rather taken the soul out of the place despite one or two pretty old cottages. The consolation is that it is not too far from the Way. It is best reached by ignoring the obvious route down the busy main road and continuing, instead, to the farm buildings ten minutes east of this road and following the farm track north down the hill which ends up by the post office in the village.

Services

The **post office/shop** (☎ 01730-817867, 🖳 www.cockingstores.co.uk; post office Mon-Fri 9am-5pm, Sat 9am-noon; shop Mon-Fri 7am-6.30pm, Sat 7am-4pm, Sun 8am-4pm) is on the corner of the main road with Mill Lane. They sell tea, coffee and sandwiches – which you can eat on one of their benches outside.

The **bus stop** is on the main road and Stagecoach's No 60 passes through regularly on its route between Chichester and Midhurst; see the public transport map p45.

Where to stay, eat and drink

The most convenient place to stay is *Hilltop Cottages* (☎ 01730-814156; 1D/1T; WI-FI), part of Manor Farm, because it is right on the Way; it offers B&B from £30 per person (single occupancy £40), with one bathroom (☛: no shower) shared between the two rooms. Packed lunches (about £3) are available on request. They now have a farm shop (open Fri-Sun 11am-4pm) selling produce from the farm, including their home-made sausages as well as sandwiches, drinks, snacks and ice cream. They also offer basic **camping** at £8 per tent (assuming two in a tent).

If this place is full you will need to go down to the village where there are several places to choose from: *Manor Farm Cottage* (☎ 01730-812784; 1D/1T shared bathroom; ☛; 🐾) is run by the parents of the owners of Hilltop Cottages, a sweet and very helpful couple who will aid you in finding alternative accommodation if they are full (and are thus very useful people to contact during the Goodwood Festival of Speed; see box above). They offer a great

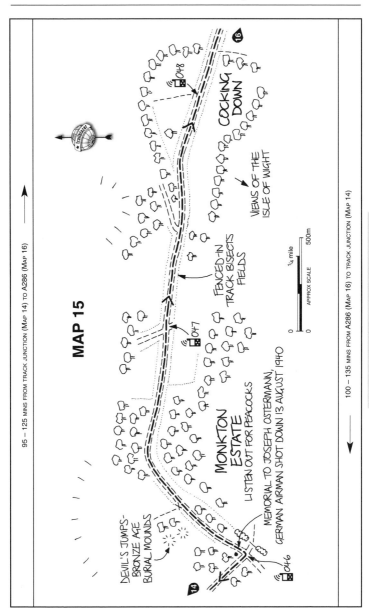

95 – 125 MINS FROM TRACK JUNCTION (MAP 14) TO A286 (MAP 16)

MAP 15

DEVIL'S JUMPS-
BRONZE AGE
BURIAL MOUNDS

MONKTON
ESTATE

LISTEN OUT FOR PEACOCKS

MEMORIAL TO JOSEPH OSTERMANN,
GERMAN AIRMAN SHOT DOWN 13 AUGUST 1940

FENCED-IN
TRACK BISECTS
FIELDS

VIEWS OF THE
ISLE OF WIGHT

COCKING
DOWN

APPROX SCALE

¼ mile

0   500m

100 – 135 MINS FROM A286 (MAP 16) TO TRACK JUNCTION (MAP 14)

breakfast with ingredients sourced, where possible, from the farm. Rates are £30 per person, up to £35 for single occupancy.

There is always a warm welcome for walkers at ***Moonlight Cottage Tea Rooms*** (☎ 01730-813336, 🖳 www.moonlightcottage.co.uk; 1D or T/1T/1D/1S; ☕; 🐕; WI-FI) with B&B from £65, or £50 for single occupancy. The double, twin and single share a bathroom; the other room has en suite facilities. As the name suggests, there is a **tea room** here too: they are open for light lunches and afternoon teas (Mar-Oct, Wed-Sun 10.30am-5.30pm, weekends only in winter). Directly opposite and owned by the same people, the sixteenth-century ***Malthouse*** (see Moonlight Cottage for phone number, 🖳 www.malthousecocking.co.uk; 1T/1D/1F en suite or with private bathroom; ☕; WI-FI) has rooms for £85 (single occupancy £65).

On Bell Lane there's also ***Downsfold*** (☎ 01730-814376, 🖳 www.downsfold.co.uk; 1D/1T, shared bathroom), with B&B from £30, or £39 for single occupancy.

The ***Bluebell Inn*** (☎ 01730-810200, 🖳 www.thebluebell.biz; 1T/1D/2D or F/1F, en suite; WI-FI) has now reopened as a pub-restaurant (Mon-Fri noon-2.30pm & 6-9pm, Sat noon-3pm & 6-9.30pm, Sun noon-3pm & 6-9pm) with five well-appointed en-suite rooms with room prices ranging from £70 to £105.

COCKING TO AMBERLEY — MAPS 16-22

It is **11½ miles (18.5km, 3¾-5¼hrs)** from the Cocking turnoff to the Amberley turnoff. From the main road south of Cocking the Way follows a chalk lane, climbing steadily through fields to rejoin the high escarpment. There is a water tap by the farm buildings (see Map 16). Just after that you will notice that the window frames on the cottages here, including Hilltop Cottages (see p102), are painted yellow; this shows they are part of the Cowdray Estate (see box below).

The track here used to be bordered on one side by dense woodland and on the other by a high hedge so the view was somewhat obscured in parts but the former South Downs Joint Committee and Graffham Down Trust created a wildlife corridor in order to link up two rich grassland sites – Heyshott Down (Map 17) and Graffham Down (Map 18). **Heyshott Down** is one of the nature reserves in this area which is managed by the Murray Downland Trust (see p59) – making it easier for a lot of the flora and fauna here to survive. The best view is probably from the trig point (Map 17), about 50m off the path.

❏ The two Cowdray Gold Cups

The Cowdray Estate is probably best known for the Polo Club and the polo matches (both national and international) held there during the year; the main event is the Gold Cup which is held in July.

The second Gold Cup refers to the colour of the paint seen on the window frames and doors of cottages and buildings that are part of the estate, particularly around Midhurst. The 'cowardy custard' yellow, as some locals call it, was first used on the cottages by the 2nd Viscount Cowdray who was a Liberal MP (yellow being the colour particularly associated with the Liberal Party), thus it was a good way of promoting the Liberal party. The paint was made specially for the Viscount and was originally called Cowdray Gold but is now known as Gold Cup, though it is not exactly the same shade as the original colour.

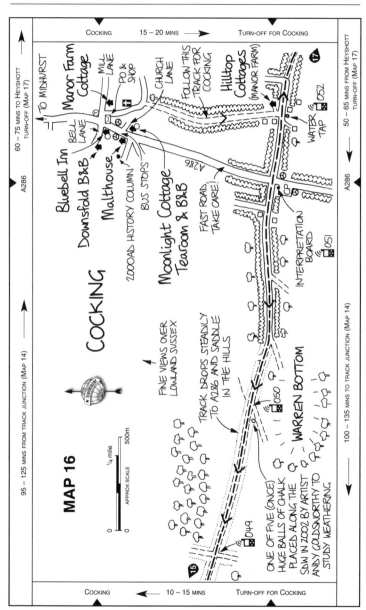

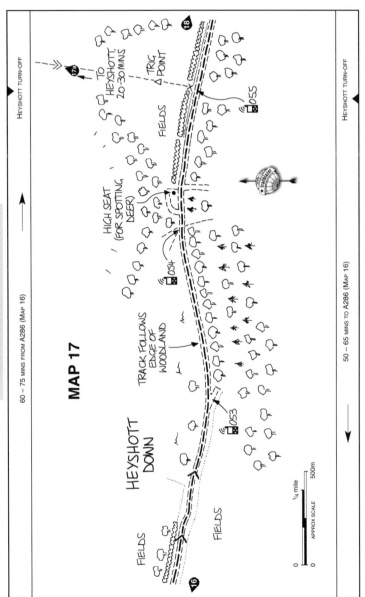

MAP 17

HEYSHOTT TURN-OFF

HEYSHOTT TURN-OFF

60 – 75 MINS FROM A286 (MAP 16)

50 – 65 MINS TO A286 (MAP 16)

HEYSHOTT DOWN

FIELDS

FIELDS

FIELDS

TRACK FOLLOWS EDGE OF WOODLAND

HIGH SEAT (FOR SPOTTING DEER)

TO HEYSHOTT, 20-30 MINS

TRIG POINT

FIELDS

¼ mile

APPROX SCALE

500m

HEYSHOTT   MAP 17a

There's just a pub and a B&B here to justi-
fy the steep and sometimes muddy descent
from the Way. *Little Hoyle* (☎ 01798-
867359, 🖥 www.littlehoyle.co.uk; 1D en
suite; WI-FI) on Hoyle Lane is 1½ miles off
the Way and offers B&B at £75 for the
room, with a reduction for single occupancy. Packed lunches (from £3.50) are available if requested in advance and they have
a drying room.

A little way to the west of the village is
The Unicorn Inn (☎ 01730-813486, 🖥 www
.unicorn-inn-heyshott.co.uk; food Tue-Sat
noon-10pm, Sun noon-4pm, winter Tue-Sat
noon-2pm & 6-9pm, Sun noon-4pm), a smart
country pub with excellent food. Main dishes, which include ale-battered cod with chips
and peas, start from £9.95 but the great views
across the hay meadows to the Downs
escarpment are free. The pub is closed on
Sunday evenings and all day on Mondays.

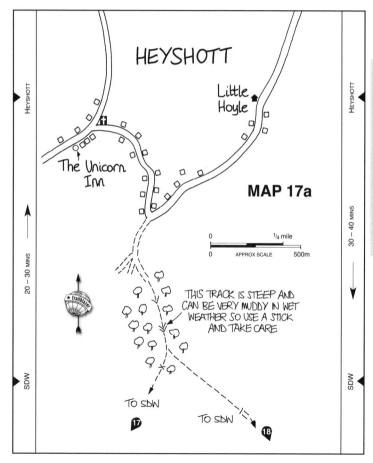

ROUTE GUIDE AND MAPS

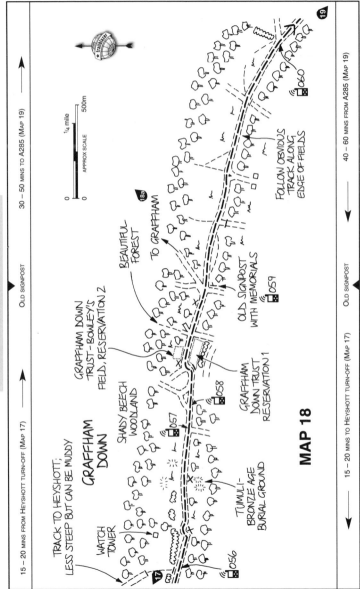

15 – 20 MINS FROM HEYSHOTT TURN-OFF (MAP 17)

OLD SIGNPOST

30 – 50 MINS TO A285 (MAP 19)

15 – 20 MINS TO HEYSHOTT TURN-OFF (MAP 17)

OLD SIGNPOST

40 – 60 MINS FROM A285 (MAP 19)

¼ mile

500m

APPROX SCALE

TRACK TO HEYSHOTT;
LESS STEEP BUT CAN BE MUDDY

WATCH
TOWER

GRAFFHAM
DOWN

SHADY BEECH
WOODLAND

GRAFFHAM DOWN
TRUST - BOWLEY'S
FIELD, RESERVATION 2

BEAUTIFUL
FOREST

TO GRAFFHAM

GRAFFHAM DOWN TRUST
RESERVATION 1

OLD SIGNPOST
WITH MEMORIALS

FOLLOW OBVIOUS
TRACK ALONG
EDGE OF FIELDS

TUMULI-
BRONZE AGE
BURIAL GROUND

MAP 18

056

057

058

059

060

17

18a

19

> ❏ **Tumuli**
> All along the crest of the Downs are numerous burial mounds known as tumuli. These
> are in the region of 4000 to 4500 years old. Some are overgrown or are not particu-
> larly distinct but many are surprisingly well preserved. A glance at an Ordnance
> Survey map of the area will indicate exactly where they are. Next time you stop for
> lunch on that nice grassy hump just remember you may be sitting on the grave of
> someone who has been dead for 4500 years.

The path then continues past a **Bronze Age burial ground** (Map 18) with
tumuli clearly visible among the tussocks of grass. The track continues on
through a mixture of woodland and grassland, passing the turn-off for Graffham.

GRAFFHAM   MAP 18a, p110

There is little to see in Graffham but it has
a lazy, peaceful air about it, being well
away from any major roads.

There's a very well-stocked **shop**
(Mon-Fri 7am-7pm, Sat 8am-5pm) where
you can also get hot drinks and snacks, next
to the village hall. The **post office** is next
door.

B&B can be found on Selham Rd at
Brook Barn (☎ 01798-867356; 1D en
suite; ✿; 🐾; WI-FI) for £75-85, or £55 for
single occupancy. A camp bed can be put
in the room for a third (and indeed fourth)
person. Dogs (and horses!) are welcome,
too.

In the centre of the village, **The
Foresters Arms** (☎ 01798-867202, 🖳 www.
forestersgraffham.co.uk; 3D en suite; 🐾;
WI-FI in main building) has comfortable,
well-equipped rooms and charges £85-99
per room (the exact price depending on
whether it's midweek or a weekend) with
full breakfast included.

Campers should head up the road for
about a mile to the **Graffham Camping &
Caravan Site** (☎ 01798-867476; end Mar-
end Oct) where a pitch is £9.35 per person
in high season.

There are two good pubs serving food:
the first, **The White Horse** (☎ 01798-
867331, 🖳 www.thewhitehorsegraffham
.co.uk/; food Tue-Fri noon-2pm & 6-9pm,
Sat noon-2.30pm & 6-9pm, Sun noon-6pm)
is just outside the village close to the
Downs. It's a friendly place with some
interesting real ales, a quiet garden and
spectacular views onto the hills. It's open
all day at weekends, evening only on
Mondays, and is closed between 3 and 6pm
during the week.

The Foresters Arms (see above; food
Tue-Sat noon-2.30pm & 6.15-9.15pm, Sun
noon-2.30pm & 6.15-8pm) has a lunchtime
and evening menu in their cosy restaurant
area. They serve locally-sourced home-
made food and have a constantly changing
range of dishes to reflect the seasons. They
also have good real ales on tap.

After the Graffham turn-off the Way eventually drops down across pasture
to the A285 main road (Map 19). Compass's No 99 **bus** service calls here if
booked in advance; see public transport map and table, pp44-6.

Climbing back up towards Bignor Hill the views open out spectacularly to
the south. The rather outlandish-looking tent structure visible by the coast is the
Butlins holiday complex at Bognor Regis. Of far greater interest is **Stane St**
(Map 20, p112), the Roman road built around 50AD to connect Noviomagus
(Chichester) with Londinium (London).   *(cont'd on p113)*

ROUTE GUIDE AND MAPS

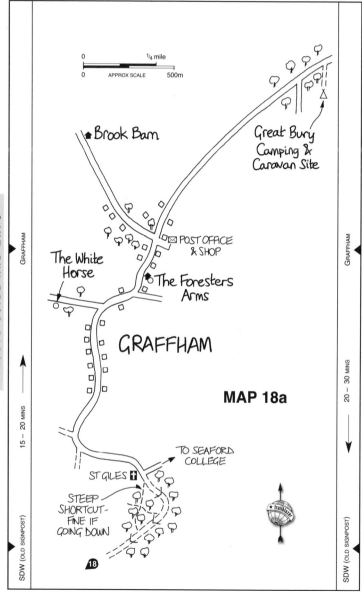

ROUTE GUIDE AND MAPS

GRAFFHAM

GRAFFHAM

15 – 20 MINS

20 – 30 MINS

SDW (OLD SIGNPOST)

SDW (OLD SIGNPOST)

Brook Barn

Great Bury Camping & Caravan Site

POST OFFICE & SHOP

The White Horse

The Foresters Arms

GRAFFHAM

MAP 18a

TO SEAFORD COLLEGE

ST GILES

STEEP SHORTCUT-FINE IF GOING DOWN

18

0   ¼ mile
0   APPROX SCALE   500m

trailblazer

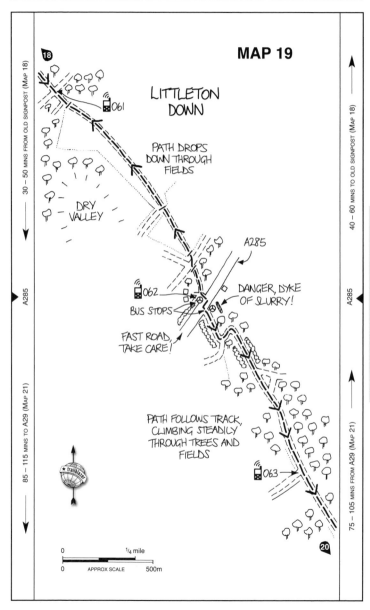

MAP 19

LITTLETON DOWN

18

061

30 – 50 MINS FROM OLD SIGNPOST (MAP 18)

40 – 60 MINS TO OLD SIGNPOST (MAP 18)

PATH DROPS
DOWN THROUGH
FIELDS

DRY
VALLEY

A285

A285

062

DANGER, DYKE
OF SLURRY!

BUS STOPS

FAST ROAD,
TAKE CARE!

PATH FOLLOWS TRACK,
CLIMBING STEADILY
THROUGH TREES AND
FIELDS

063

85 – 115 MINS TO A29 (MAP 21)

75 – 105 MINS FROM A29 (MAP 21)

ROUTE GUIDE AND MAPS

trailblazer

0   ¼ mile

0   APPROX SCALE   500m

20

85 – 115 MINS FROM A285 (MAP 19) TO A29 (MAP 21) →

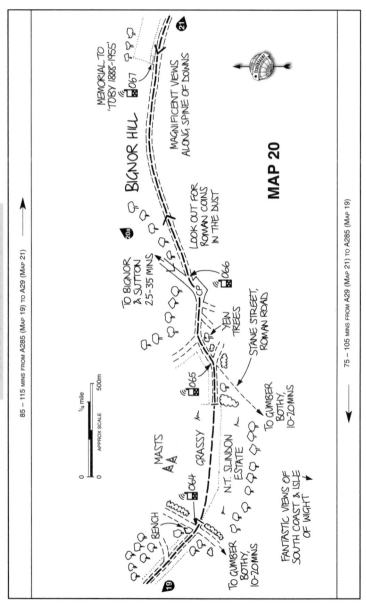

MEMORIAL TO
'TOBY 1888-1955'
067
21
BIGNOR HILL
MAGNIFICENT VIEWS
ALONG SPINE OF DOWNS

MAP 20

LOOK OUT FOR
ROMAN COINS
IN THE DUST
066
20a

TO BIGNOR
& SUTTON
25-35 MINS
CP
YEW TREES
STANE STREET,
ROMAN ROAD
065
TO CUMBER
BOTHY,
10-20 MINS

MASTS
GRASSY
064
N.T. SLINDON
ESTATE

¼ mile
500m
0
APPROX SCALE

BENCH
19
TO CUMBER
BOTHY,
10-20 MINS
FANTASTIC VIEWS OF
SOUTH COAST & ISLE
OF WIGHT

← 75 – 105 MINS FROM A29 (MAP 21) TO A285 (MAP 19)

SUTTON & BIGNOR   MAP 20a

The main reason for dropping off the hills to these twin villages is to see the fabulous mosaics at **Bignor Roman Villa** (see p114) but you can also stay comfortably here and eat well. There's a *teashop* at the villa.

The **church** at Sutton dates from the 11th century; publisher John Murray (1909-95) is buried in the churchyard.

Very close to the Roman Villa is an excellent B&B, *Stane House* (☎ 01798-869454, 🖳 www.stanehouse.co.uk; 2D/1T all en suite or with private facilities; ☕;

WI-FI), with rooms from £75 (£60 sgl occ). A mile further on is *The White Horse Inn* (☎ 01798-869221, 🖳 www.whitehorse-sutton.co.uk; 5D all en suite; ☕; WI-FI); food daily noon-2pm, eves Tue-Sat 6-9pm), a magnificent isolated country pub with B&B (£65-85 for a double, single occupancy £65) and a large restaurant. The food is exquisite: all home cooked and sourced locally, with the bread, sausages and ice cream all made on the premises. Packed lunches on request. The pub is closed between 3pm and 6pm and on Sunday and Monday evenings.

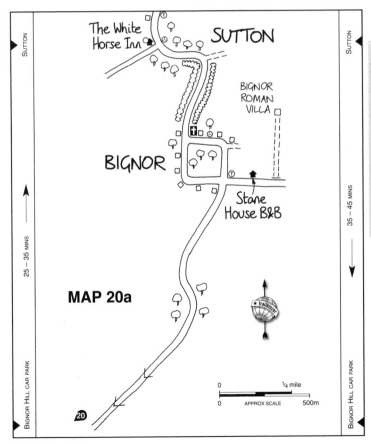

ROUTE GUIDE AND MAPS

Close to Bignor Hill, a mile south of the Way, is the excellent National Trust camping barn **Gumber Bothy** (see Map 20; ☎ 01243-814484; open Mar-Oct) which has simple accommodation for £10. They also allow **camping** here for the same price. Facilities include showers, toilets, a basic kitchen and a pay phone. Booking in advance is preferred and indeed recommended.

The Way follows part of the old Roman road over **Bignor Hill**. Look out for the signpost in Latin in the car park (not actually of Roman origin!) and look out, too, for any Roman coins that may be buried among the flint and chalk. It's well worth going down to **Bignor** (see p113) from here to see the mosaics at **Bignor Roman Villa**.

❏ **Bignor Roman Villa**   **Map 20a, p113**
Just off the old Roman road of Stane Street are the remains of Bignor Roman Villa (☎ 01798-869259, 🖥 www.bignorromanvilla.co.uk; daily Mar-May & Sep-Oct 10am-5pm, June-Aug 10am-6pm; admission £6). It was discovered by a farmer, George Tupper, who was ploughing his field in 1811.

Believed to date from the 3rd century AD, Bignor Villa was one of the biggest in England and probably home to a wealthy farmer considering its enviable position on fertile land close to the main road between Chichester and London. Bignor is most famous for the superb floor mosaics, said to be some of the world's best-preserved examples. Many are in near perfect condition, including a 24-metre length of the 70-metre corridor. This is the longest mosaic on display in Britain.

There's also a **teashop** here (open the same hours as the villa), serving teas and light lunches.

BURY   **MAP 21**
This unassuming village offers accommodation, food and a **post office** (☎ 01798-873351, open Mon, Tue & Thur 2-5pm).
Harkaway (☎ 01798-831843, 🖥 www.harkaway.freeuk.com; 1D en suite, 1S/1T share a bathroom; ●; WI-FI), on Houghton Lane, offers B&B: a room for two sharing costs from £55, or it's £60 in the en-suite double and £28 in a single.

The Squire & Horse Inn (☎ 01798-831343, 🖥 www.squireandhorse.co.uk; food Mon-Sat noon-2pm & 6-9pm, Sun noon-8.30pm), by the main road, is a freehouse with an award-winning chef and a busy restaurant. Main dishes in the restaurant include South Downs lamb for £12.95. The pub is closed Mon-Sat between 3 & 6pm.

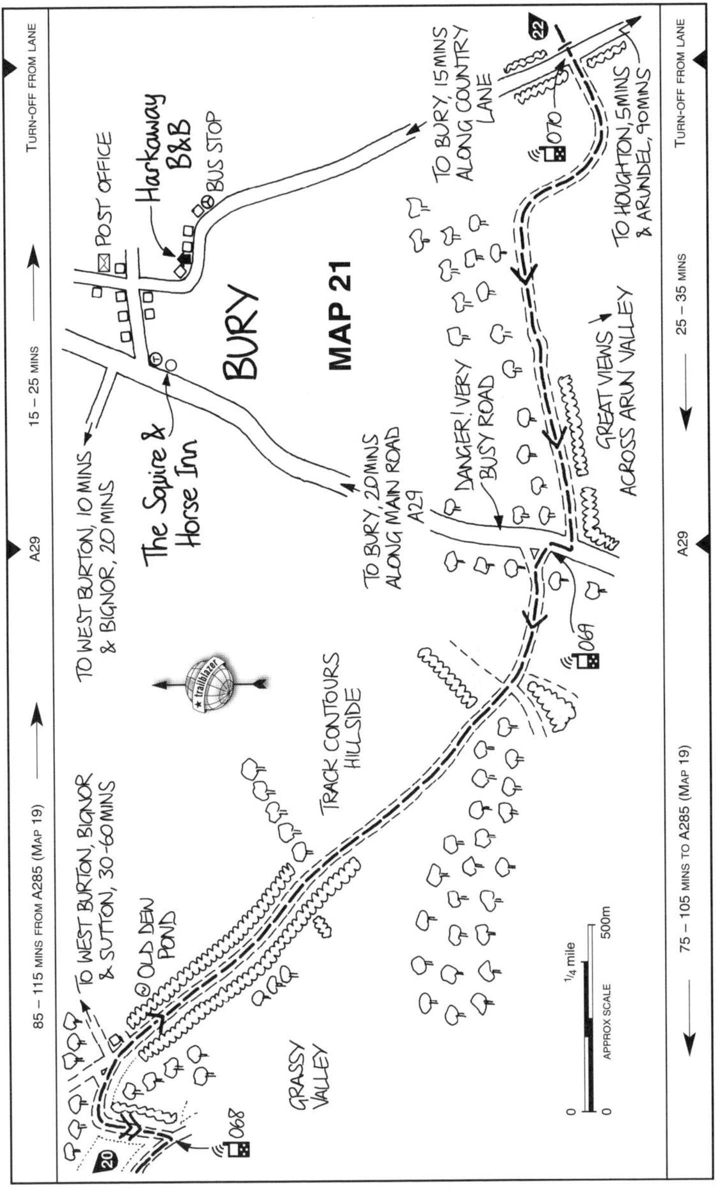

TURN-OFF FROM LANE

15 – 25 MINS

A29

85 – 115 MINS FROM A285 (Map 19)

POST OFFICE

Harkaway B&B

BUS STOP

BURY

MAP 21

The Squire & Horse Inn

TO WEST BURTON, 10 MINS & BIGNOR, 20 MINS

TO WEST BURTON, BIGNOR & SUTTON, 30-60 MINS

TRACK CONTOURS HILLSIDE

OLD DEW POND

GRASSY VALLEY

TO WEST BURTON, BIGNOR & SUTTON, 30-60 MINS

20

068

TO BURY, 20 MINS ALONG MAIN ROAD A29

DANGER! VERY BUSY ROAD

GREAT VIEWS ACROSS ARUN VALLEY

TO BURY, 15 MINS ALONG COUNTRY LANE

22

TO HOUGHTON, 5MINS & ARUNDEL, 9MINS

070

06A

TURN-OFF FROM LANE

25 – 35 MINS

A29

75 – 105 MINS TO A285 (Map 19)

¼ mile

500m

APPROX SCALE

0

0

ROUTE GUIDE AND MAPS

Continuing along the Way, there are sensational views to the east along the length of the Downs.

Follow the route across the main road and down into the Arun valley for the villages of **Houghton Bridge** and **Amberley**. If you have time it is well worth visiting **Arundel** (see p119), about a mile further south along the River Arun. You can reach it by following the riverside footpath but the easier route is to jump on the train at Houghton Bridge.

HOUGHTON BRIDGE   MAP 22

The village of Houghton Bridge can easily be reached from the SDW as the trail almost passes through it. The **train station** (called, a little confusingly, Amberley Station) has regular services to London Victoria and south to Arundel and beyond; see the public transport map and table, pp44-6. There are, however, no useful bus services.

Right by the station you'll find the entrance to **Amberley Working Museum** (☎ 01798-831370, 🖳 www.amberleymuseum.co.uk; open mid Feb to end Oct, Tue-Sun & Bank hols, plus every day during school holidays 10am-5.30pm, last entry 4.30pm; admission £9.30; call for details), situated in an old chalk pit. This extensive museum features a blacksmith's and foundry, as well as workshops producing traditional items such as brooms and walking sticks. The quarry tunnel at Amberley was actually used as a film location in the James Bond film *A View To A Kill* in 1984.

You can get teas and light lunches at *Riverside Café & Bistro* (☎ 07765-790414, 🖳 www.riversidetearooms.co.uk; mid-Mar to Oct daily 10am-5pm, to 6 or 7pm at weekends; Nov to mid-Mar Fri, Sat & Sun only from 10am). This café is especially popular when the weather is good as they have a riverside garden where they serve breakfasts, jacket spuds and cakes amongst other items, all of which are home-made. The premises are licensed.

For B&B, there's *Cherry Tree Cottage* (☎ 01798-831052 or 07814-944110; 1T), right by the railway bridge, with just one room with private bathroom. A stay in this family home costs £35 per person. They have dogs but at the time of writing can't accept visiting dogs.

Just across the road is *The Bridge Inn* (☎ 01798-831619, 🖳 www.bridgeinnamberley.com; lunch Mon-Fri noon-2.30pm, Sat & Sun noon-4pm, eves Mon-Sat 6-9pm, Sun 5.30-8pm). It's relaxed but busy on summer evenings and serves very good food. The chef is from Corfu and there are often delicious Greek specialities on the menu, such as *afelia* (slow-cooked pork stew).

Opposite is *The Boathouse Brasserie* (☎ 01798-831059; Mon-Sat 9am-2pm & 6-9pm, Sun two sittings for lunch: noon & 2pm) does breakfasts, teas and full meals with a three-course lunch or dinner for £21.50, including a roast meats carvery.

AMBERLEY   MAP 22

Perched on a sandstone ridge below the chalk Downs with the wild marshland of **Amberley Brooks** stretching to the north, Amberley claims to be the prettiest village on the Downs and it would be hard to argue otherwise.

The quiet lane leading to the church and castle is lined with thatched cottages; hollyhocks and foxgloves bloom in the small front gardens in the summer months. Unlike other downland villages where local flint is prominent in the architecture, many of Amberley's cottages were built using local sandstone, making the village distinctive.

There are records referring to Amberley dating back to 680AD. The pretty **church** was built by Bishop Luffa between 1091 and 1125. Next to the church is the **castle** (now a hotel, see Where to stay) which used to be the bishop's residence until it was recognised as a castle upon completion of the walls in 1377. More information on the history of the village

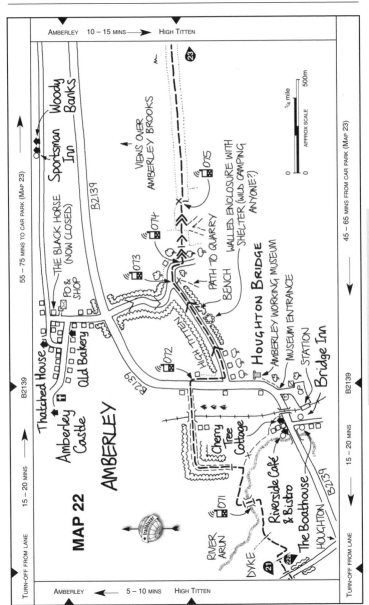

MAP 22

AMBERLEY

Woody Banks

Sportsman Inn

THE BLACK HORSE (NOW CLOSED)

PO & SHOP

B2139

VIEWS OVER AMBERLEY BROOKS

Thatched House

Amberley Castle

Old Bakery

073

074

075

23

B2139

55 – 75 MINS TO CAR PARK (MAP 23)

PATH TO QUARRY

BENCH

WALLED ENCLOSURE WITH SHELTER (WILD CAMPING ANYONE?)

072

HOUGHTON BRIDGE

AMBERLEY WORKING MUSEUM

MUSEUM ENTRANCE

STATION

Bridge Inn

HIGH TITTEN

Cherry Tree Cottage

45 – 65 MINS FROM CAR PARK (MAP 23)

071

Riverside Café & Bistro

The Boathouse

RIVER ARUN

DYKE

21

22

HOUGHTON

B2139

¼ mile

500m

0

0

APPROX SCALE

B2139

B2139

15 – 20 MINS

15 – 20 MINS

TURN-OFF FROM LANE

TURN-OFF FROM LANE

ROUTE GUIDE AND MAPS

Built in the 12th century, Amberley Castle was fortified in 1377 and used by the bishops of Chichester. In 2007 it was converted into a luxury hotel.

and the local area can be found at Amberley Working Museum (see p116).

There is a very good community-run village **shop** (🖳 www.amberleyvillagestores.co.uk; Mon-Sat 7am-5pm, Sun & bank hols 8am-5pm) **and post office** (Mon, Thur & Fri 9am-1pm, Tue 9am-noon).

In term time Compass Travel operate two school **buses**, Nos 601 and 619, that the public are welcome to use: in the morning buses go from Houghton/Amberley to Thakeham/Steyning via Storrington and in the afternoon from Steyning/Thakeham to Houghton via Storrington/Amberley.

Where to stay and eat

The Thatched House (☎ 01798-831329, 🖳 www.thatchedhouseamberley.co.uk; 1D/1F with private bathroom; 🛥) isn't actually thatched but is nonetheless an excellent place to stay. B&B is from £90 per room (£60 sgl occ).

The Old Bakery (☎ 01273-252272, 🖳 www.amberleybedandbreakfast.co.uk; 1D en-suite; 🛥; WI-FI), Church St, gets rave reviews so you'll need to book well ahead to stay here. The accommodation is in a self-contained suite with bathroom and a sitting area and costs £80 (£60 sgl occ). It's also possible to have an extra bed in the suite. Dinner (£20 for three courses) is available if ordered in advance, as are packed lunches (from £5).

Away from the village, about a mile down the lane at Crossgates is *The Sportsman Inn* (☎ 01798-831787, 🖳 www.thesportsmaninn.org.uk; 1T/3D/1F, all en suite; food Mon-Thur noon-2pm & 7-9pm, Fri noon-2pm & 7-9.30pm, Sat noon-2.30pm & 7-9.30pm, Sun noon-2.30pm & 7-9pm), a pleasant place which offers B&B for £80, or £55 for single occupancy. It's a popular pub serving real ales from local breweries. There's a wide choice of pub food but you may need to book in advance at weekends. They also serve cream teas (3-5pm). Next door is *Woody Banks* (☎ 01798-831295, 🖳 www.woodybanks.co.uk; 1D/1T private bathroom) with B&B from £70 (single occupancy £45).

If you're celebrating getting this far and can afford it, there's every luxury at *Amberley Castle* (☎ 01798-831992, 🖳 www.amberleycastle.co.uk; 19D all en suite; 🛥; WI-FI). A double room with a Jacuzzi bathroom will cost from around £315 for a room, though it is always worth enquiring about special offers. There's a grand restaurant (with a dress code) serving a tasting menu for £87.50 or two courses for £55. Afternoon tea is £30.

Unfortunately the quirky and eccentric pub, The Black Horse, has had to close.

❏ **Important note – walking times**
Unless otherwise specified, **all times in this book refer only to the time spent walking**. You will need to add 20-30% to allow for rests, photography, checking the map, drinking water etc. When planning the day's hike count on 5-7 hours' actual walking.

ARUNDEL   MAP 22a, p121

The town of Arundel is about an hour and a half from the South Downs Way via the riverside path from Houghton Bridge or a five-minute train ride from Amberley station. Those who are walking the entire South Downs Way in one trip will find that a visit to this historic town makes an ideal rest day.

Arundel boasts a fine cathedral but it is the perfectly preserved castle with its grand turreted walls that really catches the eye. **Arundel Festival** (🖳 www.arundelfestival.co.uk) is held in the castle in August.

What to see and do

This gothic **cathedral** (🖳 www.arundelcathedral.org) is somewhat upstaged by the immense castle down the road but is still a fine building in its own right. Founded by Henry, the 15th Duke of Norfolk, the cathedral is relatively new, dating back to 1873. A good time to visit is during the annual Corpus Christi festivities in early June when the main aisle of the cathedral is covered in a spectacular carpet of flowers.

The **castle** (☎ 01903-882173, 🖳 www.arundelcastle.org; Easter to early Nov Tue-Sun 10am-5pm, plus Mon during Aug and bank holidays) is the centrepiece of this historical town. Rising grandly from the trees it looms over the Arun Valley and is everything you imagine an English castle to be, complete with imposing walls, turrets and winding stone staircases. Of Norman origin it is now home to the dukes of Norfolk but is open to the public most of the year.

There are four levels of ticket ranging from Bronze (grounds and chapel only £8) to Gold Plus (castle rooms and bedrooms, castle keep, chapel and grounds £17).

The **Arundel Museum** (☎ 01903-882456, 🖳 www.arundelmuseum.org.uk; Easter-Oct daily 11am-3pm, Nov-Easter 11am-3pm subject to both the availability of volunteers and the weather; free admission) is currently housed just off River Rd by the car park. The museum's exhibits focus on local history, archaeology and agriculture. Of particular interest are the fine old photographs portraying local life

through the years. However, only part of their collection is on display as they are in the process of moving to a new location nearby. Contact them for further details and also for information about their guided walks around Arundel or their notes for self-guided walks.

The **Arundel Wildfowl and Wetlands Trust Centre** (☎ 01903-883355, 🖳 www.wwt.org.uk; daily summer 9.30am-5.30pm, rest of year 9.30am-4.30pm; admission £10.90, free for WWT members) is a natural wetland site bordered by ancient woodland and is a perfect diversion for anyone interested in birds. The hides provide opportunities for viewing a variety of warblers and waders as well as the odd buzzard circling above the oak trees.

Services

There's a **tourist information point** (☎ 01903-737838, 🖳 www.sussexbythesea.com; daily 10.30am-3pm) just off River Rd in the museum. For public **internet** access, the **library** (Mon-Wed 1-5pm, Thur-Sat 9am-1pm; £1.25 for 30mins) is at the western end of Tarrant St.

Food supplies can be found at the small **shop**, Martins, near the bridge at the bottom of the High St, while across the bridge is a Co-op (Mon-Sat 7am-10pm, Sun 8am-10pm).

The **post office** (Mon-Fri 9am-5.30pm, Sat to 12.30pm) lies just across the road from Martins, while **Lloyds Pharmacy** (Mon-Fri 8.30am-6pm, Sat 9am-5pm) sits further up the hill on the same street, and there are several **banks** on the same strip. Chocoholics will be pleased to know that Arundel is home to **Castle Chocolates** (☎ 01903-884419; daily 10am-5.30pm), 11 Tarrant St, who claim to produce what is 'probably the finest confectionery, chocolate and fudge in the South of England'. Tuck in.

Arundel is also home to **Pegler's Outdoor Shop and Expedition Advisers** (☎ 01903-883375, 🖳 www.peglers.co.uk; daily 9am-6pm), a local family-run business. They have shops throughout the town, each one specialising in a different aspect of outdoor adventure from canoeing to trekking. The main shops are on the High St and are well worth a visit. However, if you need another pair of walking boots you will need to go to their branch at 69 Tarrant St. There is a vast range of stock and the staff really know what they are talking about.

Those coming to Arundel by **train** from Amberley will find that the **station** is a ten-minute walk from the town centre; other rail services from here are to London, Pulborough and Chichester. One route on Stagecoach's No 700 Coastliner service runs from here to Brighton. Compass Travel's **bus** No 84/85 is the best choice for travel to Chichester; see the public transport map and table, pp44-6. The bus stop is near the bridge.

Where to stay
The cheapest accommodation is at *Arundel Youth Hostel* (☎ 0800-0191700, 🖳 arun del@yha.org.uk; members from £20, breakfast included, 62 beds), which is not far from the train station but a good 15-minute walk from the town centre. In addition to the standard facilities this hostel has a restaurant, internet access and a games room with table tennis, a pool table and bar football.

On the road leading from the town centre to the train station is *Arundel Park Hotel* (☎ 01903-882588, 🖳 www.arundel parkhotel.co.uk; 1S/9D/3T/2F, all en suite; WI-FI); it has plenty of rooms and a laid-back unpretentious style. Prices start at £65 for a double room, from £55 for the single and from £95 for a family room. All rates include breakfast.

In the town centre there are several options but you must book well in advance. *Arundel House* (☎ 01903-882136, 🖳 arun delhousearundel.co.uk; 5D all en suite; WI-FI), near the post office at 11 High St, is an intimate little boutique guesthouse with a brasserie. It's in a good location and a gorgeous place to stay. B&B costs from £75 to £160 for a room; there is a single occupancy rate of £75 Sun-Thur only.

Nearby is the elegant *Swan Hotel* (☎ 01903-882314, 🖳 www.fullershotels.com; 4T/7D/3D or F, all en suite; WI-FI) with prices from £75 for single occupancy, to

£115 depending on the day of the week and the size of the room.

The Town House Hotel (☎ 01903-883847, 🖳 www.thetownhouse.co.uk; 4D, all en suite; 🍽; WI-FI) opposite the castle at the top of the High St (No 65) is a very attractive place with immaculate and stylish rooms equipped with flat-screen TVs. Prices start at around £95 for two sharing. It also has an excellent restaurant (see Where to eat and drink).

On Queen's Lane, a few minutes from the centre, is *Arden Guest House* (☎ 01903-882544, 🖳 www.ardenguesthouse.net; 1S/4D/2T/1T or D; WI-FI in some rooms). Some rooms are en suite but the others share a shower room. B&B costs £65-75 (single occupancy £45-55).

Finally, *Byass House* (☎ 01903-882129, 🖳 www.byasshouse.com; 1D private bathroom/1D, T or F en suite; 🍽; WI-FI) is a beautiful red-brick Georgian townhouse at 59 Maltravers St; B&B is from £80, or £50 for single occupancy.

Where to eat and drink
Arundel is bursting with excellent pubs and restaurants. The best place to start looking is on the High St where you will find decent, filling, cheap snacks at the bottom of the hill in *The Moathouse Café and Restaurant* (☎ 01903-883297; Mon-Sat 8am-5pm, to 3pm on Thur in winter, Sun 9am-5pm) at 9 High St.

If you're looking for the ingredients for a good picnic, *Pallant of Arundel* (☎ 01903-882288; Mon-Sat 9am-6pm, to 5pm in Jan & Feb, Sun 10am-5pm) is the town's deli and specialist grocery store. They will even prepare a picnic hamper for you – at a cost of £45 or £80 for the 'very finest fare'.

Partners Café (☎ 01903 882018; Tue-Fri 8am-4pm, Sat & Sun 8am-4.30pm) 25a High St is particularly recommended for its breakfasts but also does lunches and teas.

Arundel House Brasserie (see Where to stay; Tue-Sat noon-2pm & 6-9.30pm) reopened in 2012 and offers à la carte lunches and dinners with cheaper *prix fixe* mid-week menus – £12.50 for two courses.

On the other side of the road there's a line of eateries starting with *The Red Lion*

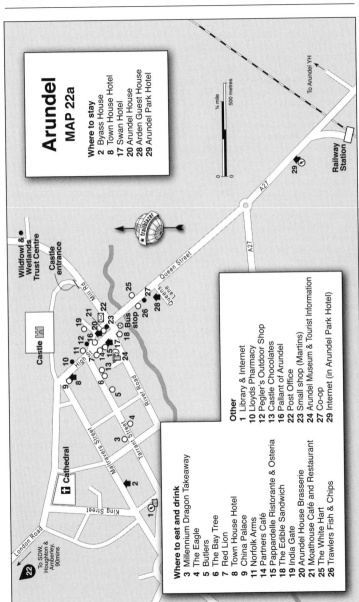

Arundel
MAP 22a

Where to stay

2 Byass House
8 Town House Hotel
17 Swan Hotel
20 Arden Guest House
28 Arundel Guest House
29 Arundel Park Hotel

Where to eat and drink

3 Millennium Dragon Takeaway
4 The Eagle
5 Butlers
6 The Bay Tree
7 Red Lion
8 Town House Hotel
9 China Palace
11 Norfolk Arms
14 Partners Café
15 Pappardelle Ristorante & Osteria
18 The Edible Sandwich
19 India Gate
20 Arundel House Brasserie
21 Moathouse Café and Restaurant
25 The White Hart
26 Trawlers Fish & Chips

Other

1 Library & Internet
10 Lloyds Pharmacy
12 Pegler's Outdoor Shop
13 Castle Chocolates
16 Pallant of Arundel
22 Post Office
23 Small shop (Martins)
24 Arundel Museum & Tourist Information
27 Co-op
29 Internet (in Arundel Park Hotel)

ROUTE GUIDE AND MAPS

(☎ 01903-882214; food daily noon-9pm) at No 45, a large no-nonsense pub with rear garden serving cheap and filling dishes. There's free WI-FI here.

The *White Hart* (☎ 01903-884422; food daily Mon-Sat noon-9pm, Sun noon-4.30pm) serves Harveys beers and has an interesting menu including tapas as well as the usual pub grub.

A short stagger from The Red Lion is *Pappardelle Ristorante & Osteria* (☎ 01903-882025, 🖳 www.pappardelle.co .uk). The informal Osteria downstairs is open daily 8am-11pm and serves drinks and light meals such as antipasto from £3.50 and open sandwiches (£7.50). The traditional Italian Ristorante is open Mon 6.30-10pm, Tue-Sat noon-2pm and 6.30-10pm (to 10.30pm on Sat). The pizzas are excellent.

India Gate (☎ 01903-884224; daily noon-2.30pm & 5.30-11.30pm), just off the High St at 3 Mill Lane, has all the usual curries.

Chinese food can be found at the other end of the High St at No 67: *China Palace* (☎ 01903-883702; daily noon-2.15pm & 6pm-midnight) is a smarter than average Chinese (Cantonese) restaurant.

For sandwiches and pastries for lunch there's the *Edible Sandwich* (☎ 01903-885969; Mon-Fri 5.30am-dark, Sat 7am-dark, Sun 8am-dark) just off River Rd by the big car park.

The best chippy in town is *Trawlers Fish & Chips* (open Mon-Sat 11.45am-9pm, Sun noon-9pm) on Queen St.

Those who want to find out how good English food can be should aim for *The Norfolk Arms* (☎ 01903-882101; food

daily noon-2pm & 7-9pm, shorter hours outside the tourist season), at 22 High St, which has a traditional restaurant serving English dishes.

More top-notch food can be found at the *Town House Hotel* (see Where to stay, food Tue-Sat noon-2pm & 7-9.30pm) which has a smart restaurant where two courses at lunchtime/in the evening will set you back £15.50/23.50 and three courses cost £19.50/29 taken under the fabulous 16th century Florentine carved ceiling.

The Bay Tree (☎ 01903-883679, daily 10.30am-4.30pm & 6.30-9.30pm) at 21 Tarrant St, serves contemporary British food and is consistently recommended. You may need to book for dinner. Nearby at No 25, *Butlers* (☎ 01903-882222; Mon-Sat noon-2.15pm & 7-9pm, Sun noon-2pm) offers two-course lunches for £11.95 Mon-Sat and two-course dinners for £14.95 Mon-Fri. On Sundays their roast lunches are popular.

One of the best pubs in town is *The Eagle* (☎ 01903-882304, 🖳 www.the eaglearundel.co.uk; daily 11am-11pm), on Tarrant St. They serve an excellent array of beers and sometimes have live music at weekends. It's a popular place: locals spill out onto the pavement on warm summer evenings. There's a Cellar Restaurant and they do bar snacks every day at lunchtime and a roast on Sunday. The wild boar sausages are recommended.

After supping the final pint most punters stumble over the road to *The Millennium Dragon Takeaway* (☎ 01903-883017; Mon, Wed, Thur 5-11.30pm, Fri & Sat 5pm-midnight, Sun 5.30-11pm), at 32 Tarrant St.

AMBERLEY TO STEYNING   MAPS 22-27a

The first half of this **10-mile (16km, 3½-5hrs)** stretch is an easy stroll along the high crest of the Downs with great views over the swamp-like **Amberley Wild Brooks** and the Low Weald. The quickest way to Storrington (Map 24) is along the path leading off the Way at GPS Waypoint 079. Alternatively take the road leading off from the Rackham Hill car park.

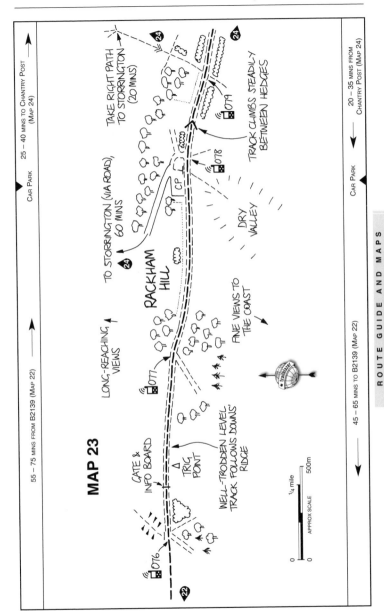

MAP 23

25 – 40 MINS TO CHANTRY POST (MAP 24)

CAR PARK

55 – 75 MINS FROM B2139 (MAP 22)

TAKE RIGHT PATH TO STORRINGTON (20 MINS)

24

24

079

TRACK CLIMBS STEADILY BETWEEN HEDGES

TO STORRINGTON (VIA ROAD), 60 MINS

24

078

CP

DRY VALLEY

RACKHAM HILL

LONG-REACHING VIEWS

077

FINE VIEWS TO THE COAST

GATE & INFO BOARD

TRIG POINT

WELL-TRODDEN LEVEL TRACK FOLLOWS DOWNS' RIDGE

076

22

20 – 35 MINS FROM CHANTRY POST (MAP 24)

CAR PARK

45 – 65 MINS TO B2139 (MAP 22)

¼ mile

500m

APPROX SCALE

0

0

STORRINGTON MAP 24

In comparison to many of the other towns and villages along the Downs the busy little town of Storrington is functional rather than attractive. It is a convenient place for topping up on supplies, getting a bite to eat or for finding a bed for the night but apart from that there is little reason to make the detour.

Services

Storrington has everything you would expect in a prosperous town. The reception at the **library** (☎ 01903-743075; Mon-Fri 9.30am-5.30pm, Sat 10am-4pm) doubles up as the **tourist information point** and they also have **internet** access (£1.25 for 30 mins). The all-important **supermarket** (Mon-Sat 8am-8pm, Sun 10am-4pm) is in a small shopping arcade just off the High St. At the other end of the High St is the **post office** (Mon-Fri 9am-5.30pm, Sat 9am-4pm) and just round the corner at 1 North St is Lloyd's **pharmacy** (Mon, Wed & Fri 9am-6.30pm, Tue & Thur 9am-5.30pm, Sat 9am-5pm). There are also three banks with **ATMs** on the High St.

Compass's **Bus** No 100 travels between Burgess Hill and Pulborough while their No 74 service goes to Horsham; see the public transport map and table, pp44-6.

Where to stay

There is a much wider choice of places to stay in Arundel (see p120) and Steyning (see p130) but if you do find yourself looking for a bed in Storrington the most accessible B&B from the Way is **Ashton House** (☎ 01903-746661, 🖳 www.ashtonhouse .net; 2D/1T, all en suite; ✍; 🐾 in 'certain circumstances'; WI-FI) on the lane leading from the Downs into the town. One of the three rooms is actually a studio with snack-making facilities. B&B in any room starts from £80 for one night, or it's £65 single occupancy; discounts for longer stays.

In the town centre, the 400-year old **White Horse Hotel** (☎ 01903-745831, 🖳 www.whitehorsestorrington.com; 10D/3F, all en suite showers; WI-FI) offers B&B starting from £115 per room, or £99 for single occupancy.

Where to eat and drink

The short High St has several cafés and pubs including **The Anchor Inn** (☎ 01903-742665; food daily noon-9pm), at the eastern end, with jacket spuds from £6.50, and the marginally more attractive **The Moon** (☎ 01903-744773, 🖳 http://themoonpub.com; food Mon-Fri noon-2.30pm & 6-9.30pm, Sat noon-3pm & 6-9.30pm, Sun noon-6pm) where the menu includes a great range of pizzas (£9.95 for small, £13.95 large) and several hearty Mexican dishes including their popular fajitas (£11.95-13.95), plus a Sunday carvery for £9.95.

Using local produce the **White Horse Hotel** (see 'Where to stay'; food Mon-Sat noon-2.30pm & 6-9.30pm, Sun noon-8pm) offers smart food in traditional surroundings, with dinner choices such as lamb tagine finished with fresh coriander and couscous (£12.95).

The best restaurant in town is the 15th-century **Old Forge** (☎ 01903-743402, 🖳 www.oldforge.co.uk; Wed, Thur, Fri & Sun lunch from 12.30pm, last reservation 1.15pm, Thur, Fri & Sat dinner from 7.15pm, last reservation 8.45pm) where the quality of the food justifies the prices. A two-course lunch including a glass of wine costs £15 and a two-course evening meal costs £21.50. It is popular with locals and tourists alike; book in advance. They have also opened a **deli** (Mon-Sat 9.30am-4pm) which serves home-made soups, sandwiches and plenty more besides.

The main rival for fine dining in Storrington sits just across the road: *13 Church Street* (☎ 01903-746964, 🖳 www.thirteenchurchstreet.co.uk; Mon-Sat 11am-3pm & 6-10.30pm) serves freshly prepared Thai specialities such as their take on the classic Pad Thai from £11.50.

For a quick, cheap snack you could try *Truffles Bakery* (☎ 01903-742459; Mon-Fri 8am-5.30pm, Sat 8am-5pm), one of a chain of bakeries, this one sitting next to the supermarket in the small shopping arcade. For something more filling, *Storrington Barracuda* (☎ 01903-742216; Mon-Thur & Sat 11.30am-2pm & 5-10pm, Fri 11.30am-2pm & 4.30-10pm, Sun 5-9pm) is the better of the two chippies in town.

ROUTE GUIDE AND MAPS

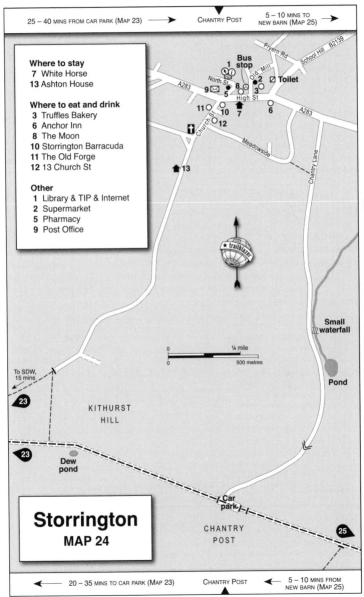

25 – 40 MINS FROM CAR PARK (MAP 23) →   CHANTRY POST   5 – 10 MINS TO NEW BARN (MAP 25) →

Where to stay
7 White Horse
13 Ashton House

Where to eat and drink
3 Truffles Bakery
6 Anchor Inn
8 The Moon
10 Storrington Barracuda
11 The Old Forge
12 13 Church St

Other
1 Library & TIP & Internet
2 Supermarket
5 Pharmacy
9 Post Office

Bus stop

Fryern Rd

School Hill B2139

Old Mill

North St

Toilet

A283

High St

Church St

Meadowside

Chantry Lane

A283

★ trailblazer

Small waterfall

Pond

¼ mile

500 metres

To SDW, 15 mins

KITHURST HILL

Dew pond

Car park

CHANTRY POST

Storrington
MAP 24

ROUTE GUIDE AND MAPS

← 20 – 35 MINS TO CAR PARK (MAP 23)   CHANTRY POST   ← 5 – 10 MINS FROM NEW BARN (MAP 25)

WASHINGTON   MAP 25

Despite the proximity of the busy A24 dual carriageway this village is a peaceful place with most of the traffic noise being absorbed by the trees. There is an alternative South Downs Way path which leads the walker directly into the village.

Next to the **village stores** (Mon-Fri 9am-1pm) you'll find good food in the welcoming, rather civilised *Frankland Arms* (☎ 01903-892220, 🖳 www.franklandarms .co.uk; food Mon-Fri noon-2.30pm & 6-9pm, Sat noon-3pm & 6-9.30pm, Sun noon-4pm). The bar here is open all day and the restaurant serves a wide range of

dishes from bangers & mash (£9.45) to tagliatelle carbonara (£8.95).

North of the village on London Rd, *Washington Caravan & Camping Park* (☎ 01903-892869, 🖳 www.washcamp.con-nectfree.co.uk) charges £6-12 per tent (depending on size of tent) plus £5 per person; dogs are free.

Stagecoach's **bus** No 1 stops here en route between Midhurst and Worthing as does Compass's No 100 (Burgess Hill to Storrington). Metrobus's No 23 (Crawley to Worthing) service also stops here. See public transport map and table, pp44-6.

The A24 dual carriageway (Map 25) is something of a blot on the landscape but it is soon forgotten once the steep climb up Chanctonbury Hill (Map 26) begins.

At the top there are the somewhat storm-ravaged remains of **Chanctonbury Ring**, a beautiful circle of beech trees that was shaken into a ragged mess during the famous storm of October 1987.

The descent for access to the beautiful small town of **Steyning** (Map 27a, p131) is a leisurely one with fine views over Steyning Bowl and down to the coastal towns of Worthing and Lancing.

❏ Chanctonbury Ring   Map 26, p128

This exposed hilltop is one of the great viewpoints of the South Downs but more significantly it is the site of an Iron Age hill-fort believed to date back to the sixth century BC. Today it is equally famous for the copse of beech trees that were planted on the site of the fort by Charles Goring in 1760 and which grew to become one of the most famous landmarks in Sussex. Sadly, the copse was badly damaged by the storm of October 1987 and despite a replanting programme the skyline has not yet recovered its distinctive crown of trees.

© HENRY STEDMAN

Chanctonbury Ring is also known for its folklore, tales of witchcraft, fairies and other mysterious goings-on. Perhaps the most famous story goes that while Satan was digging the nearby Devil's Dyke valley, spadefuls of earth landed here creating the hill you see today. The ring is also said to be haunted. It may be a beauty spot by day but it takes a brave person to spend the night there.

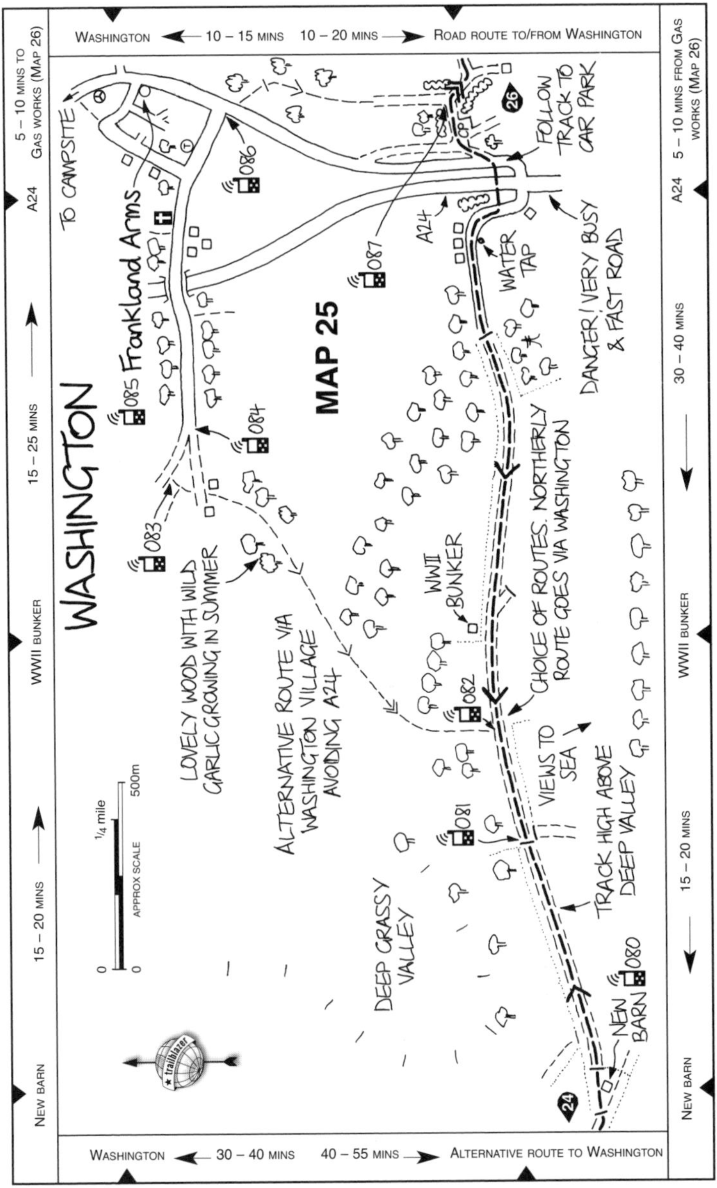

WASHINGTON ← 10 – 15 MINS   10 – 20 MINS → ROAD ROUTE TO/FROM WASHINGTON

5 – 10 MINS TO GAS WORKS (MAP 26)
5 – 10 MINS FROM GAS WORKS (MAP 26)

A24

TO CAMPSITE

085 Frankland Arms

086

087

26

FOLLOW TRACK TO CAR PARK

A24

WATER TAP

DANGER! VERY BUSY & FAST ROAD

WASHINGTON

MAP 25

084

083

15 – 25 MINS

30 – 40 MINS

WWII BUNKER

LOVELY WOOD WITH WILD GARLIC GROWING IN SUMMER

ALTERNATIVE ROUTE VIA WASHINGTON VILLAGE AVOIDING A24

CHOICE OF ROUTES: NORTHERLY ROUTE GOES VIA WASHINGTON

WWII BUNKER

082

¼ mile

500m

APPROX SCALE

0

0

VIEWS TO SEA

15 – 20 MINS

15 – 20 MINS

081

TRACK HIGH ABOVE DEEP VALLEY

DEEP GRASSY VALLEY

trailblazer

NEW BARN 080

NEW BARN

20

NEW BARN

WASHINGTON ← 30 – 40 MINS   40 – 55 MINS → ALTERNATIVE ROUTE TO WASHINGTON

ROUTE GUIDE AND MAPS

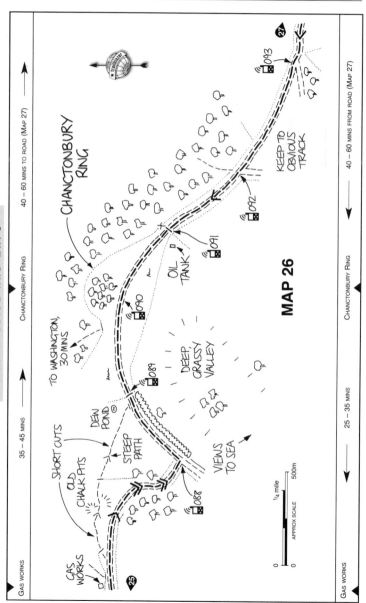

MAP 26

CHANCTONBURY RING

CHANCTONBURY RING

GAS WORKS

GAS WORKS

35 – 45 MINS

40 – 60 MINS TO ROAD (MAP 27)

25 – 35 MINS

40 – 60 MINS FROM ROAD (MAP 27)

TO WASHINGTON, 30MINS

SHORT CUTS

OLD CHALK PITS

DEW POND

STEEP PATH

GAS WORKS

VIEWS TO SEA

DEEP, GRASSY VALLEY

OIL TANK

KEEP TO OBVIOUS TRACK

¼ mile

APPROX SCALE

500m

0

0

088

089

090

091

092

093

25

27

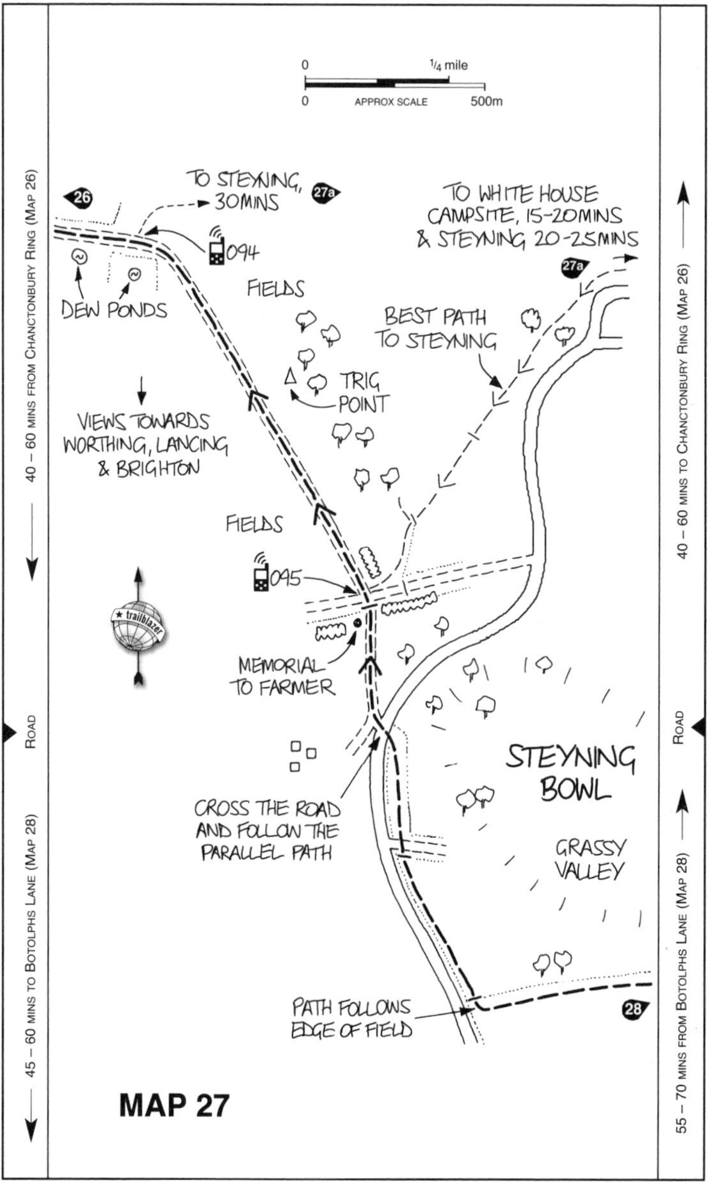

0 — 1/4 mile
0 — APPROX SCALE — 500m

TO STEYNING, 30MINS

26

27a

TO WHITE HOUSE CAMPSITE, 15-20MINS & STEYNING 20-25MINS

27a

094

DEW PONDS

FIELDS

BEST PATH TO STEYNING

VIEWS TOWARDS WORTHING, LANCING & BRIGHTON

TRIG POINT

trailblazer

FIELDS

045

MEMORIAL TO FARMER

CROSS THE ROAD AND FOLLOW THE PARALLEL PATH

STEYNING BOWL

GRASSY VALLEY

PATH FOLLOWS EDGE OF FIELD

28

MAP 27

40 – 60 MINS FROM CHANCTONBURY RING (MAP 26)

ROAD

45 – 60 MINS TO BOTOLPHS LANE (MAP 28)

40 – 60 MINS TO CHANCTONBURY RING (MAP 26)

ROUTE GUIDE AND MAPS

ROAD

55 – 70 MINS FROM BOTOLPHS LANE (MAP 28)

STEYNING   MAP 27a

Steyning, about one mile north of the path, is well worth the minor detour and not just to replenish supplies and energy. This small town has retained all the charm of a downland village and it is worth taking an afternoon off to wander around and maybe visit one or two of the sights. There are some beautiful old buildings, particularly along Church St where the **Grammar School (Brotherhood Hall)**, dating from 1614, really catches the eye with its black timber framing.

Next to the library is the small **Steyning Museum** (☎ 01903-813333, 🖳 www.steyn ingmuseum.org.uk; open Tue, Wed, Fri & Sat 10.30am-12.30pm & 2.30-4.30pm, Sun 2.30-4.30pm only, closes at 4pm Oct-Mar, open Bank Hol Mons) with displays on local history. Entrance is free.

Services

There is an **information point** in the **library** (☎ 01903-812751; Mon, Tue, Wed & Sat 9.30am-1pm & 2-5pm, Fri 9.30am-1pm & 2-7pm) which has **internet** access for £1.25/2.50 for half an hour/an hour.

For wi-fi access head to The Chequer Inn (see Where to stay). The High St has plenty of **banks** and **cash machines** and there's a **post office** (Mon-Fri 9am-5.30pm, Sat 9am-12.30pm) too. The main **supermarket**, Co-op (Mon-Sat 7am-10pm, Sun 9am-6pm) is also on the High St. Further down is a **chemist** and, virtually opposite, there is also a good **bookshop** on the High St that sells maps.

Compass's **bus** No 100 (Burgess Hill to Storrington) continues to Pulborough (for trains to London and the south coast) and the towns in-between. Brighton & Hove Buses' services Nos 2a and 20 head in the other direction to Brighton via Upper Beeding; see the public transport map and table, pp44-6.

Where to stay

Just to the south-west of town off Newham Lane is the **White House Caravan and Campsite** (☎ 01903-813737; open end Mar-Oct) with camping pitches from £8 for up to two people. Note that there is no shower block and only one toilet here. The walk into town takes about eight minutes.

A good hotel to try is **Springwells Hotel** (☎ 01903-812446, 🖳 www.spring wells.co.uk; 2S/5D/2D or T, two with four posters; 🐾 in only one room; 🐶; WI-FI), 9 High St, built in 1772, with B&B from £72/43 for the double/single with shared bathrooms; the other single is en suite and costs £61, and the other rooms, with en-suite facilities, cost £98. Packed lunches are available if booked in advance. One of the main delights of this lovely hotel is the swimming pool, heated by the spring, in the old walled garden.

If you can bear the noise from the bar, **The Chequer Inn** (☎ 01903-814437, 🖳 www.chequerinnsteyning.co.uk; 1D/1T/1F, all en suite; WI-FI), at 41 High St, offers comfortable B&B from £90, or £50 for single occupancy.

A cheaper option a little further from the centre is **5 Coxham Lane** (☎ 01903-812286; 1S/2T; shared bathroom; 🐶; 🐾) charging from £23 per person.

Where to eat and drink

The High St is the place for food. Cheap eats can be had at **Truffles** (☎ 01903-816140; Mon-Sat 7.30am-5.30pm, Sun 8am-5pm; the café open 30 mins later than the shop, and during the week closes an hour earlier), a chain bakery offering cooked breakfasts from £4.14.

A classier place is **The Steyning Tea Rooms** (☎ 01903-810064; daily 10am-6pm), which does very good breakfasts – including traditional bacon sandwiches or scrambled eggs with smoked salmon – as well as light lunches and cream teas.

For lunch packs there are takeaway buns, cakes and savouries at the **Model Bakery** (☎ 01903-813785; Mon-Fri 8.30am-5pm, Sat 8.30am-1pm), on Church St, with a second branch (☎ 01903-813126; Mon-Fri 8.30am-5pm, Sat 8.30am-3pm) at the northern end of the High St.

Probably the best place to eat in Steyning is the **Sussex Produce Company** (☎ 01903-815045, 🖳 www.thesussexpro ducecompany.co.uk; open Mon-Thur 8am-6pm, Fri & Sat 8am-8.30pm & Sun 10am-

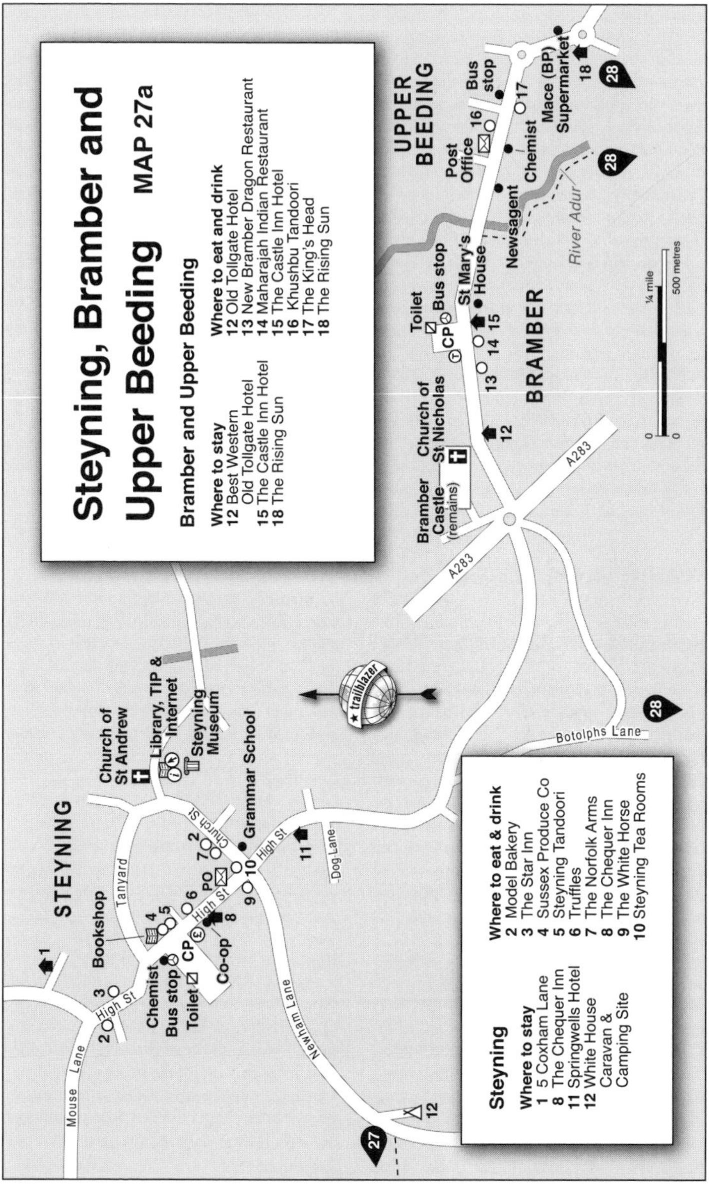

Steyning, Bramber and Upper Beeding MAP 27a

Bramber and Upper Beeding

Where to stay
12 Best Western
   Old Tollgate Hotel
15 The Castle Inn Hotel
18 The Rising Sun

Where to eat and drink
12 Old Tollgate Hotel
13 New Bramber Dragon Restaurant
14 Maharajah Indian Restaurant
15 The Castle Inn Hotel
16 Khushbu Tandoori
17 The King's Head
18 The Rising Sun

Steyning

Where to stay
1 5 Coxham Lane
8 The Chequer Inn
11 Springwells Hotel
12 White House
   Caravan &
   Camping Site

Where to eat & drink
2 Model Bakery
3 The Star Inn
4 Sussex Produce Co
5 Steyning Tandoori
6 Truffles
7 The Norfolk Arms
8 The Chequer Inn
9 The White Horse
10 Steyning Tea Rooms

STEYNING

Church of St Andrew

Library, TIP & Internet

Steyning Museum

Grammar School

Bookshop

Chemist

Bus stop

Toilet

Co-op

Church St

High St

Tanyard

Mouse Lane

High St

Newham Lane

High St

Dog Lane

UPPER BEEDING

Post Office

Chemist

Mace (BP) Supermarket

Bus stop

Newsagent

River Adur

BRAMBER

Church of St Nicholas

Bramber Castle (remains)

Toilet

Bus stop

St Mary's House

Botolphs Lane

A283

¼ mile

500 metres

★ trailblazer

27

28

28

28

4pm). This award-winning deli and local produce shop has an excellent café serving steak from Sussex Longhorn cattle and fish from the local port of Newhaven among all the other locally-sourced ingredients. There's Harvey's beer, Fairtrade coffee and if all you want is ingredients for a picnic how about a couple of pork & cranberry pies (2 for £5)? To eat in the restaurant on Friday or Saturday evening you'll need to book several days in advance.

The White Horse (☎ 01903-812347, 🖳 www.whitesbarkitchen.co.uk; food: bar daily 10am-11pm, to midnight on Sat; restaurant noon-2.30pm & 6-9.30pm), also known as Whites Bar & Kitchen, is a gastro-pub at the crossroads on the High St. The restaurant is currently Italian themed with pizza from £8.50 and pasta from £10. The pub can get quite lively in the evening; the restaurant section is quieter.

The Chequer Inn (see Where to stay; food Mon-Sat 10am-2pm & 6.30-9pm, Sun 10am-2.30pm), is a more traditional pub. Saturday is karaoke night. There's free WI-FI here. At the bottom end of the High St there is another traditional pub, *The Star Inn* (☎ 01903-813078; food daily noon-2pm & 6.30-9pm) serving dishes such as steak and ale pie for £9.45.

There is also an Indian restaurant in the village: *Steyning Tandoori* (☎ 01903-813533; Sun-Thur noon-2pm & 5.30-11pm, Fri & Sat noon-2pm & 5.30-11.30pm) serves all the usual Indian and Nepali dishes with the vegetable dansak (£6.50) being particularly tasty. There's also a *fish and chip shop*, though it's open two days a week only (Wed & Fri noon-2pm & 5-9pm).

Finally, for a straightforward pint of real ale, head to *The Norfolk Arms* (☎ 01903-812215) at 18 Church St. This is a real old-style pub where you go for a drink or three.

BRAMBER & UPPER BEEDING
MAP 27a

Acting almost as suburbs of Steyning, the twin villages of Bramber and Upper Beeding lie either side of the River Adur.

The main attraction is **Bramber Castle** (free, dawn to dusk). It was built by William de Broase in 1073 on a prominent knoll behind the village. In truth there is not much left of it, save for a few old ramparts and some collapsed sections of wall but the old moat, despite now having no water and having been taken over by trees, is still clearly visible. The only surviving part of the castle that's still in use is the **Church of St Nicholas** which was built around the same time.

St Mary's House (☎ 01903-816205, 🖳 www.stmarysbramber.co.uk; open May-Sep Thur, Sun & bank holidays 2-6pm; admission £7.50, concessions £7) is a magnificent place which claims to be the finest example of a 15th-century (built c1470) timber-framed house in Sussex. The perfectly manicured front garden, with its topiary and fish ponds, only adds to the charm.

Despite the house being a private residence the owners do allow visitors in to admire the antiques, an Elizabethan *trompe l'oeil* painted room, four-poster beds, a 'mysterious, ivy-clad monks' walk' and octagonal dining-room. It is a popular location for TV dramas, most notably *Dr Who*.

Services
On the main street in Upper Beeding there is a **newsagent** (Mon-Fri 5.30am-5pm, Sat 5.30am-1pm, Sun 6am-noon) as well as a **chemist** (Mon-Fri 9am-1pm & 2-5.30pm, Sat 9am-12.30pm) and small **post office** (Mon-Fri 9am-5.30pm, Sat 9am-12.30pm). There's also a small **shop** (daily 7am-10pm), part of the garage on the way out of town near The Rising Sun (see Where to stay).

Brighton & Hove Buses' **bus** Nos 2a and 20X pass through Bramber and Upper Beeding on their way to Brighton from Steyning, and Compass Bus No 100 calls in at both on its way between Storrington and Burgess Hill; see the public transport map and table, pp44-6.

Where to stay

In **Upper Beeding** close to the Downs is *The Rising Sun* (☎ 01903-814424, 💻 www.therisingsunupperbeeding.co.uk; 3S/ 2D or T; doubles are en-suite with showers; singles share a bathroom; 🛏; WI-FI), an inn with simple, clean and newly renovated rooms with B&B from just £35 for a single or £60 for a double.

In **Bramber**, *The Castle Inn Hotel* (☎ 01903-812102, 💻 www.castleinn hotel.co.uk; 5D/7D or T; all en suite; 🛏; 🐾 £10; WI-FI) has B&B from £55 to £80, or from £40 if you're on your own. It can get a little noisy in the evenings as the drinkers stagger home but the rooms are comfortable.

If you have cleaned the mud from your boots you could splash out on the extravagant *Best Western Old Tollgate Hotel* (☎ 01903-879494, 💻 www.oldtoll gatehotel.com; 34D, two with four posters/ 4T, all en suite; 🛏; WI-FI) which incorporates a smart restaurant and lots of pristine rooms and charges from around £80 per room, though they can drop as low as £55 in winter.

Where to eat and drink

In **Bramber** there are a surprising number of food outlets for such a small village. One of the best places is *The Castle Inn Hotel* (see above; food Mon-Fri noon-2.30pm & 6-9pm, Sat noon-9pm, Sun noon-4pm & 6-

9pm); they serve standard pub food and also have a specials board which changes daily – most mains cost around £10.

Eating at the *Old Tollgate Hotel* (see above; food: Mon-Fri 7-9.30am, Sat & Sun 8-10am; Mon-Sat noon-2pm, Sun noon-9.30pm; daily 6-9.30pm) is a classy experience with a three-course dinner (including dessert and a cheeseboard) for £26.25.

For a cheaper night out head for *New Bramber Dragon Restaurant* (☎ 01903-812408, 💻 www.thenewbramberdragon .co.uk; daily noon-2.30pm & 5.30-11pm) where a typical Chinese dish such as sweet and sour pork will cost £5.70.

The *Maharajah Indian Restaurant* (☎ 01903-814746; Mon-Fri noon-2pm & 5.30-11.30pm, Fri & Sat 5.30pm-midnight) claims to be the 'largest and most famous Indian restaurant in Sussex'. The chicken dopiaza is only £5.95 while the speciality pathia dishes start at £7.95.

Moving into **Upper Beeding** there is more food from the Indian subcontinent to take away at *Khushbu* (☎ 01903-816646; daily 5.30-11pm). *The King's Head* (☎ 01903-812196; food Mon-Fri noon-2.30pm & 6-9pm, Sat & Sun noon-3pm & 6-9pm) does some fine grub too.

There is also pub food at *The Rising Sun* (see above; food daily noon-2.30pm, Thurs-Sat 6-9pm) at the far end of the village. Scampi and chips cost £7.95 as does the fresh vegetarian bake.

STEYNING TO PYECOMBE

MAPS 27a-32

The going is easy for most of this **10 mile (16km, 4-5½hrs)** section with a good track leading the way along the level escarpment of the Downs. There are, once again, great views in all directions but particularly to the north across the Weald.

Despite the ugly pub and car park at the top of the hill the highlight of this stretch has to be **Devil's Dyke** (Map 31, p139), a spectacular dry valley said to have been carved out by Satan himself in order to let the sea flood over the lowland Weald and destroy all the churches. Geologists have blown this theory out of the water by proving that it is in fact a result of folding of the chalk strata due to pressure building between the African and Eurasian plates.

After leaving Devil's Dyke the Way drops down to a farm and then over the flanks of **Newtimber Hill**, a National Trust property and a veritable oasis of calm after the crowds that flock to Devil's Dyke.

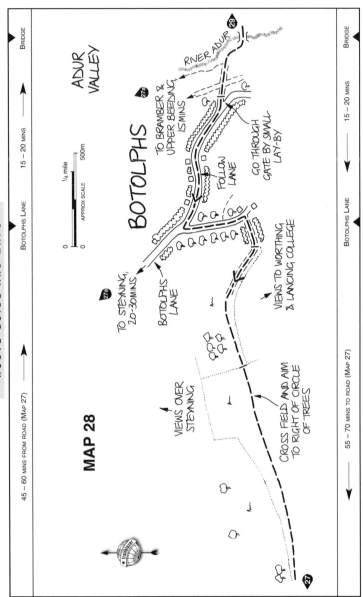

MAP 28

BRIDGE

15 – 20 MINS

BOTOLPHS LANE

45 – 60 MINS FROM ROAD (MAP 27)

ADUR VALLEY

RIVER ADUR

TO BRAMBER & UPPER BEEDING, 15 MINS

BOTOLPHS

GO THROUGH GATE BY SMALL LAY-BY

FOLLOW LANE

TO STEYNING, 20-30MINS

BOTOLPHS LANE

VIEWS TO WORTHING & LANCING COLLEGE

VIEWS OVER STEYNING

CROSS FIELD AND AIM TO RIGHT OF CIRCLE OF TREES

¼ mile
APPROX SCALE
500m
0

BRIDGE

15 – 20 MINS

BOTOLPHS LANE

55 – 70 MINS TO ROAD (MAP 27)

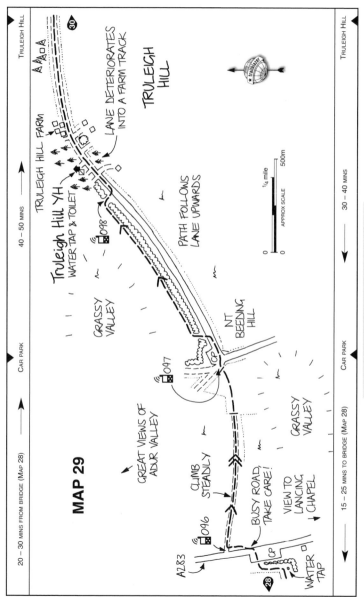

MAP 29

20 – 30 MINS FROM BRIDGE (MAP 28) ← CAR PARK ← 40 – 50 MINS ← TRULEIGH HILL ►

TRULEIGH HILL ►

Truleigh Hill YH
WATER TAP & TOILET

TRULEIGH HILL FARM

LANE DETERIORATES
INTO A FARM TRACK

TRULEIGH
HILL

30

▲☗◭

📷 098

PATH FOLLOWS
LANE UPWARDS

GRASSY
VALLEY

NT
BEEDING
HILL

📷 047

1/4 mile

APPROX SCALE

0 ——— 500m

30 – 40 MINS

CAR PARK ◄ TRULEIGH HILL ◄

GREAT VIEWS OF
ADUR VALLEY

CLIMB
STEADILY

BUSY ROAD,
TAKE CARE!

VIEW TO
LANCING
CHAPEL

GRASSY
VALLEY

📷 096

A283

WATER TAP

28

15 – 25 MINS TO BRIDGE (MAP 28)

TRULEIGH HILL   MAP 29, p135

By the South Downs Way is *Truleigh Hill Youth Hostel* (☎ 0845-371 9047, 🖳 truleigh@yha.org.uk; beds from £14 and some private rooms from £37). The purpose-built hostel has all the usual facilities and serves breakfast, packed lunches and evening meals but also has a shop and kitchen for those preferring to self cater. There's a day room with toilet open all day.

FULKING   MAP 30

Fulking is a tiny village with little of specific interest to the walker except for the delightful *Shepherd & Dog Inn* (☎ 01273-857382; food Mon-Sat noon-9pm, Sun noon-8pm). It's everything that a proper country pub should be with plenty of real ales and good food and a beer garden with views of the downs. The pub gets its name from Fulking's reputation for having a rather large population of sheep: in the early 19th century the village was home to ten times as many sheep as people and the pub was the place where the shepherds would meet after a hard day's shearing to spend their earnings on the local brew.

Next to the pub car park is the locally famous **Victorian fountain**, placed there in memory of John Ruskin, the man responsible for installing the village's water supply.

POYNINGS   MAP 31

The hidden leafy village of Poynings sits at the foot of the escarpment away from the hustle and bustle high above at the beauty spot of Devil's Dyke. Poynings is a scenic two-mile walk from the Dyke.

Brighton & Hove Buses' **bus** service No 77 from Devil's Dyke to Brighton is the most convenient public transport link from this village; see the public transport map and table, pp44-6.

Where to stay and eat

Saddlescombe Farm (☎ 01273-857712, 🖳 saddlescombefarmcampsite@national trust.org.uk; open Apr-Sep; 🐾) is a five-acre natural (ie basic – there are no showers just washbasins and a toilet) **campsite** run by the National Trust. It's just over a mile from Poynings beside the Way. They charge £5 per person. At the farm, there's a *tearoom* (closed Wed) serving cream teas, cakes, sandwiches and snacks.

Dyke Lane Cottage (☎ 01273-857335, 🖳 jakeamber@dykelane.freeserve.co.uk; 1T shared bathroom/2D en suite) is walker and cyclist friendly and offers B&B from £30 per person with a supplement for single occupancy.

Set in the heart of the village, *The Royal Oak* (☎ 01273-857389; 🖳 www.royaloakpoynings.biz; food daily noon-9.30pm) serves fabulous food, not least the Harvey's beer battered deep-fried fish, triple-cooked chips and mushy peas.

If descending to The Royal Oak does not appeal, the only other choice is the characterless and completely out-of-place *Devil's Dyke* pub (☎ 01273-857256; food Mon-Sat 11.30am-10pm, Sun noon-10pm) at the top of the hill, whose only redeeming feature is its proximity to the Way. Main courses cost £6-10. You can sit outside and watch the hang-gliders if the conditions are right and people are flying.

❏ **Important note – walking times**
Unless otherwise specified, **all times in this book refer only to the time spent walking**. You will need to add 20-30% to allow for rests, photography, checking the map, drinking water etc. When planning the day's hike count on 5-7 hours' actual walking.

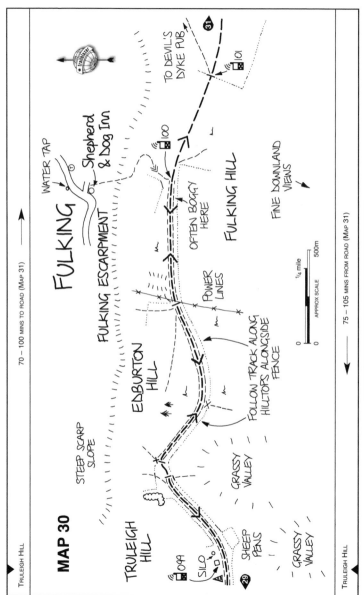

70 – 100 MINS TO ROAD (MAP 31)

MAP 30

TRULEIGH HILL

SILO

SHEEP PENS

GRASSY VALLEY

GRASSY VALLEY

GRASSY VALLEY

FOLLOW TRACK ALONG HILLTOPS ALONGSIDE FENCE

EDBURTON HILL

STEEP SCARP SLOPE

FULKING ESCARPMENT

POWER LINES

¼ mile

APPROX SCALE

500m

FULKING

WATER TAP

Shepherd & Dog Inn

OFTEN BOGGY HERE

FULKING HILL

FINE DOWNLAND VIEWS

TO DEVIL'S DYKE PUB

75 – 105 MINS FROM ROAD (MAP 31)

PYECOMBE   MAP 32, p141

Pyecombe, like many a downland village, has some very pretty ivy-clad flint houses but the peace and tranquillity that this place evidently once had has been somewhat spoilt by the constant hum of traffic from the A23 which converges with the equally unappealing A273 just below the village. The trees hide the roads from view but struggle to do the same with the constant drone. Nevertheless, a little wander through the lanes of Pyecombe is pleasant enough and it's a convenient place to stay being right on the Way and with several B&Bs and a pub.

If you're looking for a picnic lunch, the BP petrol station just south of the village has an **M&S food outlet** stocked with treats.

Metrobus's No 273 (Brighton to Crawley) stops here; see the public transport map and table, pp44-6.

Where to stay and eat

Right on the Way, *Hobbs Cottage* (☎ 01273-846150, 🖳 wendy.desborough @btinternet.com; 2T, 1 en suite; ☞; WI-FI) couldn't be better located. It's a well-run, friendly place charging £70 for two in the en suite twin and £60 for the twin room

with shared bathroom. If you have a larger group they can accommodate up to seven people with folding beds.

The White House (☎ 01273-846563, 🖳 louloua@onetel.net; 1S/2D or T shared bathroom; ☞) charges £35 for the single and £70 for two in a double. In addition to the rooms they also have a **caravan** outside for smokers or those who want to come in late without disturbing the owner. Both walker and dog friendly, this is a nice place.

There's also *1 Church Cottages* (☎ 01273-844036, 🖳 eandacorbett@hotmail .co.uk; 1F en suite; ☞), a comfortable B&B charging £70 for two using the room as a twin or £100 as a family room with an additional folding double bed.

The only pub in the vicinity is *The Plough Inn* (☎ 01273-842796; food Mon-Fri 11.30am-10pm, Sat & Sun noon-10pm) located at the southern end of the village and commanding unenviable views of the commuter traffic hurtling down the A23 to and from Brighton. Despite this it is a good pub with tasty pub meals and the bar is open all day, every day. They also do takeaways.

CLAYTON   off MAP 32, p141

The main attraction of Clayton is not the small village at the foot of the hill but the two windmills (see box below) sitting conveniently at the top just two minutes from the path.

There's no B&B in the village itself but out on the bend on the main road, about five minutes' walk away, is the *Jack & Jill*

Inn (☎ 01273-843595, 🖳 www.thejackand jillinn.co.uk; 3T/1D all en suite; food Mon-Thur noon-2pm & 6-9pm, Fri, Sat & Sun noon-9pm) with B&B for £65, or £40 for single occupancy (less £5 if you don't want breakfast). The bar is open all day, every day and serves a selection of real ales with regularly changing guest beers.

❏ Jack and Jill Windmills

The twin windmills above Clayton, known as Jack and Jill (Map 32), are famous local landmarks that can be seen for miles around. There is evidence that suggests the first windmill was erected way back in 1765. The names of the windmills are said to originate from the 1920s when tourists first came to visit. The post mill Jill, the white windmill, has been fully restored and occasionally grinds out some wholemeal flour. It is the only one of the two that is open to the public (🖳 www.jillwindmill.org.uk; May-Sep, most Sun & bank hols 2-5pm). Admission is free and there is a *tea shop*.

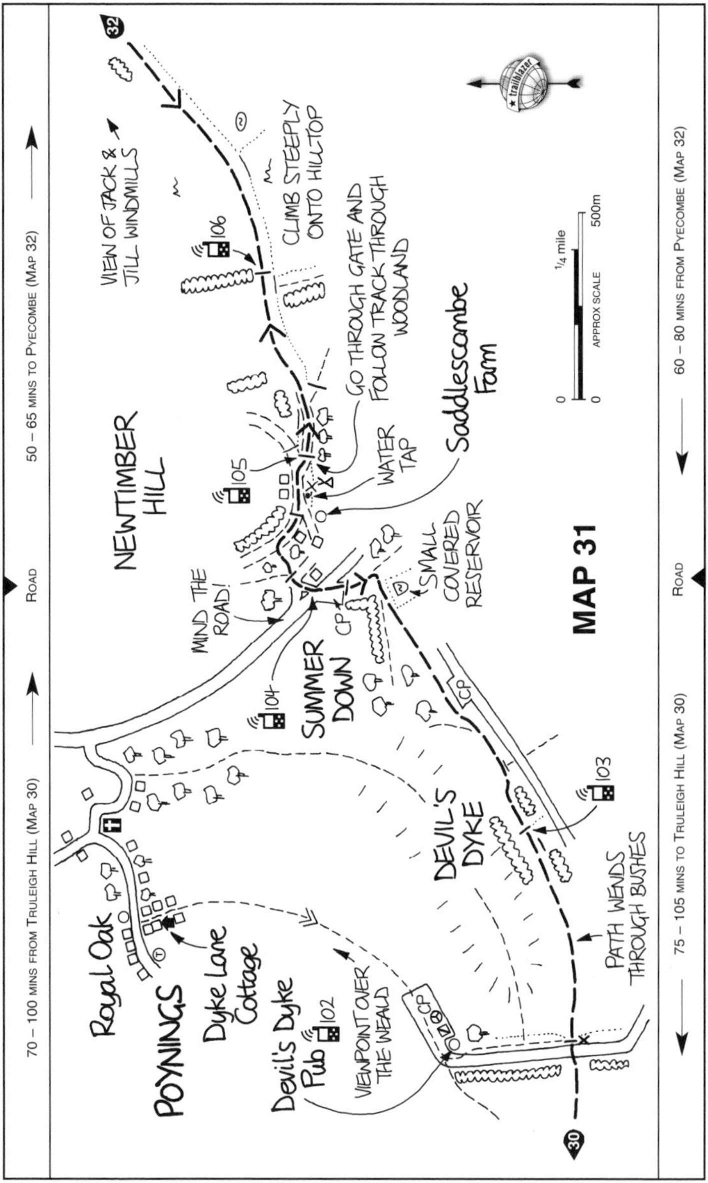

VIEW OF JACK & JILL WINDMILLS

CLIMB STEEPLY ONTO HILLTOP

GO THROUGH GATE AND FOLLOW TRACK THROUGH WOODLAND

📷 106

Saddlescombe Farm

WATER TAP

NEWTIMBER HILL

📷 105

MIND THE ROAD!

SMALL COVERED RESERVOIR

MAP 31

SUMMER DOWN

CP

📷 104

DEVIL'S DYKE

📷 103

CP

PATH WENDS THROUGH BUSHES

Royal Oak

POYNINGS

Dyke Lane Cottage

Devil's Dyke Pub 📷 102

VIEWPOINT OVER THE WEALD

CP

¼ mile
APPROX SCALE
0   500m

50 – 65 MINS TO PYECOMBE (MAP 32)

60 – 80 MINS FROM PYECOMBE (MAP 32)

70 – 100 MINS FROM TRULEIGH HILL (MAP 30)

75 – 105 MINS TO TRULEIGH HILL (MAP 30)

ROAD

ROAD

32

30

PYECOMBE TO SOUTHEASE   MAPS 32-38

This reasonably long stretch, **14¹/₂ miles (23.5km, 5-7hrs)** provides sweeping views north. The high ground in the distance is the High Weald, a large area of sandstone incorporating Ashdown Forest, the home of Winnie the Pooh, while to the south is Brighton and the English Channel.

The high point of this section is **Ditchling Beacon** (Map 33, p143). The name refers to the pyres that were burnt here and at other sites along the Downs such as Beacon Hill (see p85) in Hampshire. The beacons were lit to warn of impending attack, most notably during the time of the Spanish Armada. More recently they were used for celebrating Millennium Eve and the Queen's Diamond Jubilee in 2012.

Ditchling Beacon is another National Nature Reserve but is also a popular tourist spot. Access is made particularly easy by the road that winds in hairpins up the escarpment from Ditchling village; Brighton & Hove Buses bus No 79 runs between the car park at Ditchling Beacon and Brighton Railway station; see public transport map and table, pp44-6.

After leaving the hustle and bustle of the Beacon the route continues towards **Black Cap** (Map 34, p144) where the track takes a sharp right-hand turn. Those wishing to visit **Lewes** (see p145) should head straight on at this point: however, it is important to note that it is at least an hour's walk from here.

For those continuing on the Way, once over the A27 dual carriageway the path returns to the ridge of the Downs before crossing the Greenwich Meridian to reach the villages of **Rodmell** and **Southease** (Map 38, p155) where the smell of the sea will probably be prevalent and the chalk cliffs of Seaford Head can be seen in the distance.

DITCHLING   MAP 33a, p142

It is about a mile from the Downs to this village but if you are trying to decide on a place to spend the night this is a good choice and worth the short detour. Ditchling is among the prettiest of the pretty, perhaps bettered only by Alfriston and Amberley. There is a multitude of historic buildings centred around the crossroads but the oldest of all is the fine 13th-century Norman **St Margaret's Church**.

Opposite the church you can still see the house, **Wings Place**, bought by Henry VIII for his fourth wife, Anne of Cleves (see Plumpton p142 and p145), as part of a 'pay off' at the end of their marriage.

Not far from the church, in the old Victorian village school, **Ditchling Museum** (☎ 01273-844744, 💻 www.ditchling-museum.com) is currently closed for refurbishment; they hope to be open again by 2013. They have a wealth of information on local history. The emphasis, however, is put on Ditchling's renown as the home of famous artists such as the sculptor Eric Gill and the painter Sir Frank Brangwyn.

Services

There are two small **village shops** with limited provisions. One is a short way up the High St next to Church Lane while the other, incorporating the **post office** (☎ 01273-842736; post office Mon-Fri 9am-1pm & Sat 9am-12.30pm, shop Mon-Fri 8am-1pm & 2.15pm-6pm, Sat 8am-1pm, Sun 8am-2pm), is at the crossroads in the centre of the village.

Close by is **Ditchling Pharmacy** (Mon-Thur 9am-1pm & 2-5.30pm, Fri 9am-1pm & 2-6.30pm).

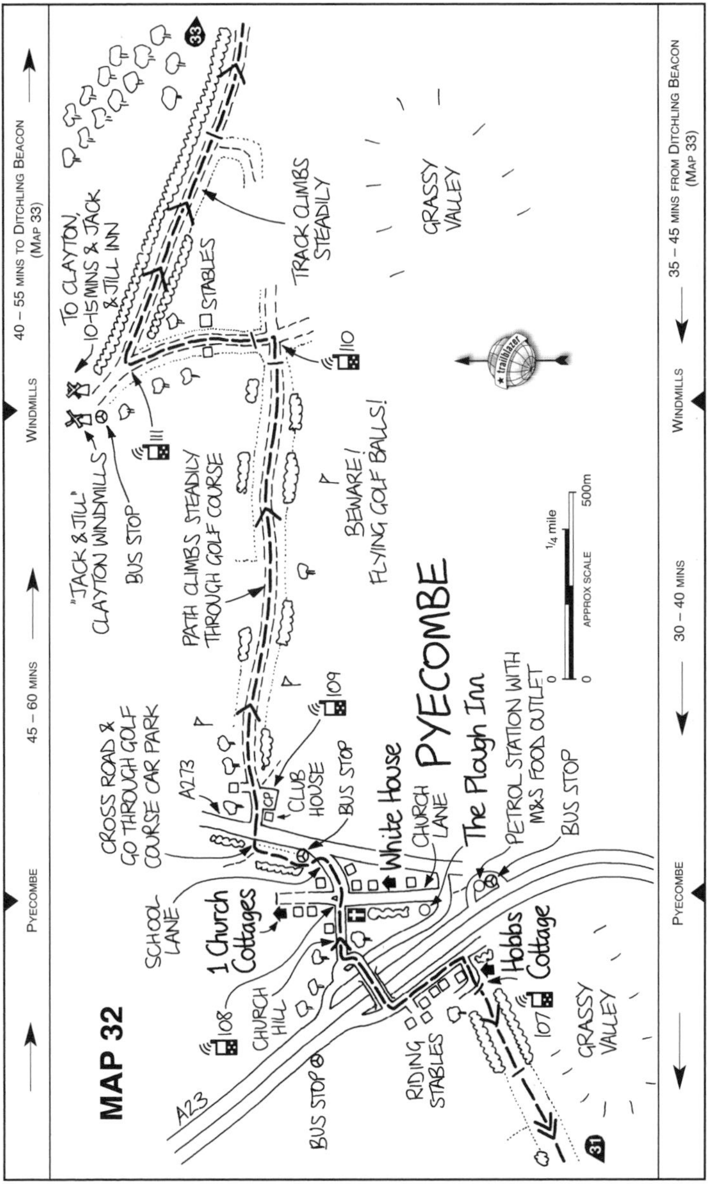

MAP 32

Where to stay and eat

The wonderful old **Bull Inn** (☎ 01273-843147, ☐ www.thebullditchling.com; 4D en suite, food Mon-Fri noon-2.30pm & 6-9.30pm, Sat noon-9.30pm, Sun noon-9pm; ☛; WI-FI), on the High St, has B&B from £100, rising to £120 at weekends.

There's also **The White Horse** (☎ 01273-842006; ☐ www.whitehorseditchling.com; 3D/4T most en suite, food Mon-Fri noon-3pm & 6-9.30pm, Sat noon-9.30, Sun noon-4pm & 6-9pm; ☛; ☜; WI-FI). Charges for two in a room range from £70 to £110. They offer pub fare and a restaurant menu that includes Sussex free range chicken & mustard pie (£12) or local sausages and truffled mash (£10).

If staying in a pub does not appeal to you there are more peaceful options away from the busy main road that runs through the village centre. There are beds from £40 at **2 South Cottage** (☎ 01273-846636, ☐ soniastock@btinternet.com; 1D/1T, shared bathroom; ☛; ☜) which can be found down a rough track. It's a nice quiet place to stay. There's also the **White Barn** (☎ 01273-842920, ☐ www.thewhitebarnbandb.co.uk; 1D private bathroom; ☛), on Lodge Hill Lane, with B&B for £75, single occupancy £45. The big double bed is extremely comfortable!

The most luxurious accommodation in the area is also closest to the Way, at **Tovey Lodge** (Map 33; ☎ 01273-256156, ☐ www.sussexcountryholidays.co.uk; all en suite; ☛; ☜ £5; WI-FI) on Underhill Lane. There's an indoor swimming-pool, hot tub and sauna. They charge according to season and demand, with room rates ranging from £88 to £165 in summer; £62 to £135 in winter. Single occupancy is £15 less.

For breakfast and lunch try **Ditchling Tea Rooms** (☎ 01273-842708; summer daily 9am-5.30pm, winter 9am-4.30pm), where you can pick up anything from beans on toast (£4.25) or a brie & cranberry baguette (£4.95) to more substantial fare like minced beef and ale pie.

To make up a picnic visit **The Larder** (open Mon-Sat 9am-6pm), a deli stocking local produce. You can also get hot drinks to take away.

The General (☎ 01273-846638, ☐ www.thegeneralrestaurant.com; open Tue-Fri 11am-5pm & 7-11pm, Sat 9am-5pm & 7-11pm, Sun 9am-6pm) is a popular place for a coffee or a full meal. The 'modern fusion' menu is interesting and features Persian lamb stew soup (£8.95) and Sussex Rarebit with haddock or ham on sourdough (£8.95). There's a 3-course dinner menu from £21.

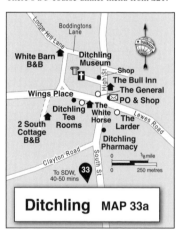

Ditchling   MAP 33a

PLUMPTON   MAP 34

Famous for its agricultural college, Plumpton is also the location for the privately owned **Plumpton Place**, a 16th-century mansion complete with moat, once owned by Anne of Cleves after it was given to her by Henry VIII. The best view of the mansion is from the Way on the top of the hill.

Countryliner's **bus** No 166 will take you to Lewes or Haywards Heath from here; see the public transport map, p45.

Campers will find pitches at two local sites. **Hackman's Farm** (☎ 01273-890348, Feb-Oct) charges £5 for a person and a tent. Campers can use the toilet at the back of the farm and there's also a water tap there.

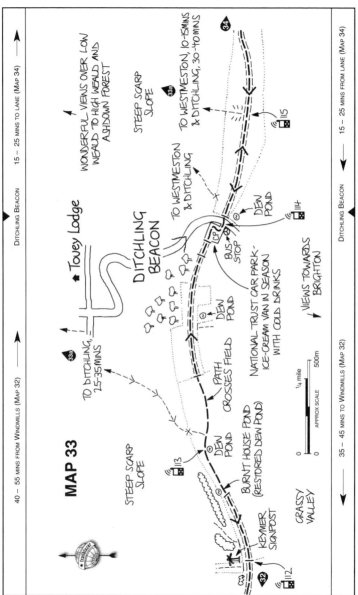

MAP 33

40 – 55 MINS FROM WINDMILLS (MAP 32) →

15 – 25 MINS TO LANE (MAP 34) →

DITCHLING BEACON ▶

WONDERFUL VIEWS OVER LOW WEALD TO HIGH WEALD AND ASHDOWN FOREST

STEEP SCARP SLOPE

Tovey Lodge

DITCHLING BEACON

TO DITCHLING, 25-35 MINS

TO WESTMESTON & DITCHLING

STEEP SCARP SLOPE

TO WESTMESTON, 10-15 MINS & DITCHLING, 30-40 MINS

DEW POND

PATH CROSSES FIELD

DEW POND

DEW POND

NATIONAL TRUST CAR PARK - ICE-CREAM VAN IN SEASON WITH COLD DRINKS

BUS STOP

DEW POND

VIEWS TOWARDS BRIGHTON

STEEP SCARP SLOPE

DEW POND

BURNT HOUSE POND (RESTORED DEW POND)

KEYMER SIGNPOST

GRASSY VALLEY

APPROX SCALE

0 — 500m

0 — ¼ mile

35 – 45 MINS TO WINDMILLS (MAP 32) →

DITCHLING BEACON ▶

15 – 25 MINS FROM LANE (MAP 34) →

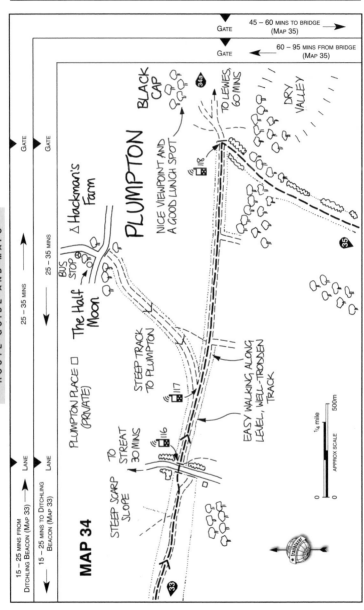

Further along the Way – and right on it – (see **Map 35**, p151) there's *Housedean Farm* (☎ 07919-668816, 🖳 www.house dean.co.uk; camping@housedean.co.uk), on a large farm. There's lots of space, flushing loos, a shower, washing-up area and places for campfires. They charge £8 per person (no charge for the tent). The bus stop for Lewes and Brighton is nearby.

The Half Moon (☎ 01273-890253; food Mon-Fri noon-3pm & 6-9pm, Sat

noon-10pm, Sun noon-6pm) is an excellent local pub with a wide selection of interesting dishes including crispy fried pig's ears with aïoli (£4), dry aged steaks from £17; and various items of game. All their meat and fish is sourced locally with food miles travelled noted. There are also real ales on tap, locally brewed and changed on a regular basis. The main kitchen is closed 3-6pm during the week but they still serve filled ciabatta sandwiches at that time.

LEWES   MAP 34a, p147
'Lewes ... lying like a box of toys under a great amphitheatre of chalky hills ... on the whole it is set down better than any town I have seen in England'   **William Morris**

Lewes, the county town of East Sussex, is still an attractive place to visit and one of the most desirable places to live in the South East. Like Totnes in Devon, it's a Transition Town (🖳 www.transitiontown lewes.org), populated by a vibrant community of people some of whom are dedicated to following this movement based on permaculture and sustainability. They've even issued their own currency (see box p148).

For the visitor it's interesting to see somewhere that's paying more than lip service to being green. It also means there's a profusion of places to buy and eat good healthy food; it's well worth spending the night here.

Lewes lies in a strategic position by the River Ouse with Mount Caburn rising steeply to the west. This did not go unnoticed by William the Conqueror who had William de Warrene fortify the town soon after the Battle of Hastings in 1066.

The town's focal point is **Lewes Castle** (see box below), which sits proudly at the very highest point on a grassy bluff.

Down the hill from the castle, **Anne of Cleves House** (☎ 01273-474610, 🖳 www.sussexpast.co.uk; Feb-Oct Tue-Sat 10am-5pm, Sun & Mon 11am-5pm; admission £4.70, or £9.60 with combined Lewes Castle ticket) is open to the public – unlike Plumpton Place (see p142) and Wing's Place (see p140) which were also given as a gift from Henry VIII to his fourth wife Anne of Cleves. This house is well worth visiting for its beautiful interior with timber beams and oak furnishings. The herb garden is also interesting.

Lewes still has some excellent bookshops, the oldest of which, the **Fifteenth Century Bookshop**, can be found at the top of the High St opposite the castle entrance. The timber-framed building that houses the shop is worth a visit in itself.

At the same end of the High St is **Bull House** where Thomas Paine, the founder of American Independence, lived between 1768 and 1774. During his time in Lewes he acted as the local tobacconist and

ROUTE GUIDE AND MAPS

❑ Lewes Castle & Barbican House Museum
This Norman **castle** (☎ 01273-486290, 🖳 www.sussexpast.co.uk; open daily year round except Mon in Jan, 10am-5.30pm or dusk if earlier; admission £6.60 or combined ticket for Anne of Cleves House £9.60) was built by Lieutenant William de Warenne shortly after the Battle of Hastings in 1066. The well-preserved castle gate and walls can be explored and the ticket also gives access to the **Barbican House Museum** opposite, which contains artefacts from the castle and an interactive display covering the history of the town and castle.

exciseman. A commemorative plaque can be seen on the outside wall.

Real-ale drinkers cannot go to Lewes without visiting **Harvey's Brewery** (☎ 01273-480209, 🖳 www.harveys.org.uk) though with a waiting list of more than a year for guided tours most fans will get no further than the shop. Phone or check the website for details. Harvey's is the oldest brewery in Sussex and has been producing real ales for well over 200 years using hops from Sussex and Kent and water from their own spring. The company is still run by the same family that founded it seven generations ago. The shop (☎ 01273-480217; Mon-Sat 9.30am-4.45pm) sells a vast array of Harvey's related paraphernalia.

Services

The **tourist information centre** (☎ 01273-483448, 🖳 lewes.tic@lewes.gov.uk; Apr-Sep Mon-Fri 9am-5pm, Sat 9.30am-5.30pm, Sun & Bank hols 10am-2pm; Oct-Mar Mon-Fri 9am-5pm, Sat 10am-2pm, closed Sun) is on the corner of Fisher St and the High St at No 187. There is no charge for accommodation booked in the Lewes area for visitors to the centre though a 10% deposit towards the cost of the first night's accommodation is taken. They also sell maps, books and guides.

The **post office** (Mon-Fri 9am-5.30pm, Sat 9am-12.30pm) is on the High St where there is also a **chemist** and there are plenty of **banks** with **cash machines**. Waitrose **supermarket** is on Eastgate St and walking equipment can be found at **The Outdoor Shop** (☎ 01273-487840; Mon-Sat 9am-5.30pm) at the lower end of the High St near the river.

Taxis can be called on ☎ 01273-483232. Convenient and regular **trains** from Lewes run south to Seaford, Eastbourne and Brighton and north to Gatwick Airport and London Victoria.

There are also several useful **bus** services: Brighton and Hove Buses' No 28 runs to Brighton and their No 29/29a service stops here en route between Brighton and Tunbridge Wells; for Plumpton or Haywards Heath you'll need to use Countryliner's No 166 and for Alfriston

their No 125 service. For Rodmell, Southease and Newhaven take Renown's No 123; see the public transport map and table, pp44-6. The bus station is on Eastgate St.

Where to stay

There is no shortage of rooms in Lewes but as with any other popular tourist town booking in advance is advised.

1 Garden Cottages (☎ 01273-473343, 🖳 www.lewesroom.co.uk; 1D/1T en suite; ☛; WI-FI), 59 South St, is an attractive B&B on the eastern edge of the town. You'll get a good breakfast and the friendly owner is a mine of information about the area. She charges £80 per room (£50 sgl occ) or £130 for the double with a sofa bed in the adjoining sitting room.

The hospitable owner of *One Harveys Way* (☎ 01273-480865, 🖳 anddrewkr37 @gmail.com; 1S/1T shared bathroom; ☛; WI-FI) charges £35 for the single and £70 for the twin with a healthy breakfast of cereal, fruit and toast. A cooked breakfast is £5 extra.

Castle Banks Cottage (☎ 01273-476291, 🖳 www.castlebankscottage.co.uk; 1S/1T, shared bathroom but basins in each bedroom; ☛; WI-FI), 4 Castle Banks, is in a quiet street near the castle. They charge £40 for the single and £80 for the double with a full cooked breakfast which you can have in the garden on sunny days.

The Old Coach House (☎ 01273-483138; 1T en suite; 🐾) is an attractive 18th century cottage centrally situated on Bull Lane. It's £40 per person for B&B.

The Prospect B&B (☎ 01273-472883, 🖳 www.theprospectbandb.co.uk; 1T/1D en suite; WI-FI) is on St Martin's Lane in the centre of town. They charge from £45 per person; the breakfasts are excellent and include home-baked bread.

Montys (☎ 01273-476750, 🖳 www .montysaccommodation.co.uk; 1D; ☛; WI-FI), Broughton House, 16 High St, charges £95 to £110 for the luxurious self-contained suite which includes a four-poster bed and free-standing bath, an en suite shower and a kitchenette. Tea, coffee, orange juice and home-made muesli are provided.

Felix House (☎ 01273-473250, 🖥 www.lewesbedandbreakfast.co.uk; 1S/2D en suite with power showers; ➡; WI-FI), 22 Gundreda Rd, is ideally placed for walkers being halfway between the Way and Lewes town centre. If you're walking in on Hill Rd, turn right onto King Henry's Rd, right again onto De Warenne Rd and Gundreda

Rd is on the right. They charge £40 per person for B&B including a full cooked breakfast.

There's also accommodation at *The Crown Inn* (☎ 01273-480670, 🖥 www .crowninnlewes.co.uk; 4D/2T/1F; ➡; WI-FI) which has been occupying a prominent position on the High St for nearly 400

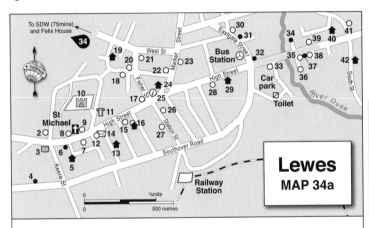

Lewes
MAP 34a

ROUTE GUIDE AND MAPS

Where to eat and drink
2 Baltica Café
7 Shanaz Indian Restaurant
8 Castle Sandwich Bar
9 Panda Garden
12 Beckworths
15 Charcoal Grill
16 Pelham House
17 Ask Italian
18 Lewes Arms
20 The Friar Fish and Chip Shop
21 Carnival Chinese Takeaway
22 Café at the Needlemakers
23 Famiglia Lazzati
26 The Royal Oak
27 Limetree Kitchen
28 Robson's of Lewes
30 Chaula's Café Restaurant
33 Forfars Bakery
35 Bill's Produce Store
36 John Harvey Tavern
38 Gardener's Arms
39 The Real Eating Company
41 Buttercup Café

Where to stay
5 The Old Coach House
13 The Prospect B&B
16 Pelham House
19 Castle Banks Cottage
24 The Crown Inn
29 Montys
40 One Harveys Way
42 1 Garden Cottages

Other
3 15th Century Bookshop
4 Anne of Cleves House
6 Bull House
10 Lewes Castle
11 Barbican Museum
14 Post Office
25 TIC
31 Waitrose supermarket
32 Chemist
34 Harvey's Brewery and shop
37 The Outdoor Shop

years. They charge from £45 for single occupancy, £75 for two sharing and £100 for the family room. Most of the rooms have an en suite bathroom.

A classy place is **Pelham House** (☎ 01273-488600, 🖥 www.pelhamhouse .com; 2S/29D; 🖝; WI-FI) and with 31 rooms if they're not booked up they may have some very good deals with B&B in doubles from as little as £60; standard room charges range up to £160.

Where to eat and drink
Most of Lewes's cafés, pubs and restaurants can be found on or just off the upper High St.

On the eastern side of town, **Buttercup Café** (☎ 01273-477664, 🖥 http://thebutter cupcafe.wordpress.com; open Mon-Fri 9.30am-4pm, Sat 9am-4pm, may also open Sun in summer) is a quirky little café serving breakfasts, lunches and teas. Set amongst an antique shop and a studio it's right at home

❏ The Lewes Pound
In 2008, Lewes town took the unusual step of issuing its own currency, to be used alongside sterling.

The idea behind the 'Lewes Pound' is to encourage demand for local goods and services, and the logic behind it is simple: money spent in shops in the town that are merely another branch of a national chain does not stay in the local economy; but money spent in shops owned by locals or on local services does. So while the Lewes Pound would not be accepted in, for example, the local outlet of a nationwide superstore, of which there are several in Lewes, it would be accepted by a local trader – who would then spend it locally with another local trader, and so on and so on. Thus, by ensuring that money is spent locally and so stays within the community, the wealth of the locals is safeguarded.

The founders of the Lewes Pound argue that there are environmental benefits, too, for supporting local businesses reduces the need to transport goods over many miles, thus minimising the carbon footprint of local people. There is also a social case to be made too, as the Pound could be seen to strengthen the relationship between shopkeepers and the local community.

The actual practicalities of circulating the pound are simple: people buy Lewes Pounds (with sterling) at one of seven issuing points (including Lewes Town Hall, Mays General Store on Cliffe High St, and Richards & Son, Butchers, on Western Rd) then spend them with participating traders.

Whilst the establishing of a new currency may seem like a highly bizarre step to take, it isn't without precedent; indeed, Lewes itself had its own currency for over a century between 1789 and 1895. The issuers of the latest Lewes Pound, however, admit that their currency is not actually legal tender, in that there is no obligation on the part of retailers to accept the pound. Nevertheless, with its own watermarks, serial numbers and other hidden security features, the current Lewes Pound note certainly looks like money.

Initially this new Lewes Pound enjoyed some success. Indeed, such was the demand for the new currency that more had to be produced. The demand for the currency was due not only to people wishing to buy local produce, but also from souvenir hunters; and some of the currency even appeared for sale on eBay.

Some residents of the town, however, see the Lewes Pound as an unnecessary complication. They argue, rightly, that they can support local traders by buying from them using good old-fashioned sterling, and don't see the need for this currency.

The project will run for at least five years. Some say that the publicity brought about by the new currency, and the issues it has raised, means that it is *already* a success. However, it doesn't seem to be quite as much in evidence as it did in the past.

here in Lewes. The menu's interesting and the food is delicious and very good value. It's worth checking the website as they sometimes do themed supper evenings and host exhibitions in the studio.

Right at the western end of town near the castle, at 145 High St, is a similarly-popular restaurant, *Baltica Café* (☎ 01273-483449, 🖥 www.baltictrader.co.uk; open Mon-Sat 9am-5pm, Sun 11am-4pm). Part of a Polish ceramics shop the menu includes some excellent Polish dishes such as pierogi filled with pork and vegetables (£9.95) and goulash (£8.95). There are also delicious pastries.

Another highly recommended place is the *Café at the Needlemakers* (☎ 01273-486258, 🖥 www.needlemakers.co.uk; open Mon-Sat 9.30am-5.30pm, also open Sun in summer). The coffee is excellent and there's a mouthwatering range of home-made cakes, scones and muffins. They also do salads and open sandwiches with most ingredients locally sourced. There are lots of interesting shops to look round at the Needlemakers.

Bill's Produce Store (☎ 01273-476918, 🖥 www.bills-website.co.uk; Mon-Thur 8am-10.30pm, Fri & Sat 8am-11pm, Sun 9am-10.30pm) is a great place with tables outside on the cobbled street. The store incorporates a very colourful fruit and veg shop as well as a café and is always busy with locals and tourists alike.

Limetree Kitchen (☎ 01273-478636, 🖥 www.limetreekitchen.co.uk; Mon-Fri 7.30am-3pm, Wed-Fri 5.30-11pm, Sat 10am-11pm, Sun 10am-3pm), 14 Station St, is an excellent café-restaurant serving coffee, drinks and light lunches as well as more substantial dishes such as fried sardines with sea beet and marinated cockles (£13).

The Real Eating Company (☎ 01273-402650, 🖥 www.real-eating.co.uk; food Mon-Fri 10am-3pm & 6-9pm, Sat 9am-3pm & 6-10pm, Sun 10am-4pm), 18 Cliffe St, is another recommended café-restaurant, serving drinks and light meals and 'modern British' cuisine. A cream tea is £4.75 and Coronation chicken salad is £10.95.

There's a good restaurant at *Pelham House* (see Where to stay; daily noon-

2.30pm & 6.30-9.30pm). For two/three courses it's £19.50/ £25.

For Italian food you could try *Ask Italian* (☎ 01273-479330; Mon-Sat 11.30am-11pm, Sun 11.30am-10pm) where all the usual pizza and pasta dishes are served in a relaxed atmosphere. Mains cost around £7.50-12. There's also *Famiglia Lazzati* (☎ 01273-479539; Mon-Fri 5-10pm, Sat & Sun noon-10pm) on Market St; it's small and cheerful and the pizzas start at £5.95.

There are several Indian restaurants. *Chaula's Café Restaurant* (☎ 01273-476 707; Sun-Thur 11am-3pm & 5-10.30pm, Fri & Sat 11am-11pm), at 6 Eastgate St near the bus station, is a cheap place to get a filling meal. There's a buffet for £6 and they do takeaway buffet boxes for £3.75. Back on the High St there's *Shanaz Indian Restaurant* (☎ 01273-488028; daily noon-2pm & 6-11pm) which has the usual range of Indian dishes.

There are numerous small cafés and takeaways. The *Charcoal Grill* (☎ 01273-471126; Sun-Thur noon-midnight, Fri & Sat noon-1am) has takeaway pizzas, kebabs and burgers. For cheap home-made pizzas, sandwiches or cakes try *Beckworths* (☎ 01273-474502; Mon-Sat 9am-5pm) which is set in a tiny timber-framed house at 67 High St: it is also a deli which serves a variety of cold meats. Further up the High St, *Castle Sandwich Bar* (☎ 01273-478080; Mon-Fri 9.30am-3pm, Sat 11am-2pm) has very reasonably priced sandwiches.

The Friar Fish and Chip Shop (☎ 01273-472016; Tue-Sat noon-1.45pm & 5-9.30pm) is on the aptly named Fisher St. On the same street there's the *Carnival Chinese Takeaway* (☎ 01273-474221; Wed-Mon 5-11pm). *Panda Garden* (☎ 01273-473235; Tue-Fri noon-2pm & daily 6-10.30pm) is on the High St near the castle.

Another place to find something quick to eat is on the lower High St by the river where *Forfars Bakery* (☎ 01273-474827; Mon-Sat 7am-5pm) has sandwiches and jacket potatoes from £3. There's also *Robson's of Lewes* (☎ 01273-480654; Mon-Sat 9am-5pm, Sun 10am-5pm) on the High St, a coffee shop and takeaway. They serve breakfasts, light lunches and teas.

With a brewery in town it's not surprising that there's a wide choice of pubs to choose from. The *John Harvey Tavern* (☎ 01273-479880; food Mon-Sat noon-2.30pm & 6-9.30pm, Sun noon-4.30pm), part of the famous brewery, is just off the High St. The menu is full of tasty-looking dishes and there is also, of course, plenty of Harveys Ale to wash it all down.

Another good spot for a pint of the local brew is *The Gardener's Arms* (☎ 01273-474808) which is conveniently situated a short way down the High St; it is a popular place with locals wanting a quiet drink.

The Lewes Arms (☎ 01273-473152; food Mon-Fri noon-8.30pm, Sat noon-9pm, Sun noon-8pm) is a lovely traditional pub with snugs and quiet corners where you can enjoy a beer; they offer good pub fare.

On Station St there's a selection of real ales and more pub grub at *The Royal Oak* (☎ 01273-474803; food Mon-Sat noon-2.30pm & 6-9pm, Sun noon-5pm). There's live music on Thursday nights (often folk music) and a steak special (two steaks and two drinks for £25).

❏ Paragliding

At certain points on the Downs, particularly around the Lewes area, colourful canopies can be seen floating effortlessly, high above the hilltops. These paragliders are attracted to the scarp slope of the Downs by thermal updrafts which develop through the course of warm summer days. Anyone can try paragliding with the following companies offering expert tuition to help fledgling fliers take their first flight. The sensation of running along a hilltop only for your feet to leave the ground and find yourself floating like a weightless feather in a cool breeze is certainly a unique way to appreciate the countryside. Popular spots for paragliding include Ditchling Beacon and Mount Caburn near Lewes.

● **Airsports Paragliding** (☎ 01903-879241, 🖳 www.airsports.co.uk) Offers five-day beginners' courses at their private site near Steyning from £495 per person.

● **Airworks Paragliding Centre** (☎ 01273-434002, 🖳 www.airworks.co.uk) One-, five- and ten-day courses for £130, £490 and £890 respectively, operated from their base at Glynde. They can also give tuition in hang-gliding.

● **Freeflight Paragliding** (☎ 01273-628793, 🖳 www.freeflightbrighton.co.uk) Offers tasters from £100 and four-day courses from £500 near Steyning.

KINGSTON-NEAR-LEWES
MAP 36, p152

Kingston-near-Lewes is one of the larger downland villages. From the top of the hill the rather out-of-place housing estate is all too obvious but once down in the village it is well hidden. The main street, lined with pretty cottages, comes as a pleasant surprise.

On The Avenue *Nightingales* (☎ 01273-475673, 🖳 nightingalesbandb.co.uk; 1D/1T, both en suite; ☛; WI-FI) offers B&B for £76-80, £50 for single occupancy. Breakfast features eggs from the owner's free-range hens and home-made bread.

The only place to eat is *The Juggs* (☎ 01273-472523; food Mon-Fri noon-2.30pm & 6-9pm, Sat & Sun noon-9pm, may soon also open for breakfasts), an excellent pub, open all day, with a pretty front garden. There are plenty of vegetarian options on the menu. The unusual name refers to the baskets once used for carrying fish from Brighton to the market in Lewes.

The only **bus** service is Renown Coaches' **bus** No 123, between Lewes and Newhaven; see the public transport map and table, pp44-6.

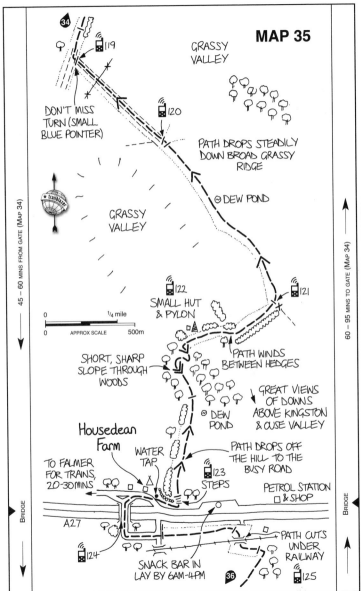

MAP 35

GRASSY VALLEY

📶 119

📶 120

DON'T MISS TURN (SMALL BLUE POINTER)

PATH DROPS STEADILY DOWN BROAD GRASSY RIDGE

⊙ DEW POND

★ trailblazer

GRASSY VALLEY

0   ¼ mile
0   APPROX SCALE   500m

📶 122

SMALL HUT & PYLON

📶 121

PATH WINDS BETWEEN HEDGES

SHORT, SHARP SLOPE THROUGH WOODS

GREAT VIEWS OF DOWNS ABOVE KINGSTON & OUSE VALLEY

⊙ DEW POND

Housedean Farm

WATER TAP

PATH DROPS OFF THE HILL TO THE BUSY ROAD

TO FALMER FOR TRAINS, 20-30 MINS

📶 123 STEPS

PETROL STATION □ & SHOP

A27

📶 124

SNACK BAR IN LAY BY 6AM-4PM

PATH CUTS UNDER RAILWAY

📶 125

BRIDGE

BRIDGE

45 – 60 MINS FROM GATE (MAP 34)

60 – 95 MINS TO GATE (MAP 34)

ROUTE GUIDE AND MAPS

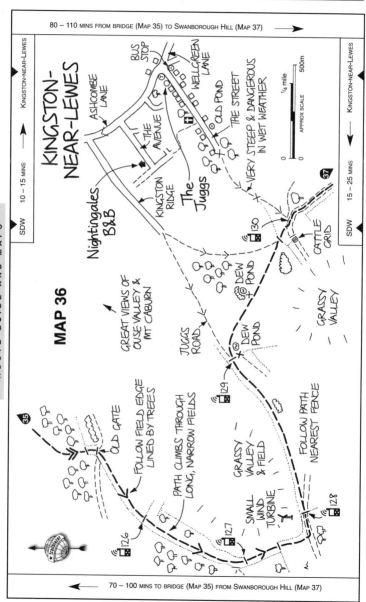

80 – 110 MINS FROM BRIDGE (MAP 35) TO SWANBOROUGH HILL (MAP 37)

KINGSTON-NEAR-LEWES

KINGSTON-NEAR-LEWES

SDW 10 – 15 MINS

SDW 15 – 25 MINS

BUS STOP

MELLGREEN LANE

ASHCOMBE LANE

THE AVENUE

OLD POND

THE STREET

VERY STEEP & DANGEROUS IN WET WEATHER

¼ mile

500m

APPROX SCALE

KINGSTON-NEAR-LEWES

The Juggs

Kingston Ridge

Nightingales B&B

130

37

CATTLE GRID

MAP 36

GREAT VIEWS OF OUSE VALLEY & MT CABURN

DEW POND

GRASSY VALLEY

JUGGS ROAD

DEW POND

35

OLD GATE

FOLLOW FIELD EDGE LINED BY TREES

PATH CLIMBS THROUGH LONG, NARROW FIELDS

129

GRASSY VALLEY & FIELD

FOLLOW PATH NEAREST FENCE

126

127

SMALL WIND TURBINE

128

70 – 100 MINS TO BRIDGE (MAP 35) FROM SWANBOROUGH HILL (MAP 37)

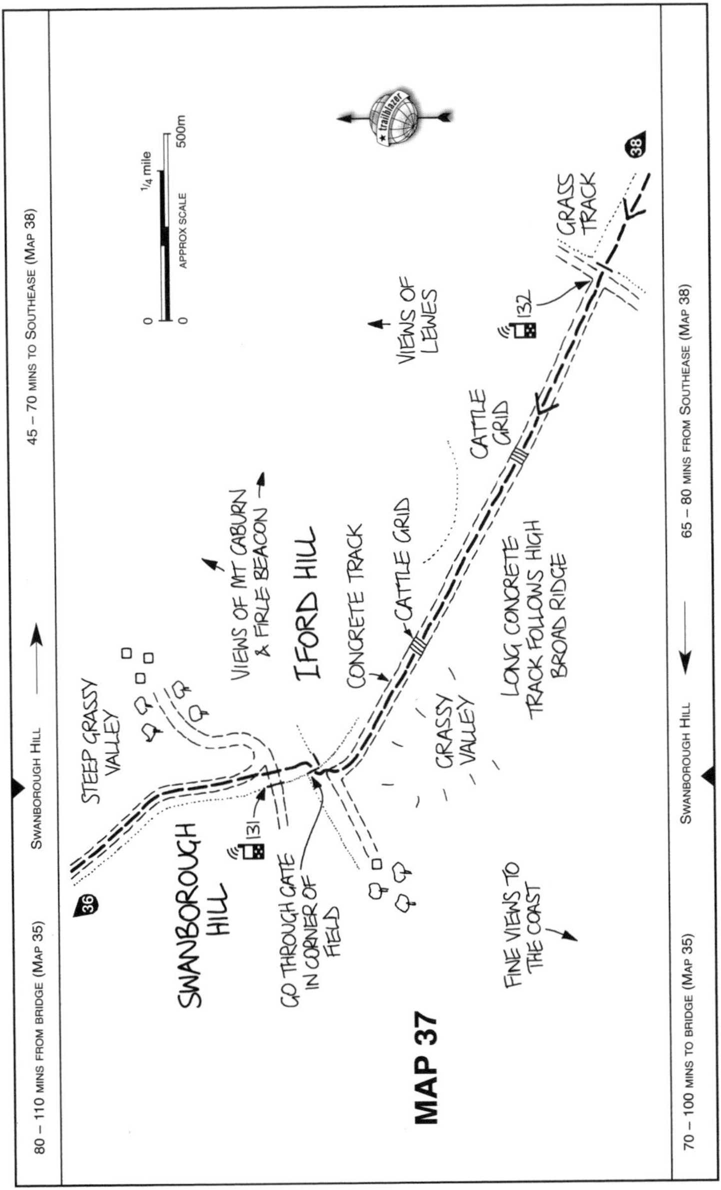
MAP 37
80 – 110 MINS FROM BRIDGE (MAP 35)
SWANBOROUGH HILL
45 – 70 MINS TO SOUTHEASE (MAP 38)
70 – 100 MINS TO BRIDGE (MAP 35)
SWANBOROUGH HILL
65 – 80 MINS FROM SOUTHEASE (MAP 38)
0
0
1/4 mile
500m
APPROX SCALE
trailblazer
36
SWANBOROUGH HILL
STEEP GRASSY VALLEY
131
GO THROUGH GATE IN CORNER OF FIELD
VIEWS OF MT CABURN & FIRLE BEACON
IFORD HILL
CONCRETE TRACK
CATTLE GRID
GRASSY VALLEY
LONG CONCRETE TRACK FOLLOWS HIGH BROAD RIDGE
FINE VIEWS TO THE COAST
CATTLE GRID
VIEWS OF LEWES
132
GRASS TRACK
38

TELSCOMBE   **off MAP 38**
Telscombe Youth Hostel (☎ 0845-371 9663, 🖥 telscombe@yha.org.uk; 22 beds from £13, rooms from £36) is best reached by leaving the South Downs Way at the farm buildings at the bottom of the steep path down Mill Hill. The hostel itself is self-catering only but there is a shop selling basic provisions.

RODMELL   **MAP 38**
Rodmell is famous for having been home to Virginia Woolf (see box below) and her husband Leonard. **Monk's House** (☎ 01273-474760, Apr-Oct Wed-Sun 1-5.30pm, £4.40 or free to NT members), where they once lived, is owned by the National Trust and open to the public. It can be found by walking towards the end of the dead-end lane. Whilst down there it is also a good idea to follow the loop in the road to admire the pretty thatched cottages.

The only **bus** service is Renown Coaches' **bus** No 123, between Lewes and Newhaven; see the public transport map and table, pp44-6.

Where to stay, eat and drink
Opposite the pub, is the friendly *Sunnyside Cottage B&B* (☎ 01273-476876; 1T or F en suite; 🐾), complete with its own goat, and B&B at £35 per person (with no extra charge for single occupancy) including a good cooked breakfast. The accommodation is like a separate flat though the entrance is through the main house.

Down the road to Monk's House is *Deep Thatch Cottage* (☎ 01273-477086; 🖥 deepthatchcottage.co.uk; 1T/2D en suite wi-fi), offering accommodation in three self-contained apartments each with bedroom, bathroom and kitchen. Everything for breakfast is supplied for you to prepare yourself. They charge £75-85 per apartment. Around the corner, *Ash Tree Cottage* B&B (☎ 01273-477982; 🖥 www.ashtreerodmellbandb.co.uk; 1D en suite; wi-fi), offers a similar approach to B&B with a self-catering apartment complete with its own patio. They charge £75 (£50 sgl occ).

The Abergavenny Arms (☎ 01273-472416, 🖥 www.abergavennyarms.com; food Mon-Sat noon-3pm & 6-9pm, Sun noon-4pm) is a great place to take a break and sit by the log fire if it's cold. The name refers to Lord Abergavenny who owned much of the land in this area and it's a freehouse with real ales and tasty meals. The filled rustic rolls (£6) make a great light lunch; main dishes are £10-17. The well inside the pub was once the main source of water for the entire village.

❏ **Virginia Woolf and the Bloomsbury Group**
Born in 1882 in London, Virginia Woolf was a highly accomplished novelist, writing such titles as *The Voyage Out*, *Night and Day*, and *Jacob's Room*. In 1912 she married Leonard Woolf. Their links with Sussex began in 1919 when they moved to the 18th-century **Monk's House** in Rodmell. Their friends included a number of famous artists and writers of the time, not least Virginia's sister the artist Vanessa Bell. Along with the poet TS Eliot and the artists Duncan Grant, Roger Fry and Clive Bell they were known collectively as the Bloomsbury Group.

Many of the paintings from the Bloomsbury Group can be seen in the gallery at the former home of Vanessa Bell and Duncan Grant, **Charleston Manor** (see p156), and also in the small church of St Michael and All Angels at **Berwick** (see p160).

Woolf's life was beset by frequent and sometimes enduring spells of mental breakdown. She tried to kill herself through defenestration (ie throwing herself from a window) before finally, on 18 March 1941, filling her pockets with stones and drowning herself in the nearby River Ouse. Her husband was left with a suicide note in which she spelt out the depths of her love for him: 'If anybody could have saved me it would have been you. Everything has gone from me but the certainty of your goodness'.

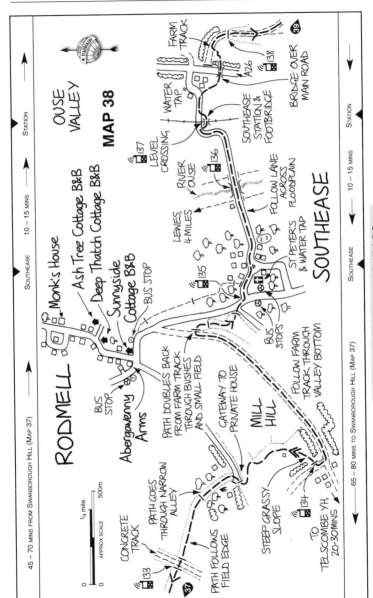

SOUTHEASE   MAP 38, p155

Not far from Rodmell and actually lying on the route of the Way is Southease. This is a very small settlement, tucked away from any main roads, with a tiny Saxon church, **St Peter's**, incorporating an unusual Norman round tower. This round tower is one of three in Sussex, all in the Ouse Valley and all built in the first half of the 12th century. Inside the church are the remains of some wall paintings which date from the 13th century and which used to cover the whole church; they were revealed again in the 1930s. The triangular village green surrounded by cottages makes an excellent lunch stop.

Because Southease is on the **train** line between Lewes and Seaford it's an ideal place to start or end a day walk; services operate approximately once an hour. Renown Coaches **bus** No 123, between Lewes and Newhaven, stops here; see the public transport map and table, pp44-6.

SOUTHEASE TO ALFRISTON   MAPS 38-42

Continuing along the crest of the escarpment, with the high point at Firle Beacon (Map 40), this stretch affords easy walking for **7¾ miles (12.5km, 2½-3½hrs)** with fine views to the coast and across the lowlands to **Mount Caburn**, probably the most grandiose name for any hill of 150 metres altitude.

Once past **Bostal Hill** (Map 41) the path drops steadily down to pretty wee Alfriston.

WEST FIRLE   off MAP 40, p158

This small village among the trees at the foot of the Downs escarpment has few facilities to attract the walker but there is **Firle Stores & Post Office** (☎ 01273 858219; Mon-Sat 9am-5.30pm, closed for lunch 1-2pm, Sat 9am-1pm and also May-Sep until 3pm on Sat and 10.30am-4pm on Sun), which offers plenty of choice for your lunchbox.

You can now stay at *The Ram Inn* (☎ 01273-858222; ☐ www.raminn.co.uk; 2D/2T en suite; ☛; 🐾; WI-FI) and they charge £90-110 for each room Mon-Thur and £110-145 Fri-Sun. Food (main dishes £10-19) is served in what was formerly the Court Room where judges once passed sentence on misbehaving villagers. The real ales are worth the detour and the bar is open 11.30am-11.30pm every day with the kitchen open Mon-Fri noon-3pm & 6.30-9.30, Sat & Sun 9-10.30am, noon-4pm & 6.30-9.30pm.

About a mile from the village is **Charleston Manor** (☎ 01323-811626, ☐ www.charleston.org.uk; Apr-Oct Wed-Sun daily 1-6pm, July & Aug from noon, admission £9.50) which houses a gallery of work by the Bloomsbury group of artists (see box p154), and hosts a festival each May (see p13). Charleston is a stop on Cuckmere Community Bus's No 25 Saturday service; see public transport map and table, pp44-6.

ALCISTON   off MAP 41, p159

Alciston is yet another beautiful but tiny downland village with little to draw the walker here apart from *The Rose Cottage Inn* (☎ 01323-870377, ☐ www.therosecottageinn.co.uk; 1S/1D, food Mon-Sat noon-2pm & 6.30-9.30pm, Sun noon-2pm & 6.30-9pm; ☛), a genuine country pub that has been around for over 350 years. Timber framing and open fires add to the charm and there is also a good choice of locally brewed ales though the bar is closed in the afternoons (3-6.30pm). There is a mouth-watering menu based on locally sourced produce: the restaurant menu contains a wide selection of fish dishes as well as standard pub fare. They offer **B&B** in two self-contained flats with a kitchen/lounge diner, toilet and shower room at £70 for the single and £120 for double: this is the total price for the **two-night** minimum stay.

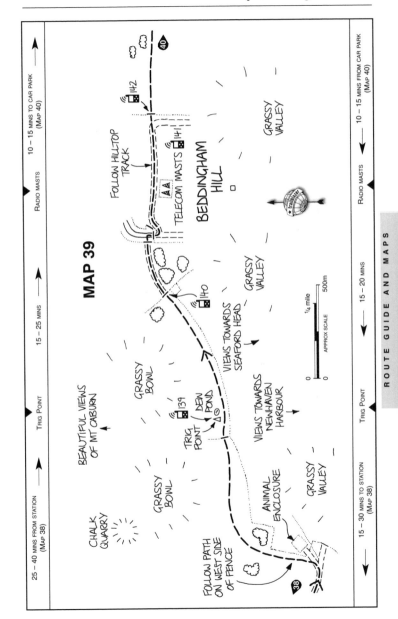

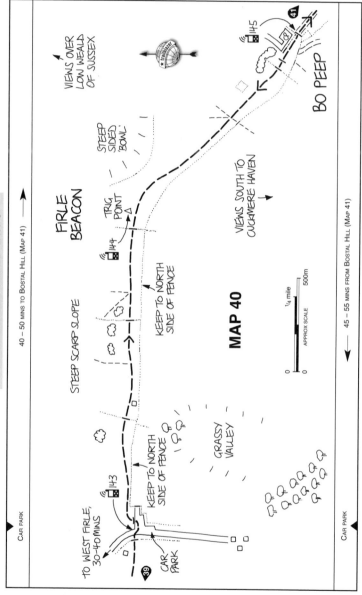

40 – 50 MINS TO BOSTAL HILL (MAP 41) →

CAR PARK

VIEWS OVER LOW WEALD OF SUSSEX

🔋145

BO PEEP

STEEP SIDED 'BOWL'

FIRLE BEACON

TRIG POINT △

🔋144

VIEWS SOUTH TO CUCKMERE HAVEN

STEEP SCARP SLOPE

KEEP TO NORTH SIDE OF FENCE

MAP 40

¼ mile
0   APPROX SCALE   500m
0

🔋143

KEEP TO NORTH SIDE OF FENCE

GRASSY VALLEY

TO WEST FIRLE, 30–40 MINS

CAR PARK

39

CAR PARK

45 – 55 MINS FROM BOSTAL HILL (MAP 41)

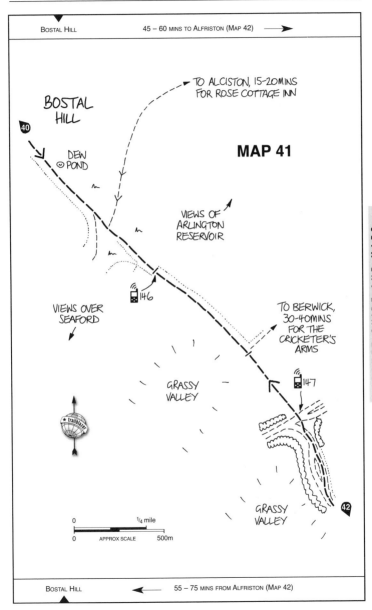

BOSTAL HILL

45 – 60 MINS TO ALFRISTON (MAP 42) ⟶

TO ALCISTON, 15-20MINS
FOR ROSE COTTAGE INN

BOSTAL
HILL

40

DEW
⊙ POND

MAP 41

VIEWS OF
ARLINGTON
RESERVOIR

146

VIEWS OVER
SEAFORD

TO BERWICK,
30-40MINS
FOR THE
CRICKETER'S
ARMS

147

GRASSY
VALLEY

trailblazer

42

GRASSY
VALLEY

0   1/4 mile

0   APPROX SCALE   500m

BOSTAL HILL   ⟵   55 – 75 MINS FROM ALFRISTON (MAP 42)

BERWICK   off MAP 41, p159

Berwick is famous for the Bloomsbury Group of Victorian artists which included Vanessa Bell, Roger Fry and Duncan Grant. Some of Vanessa Bell's work can be seen in the small **church** on the edge of the village.

For food head to *The Cricketer's Arms* (☎ 01323-870469, 🖵 www.cricketers berwick.co.uk; food Apr-Sep daily noon-9pm, mid Sep-Apr Mon-Fri noon-2.15pm & 6-9pm, Sat & Sun noon-9pm; open all day at Easter and on bank holidays).

They serve a range of salads (fresh dressed crab with granary bread, £11), sharing platters and pub favourites such as ham, eggs and chips (£9.50).

Berwick is a stop on the London to Eastbourne **train** line and Cuckmere Community **bus** operates several routes (see public transport map and table, pp44-6), most of which connect with train arrivals here, making it an ideal place to start or end a day walk.

ALFRISTON   MAP 42

Alfriston is another candidate for 'prettiest village on the South Downs Way'. However, this small collection of Tudor wood-beamed buildings slung higgledy-piggledy along a narrow main street is far from a well-kept secret. In high season coachloads of tourists come to 'ooh' and 'ahh' at the sights and have cream teas. Nevertheless, it is worth planning on spending a few hours to take it all in at a leisurely pace.

Whilst here make sure you take a look around the **church** and the **Clergy House** (see box below) by the church and the village green.

Services

The **post office** (Mon-Fri 9am-5.30pm, Sat 9am-12.30pm) on The Square doubles as the village **shop/deli** (Mon-Sat 8am-7pm, Sun 10am-5pm). It is worth a visit just to take in its almost authentic 'Olde Worlde' atmosphere. The now-forgotten 'Lamson' system of moving cash to a single cashier whereby cannisters containing the money were shot along wires and tubes is still in

place, though no longer used. The deli here is a great place to pick up the ingredients for a top class picnic.

There's an excellent independent bookshop, **Much Ado Books** (☎ 01323-871222, 🖵 www.muchadobooks.com; Wed-Sat 10am-5pm, Sun 11am-5pm) with an interesting stock of old and new books, maps and guides. Another good place to browse is **Music Memorabilia**, a record and CD shop.

For those with a sweet tooth, **Munchlicious** (daily 10am-5pm) sells a bewildering array of chocolate; anything from Columbian to organic. They sell ice creams in the summer months and also have traditional sweets if you fancy something for the next day of walking.

Cuckmere Community **bus**'s Nos 26, 42 & 47 services stop here as does Countryliner's No 125 service (Alfriston to Lewes) and Renown's No 126 service (Eastbourne to Seaford); see public transport map and table, pp44-6.

❏ **Alfriston Church and Clergy House**

The 14th-century flint church by the river sits in the middle of a well-groomed lawn and is worth a look, as is the Clergy House (☎ 01323-871961, 🖵 www.nation altrust.org.uk; daily except Thur & Fri* late Feb-mid Mar & Nov-mid Dec 11am-4pm, mid Mar-end Oct 10.30am-5pm; £4.50) next door. This beautiful 14th-century, timber-framed thatched house was the first property the National Trust bought thanks to the local vicar who in 1896 suggested the building be safeguarded for the nation. Apart from anything else it's a good spot for lunch.   *(In Aug also open Fri)

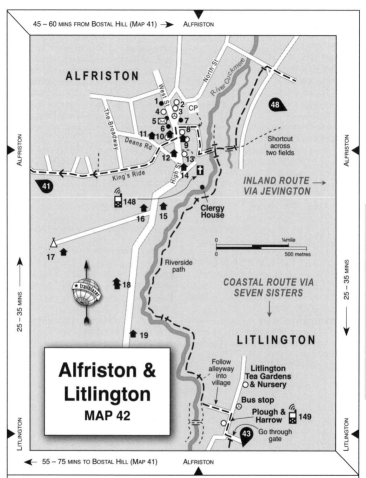

45 – 60 MINS FROM BOSTAL HILL (MAP 41) → ALFRISTON

ALFRISTON

West St

North St

River Cuckmere

48

CP

1
2
3
4
5
6
7
8
10
11
9
12
13
14

Deans Rd

The Broadway

The Broadway

King's Ride

High St

41

148

16   15

Shortcut across two fields

INLAND ROUTE →
VIA JEVINGTON

Clergy House

0   ¼mile
0   500 metres

17

COASTAL ROUTE VIA
SEVEN SISTERS

Riverside path

18

19

trailblazer

Alfriston &
Litlington

MAP 42

LITLINGTON

Follow alleyway into village

Litlington
Tea Gardens
& Nursery

Bus stop

Plough &
Harrow

149

43   Go through gate

← 55 – 75 MINS TO BOSTAL HILL (MAP 41)   ALFRISTON

ALFRISTON

ALFRISTON

25 – 35 MINS

LITLINGTON

25 – 35 MINS

LITLINGTON

Where to stay
9 The George Inn
10 The Star Inn
11 April Cottage
12 Chestnuts B&B
14 Wingrove House
15 Deans Place Hotel
16 Dacres
17 Pleasant Rise Farm
   Campsite & B&B

Where to stay (cont'd)
18 Riverdale House &
   Highcroft B&B
19 YHA Alfriston Frog Firle

Other
1 Much Ado Books
5 Village Shop/Deli & PO
6 Music Memorabilia
7 Munchlicious

Where to eat and drink
2 Badgers Tea House
3 The Singing Kettle
4 Ye Olde Smugglers Inne
   (Market Inn)
5 Deli (in Village Shop)
8 Tudor House Restaurant
9 The George Inn
10 The Star Inn
13 Moonrakers

Where to stay

For the latest information on accommodation it's worth checking the village website: 🖥 www.alfriston-village.co.uk

YHA Alfriston Frog Firle (☎ 0845-371 9101, 🖥 alfriston@yha.org.uk; 68 beds from £15, rooms from £36; WI-FI) is about a mile down the road. The hostel has all the usual facilities, offers meals and internet access is available.

Campers should also head to the southern extreme of the village where a sign points down a track to *Pleasant Rise Farm Campsite* (🖥 alfristoncampingpark@hot mail.co.uk – contact by email only); pitches cost £7 per person. There are 60 pitches. Also on the farm there's B&B at *Pleasant Rise Farm* (☎ 01323-871298, 🖥 linda@pleasant-rise-farm.co.uk; 1T/1D, en suite; 🐾). They charge £80 for the twin room and £70 for the double (£45 sgl occ).

In the village itself there are few cheap options though *Chestnuts B&B* (☎ 01323-870298, 🖥 www.chestnuts-alfriston.co.uk; 1D/2T shared bathroom; ☛; 🐾 ; WI-FI) is from £70 for two (single occupancy is £50).

Dacres (☎ 01323-870447; 1T or Tr en suite), charges from £40 per person (from £42 for single occupancy). The room is more of a studio apartment and a third bed (not a folding bed) can be moved into the sitting area. There's a lovely garden and the hospitable owner provides excellent organic cooked breakfasts.

April Cottage (☎ 01323-870536, 🖥 www.aprilcottage-alfriston.co.uk; 1S/1T/2D, with 2 guest bathrooms; ☛; WI-FI), 3 Deans Rd, charges from £70 for two and from £40 for the single room.

Riverdale House (☎ 01323-871038, 🖥 www.riverdalehouse.co.uk; 5 rooms which can be arranged as doubles, twins or triples; en suite; ☛; WI-FI), is peacefully located on the edge of the village, off Seaford Rd. It's a very comfortable B&B and rates for the rooms range from £80 to £95 (£130-140 for the suite) depending on the size of the room and the season. Transfers available. Sharing the same driveway as Riverdale next door, *Highcroft B&B* (☎ 01323-870553, 🖥

www.highcroftalfriston.co.uk; 2D/1T; en suite or private bathroom; ☛; WI-FI), charges from £75 to £95 for two people. An extra bed (£25 per adult including breakfast) can be put in one of the rooms.

Wingrove House (☎ 01323-870276, 🖥 www.wingrovehousealfriston.com; 4D/1T, all en suite; ☛; 🐾 ; WI-FI) is a 19th century colonial style house that has five luxurious rooms and a good restaurant. Prices vary according to season but start at around £50 per person.

The Star Inn (☎ 01323-870495, 🖥 www.thestaralfriston.co.uk; 2S/21D/14T, all en suite; ☛; 🐾 £7.50; WI-FI) is one of the oldest inns in England, said to date back to 1345 (see box p164). Prices for B&B vary considerably depending on season and demand and you can pay as little as £65 for two people or as much as £130. Check the website.

The George Inn (☎ 01323-870319, 🖥 www.thegeorge-alfriston.com; 1S/5D, all en suite; ☛; 🐾 ; WI-FI) is a magnificent old building with oak beams. The rates for B&B here are from £100 for two in a double; the single is from £70.

At the southern end of the village is the large *Deans Place Hotel* (☎ 01323-870248, 🖥 www.deansplacehotel.co.uk; 3S/29D or T/4F, all en suite; ☛; 🐾 £5; WI-FI) a smart 14th-century country house hotel set in a big garden with manicured lawns and a swimming-pool. Prices range from about £100 to £160 for two people in a double room but contact them to enquire if they have any special deals.

Moonrakers Restaurant (☎ 01323-871199) has one double room. See opposite for their dinner, B&B package.

Where to eat and drink

For such a small village Alfriston does well for pubs and cafés, many of which have long histories.

Badgers Tea House (☎ 01323-871336; daily 9.30am-4.30pm, food until 3.30pm) is a traditional English teashop with a little walled garden to sit in. Housed in a building dating back to 1510, they serve breakfasts (from £6.95), a selection of home-made cakes, soups served with chunky bread (£5.25), light lunches (dressed crab £8.25) and cream teas (£6.25).

Of a similar ilk is *The Singing Kettle* (☎ 01323-870723; daily 10am-5pm) which does tasty snacks such as buck rarebit (cheese on toast with a poached egg on top; £5.35) and ploughman's (£7.95).

One of the best pubs is undoubtedly *The George Inn* (see Where to stay; Mon-Sun noon-9pm) where sea bass with salsa verde costs £15.95.

Tudor House Restaurant (☎ 01323-870891, 🖳 www.tudorhouse-restaurant.co .uk; daily 10.30am-5pm, Wed-Sat 7-9.30pm) is good value: loin of pork with sage stuffing is £8.95.

The Star Inn (see Where to stay; food daily noon-2.30pm & 6-9pm, all day in holiday periods) has bar meals and a restaurant which is usually candlelit and in winter there is a roaring fire. The three-course

roast Sunday lunch menu is £21.95, but they have much cheaper bar meals and they do a decent cream tea for £5.95.

Ye Olde Smugglers Inne (aka The Market Inn; ☎ 01323-870241; food daily noon-9pm) has friendly staff and an attractive conservatory at the back. Main dishes in the restaurant range from £8.95 for pasta dishes to £16.95 for the steak. The name is derived from a famous gang of smugglers (see box p164) who once used the pub to plan smuggling ventures at Cuckmere Haven.

Moonrakers Restaurant (☎ 01323-871199, 🖳 www.moonrakersrestaurant.co .uk; Wed-Sat noon-2.30pm & 6.30-midnight, Sun noon-4pm) is a smart place with set lunch menus for £15.50/19.50 for two/three courses. The set dinner costs £35. If you want to make a real occasion of it they have a double **room** upstairs: dinner, B&B for two is £185-215.

ALFRISTON TO EASTBOURNE (COASTAL ROUTE VIA CUCKMERE)
MAPS 42-47

These **10½ miles (17km, 4¼-5¾hrs** – plus another 1½ miles to Eastbourne; see town map p179) are arguably the highlight of the whole walk, including a stretch through the beautiful **Cuckmere Valley** (Map 43, p165) which culminates in wide meanders leading to what is one of the few undeveloped river mouths in the South-East.

The final assault on Eastbourne is a spectacular roller-coaster ride over the **Seven Sisters** (or should that be eight; see Map 44, p167 & Map 45, p168), a line of chalk cliffs that are less famous than their Dover counterparts but far more spectacular.

If that was not enough the path continues to reach the final high point of the whole walk: **Beachy Head**, a spectacular chalk cliff jutting into the English Channel with 360° views (Map 47, p170). Even the sprawling mess of Eastbourne is well worth admiring from here.

The path finishes at the foot of the hill where it meets abruptly with Eastbourne's suburbs. There is accommodation and refreshments in the neighbourhood of **Meads Village** (see p171) but if you want to go into Eastbourne there is a bus (see p178) or a rather tedious half-hour walk to the town centre. Alternatively, after walking one hundred miles there is no shame in calling a **taxi** to the town centre and Eastbourne Taxis (☎ 01323-720720) have a reliable fleet.

ROUTE GUIDE AND MAPS

LITLINGTON   MAP 42, p161

Sitting on the eastern bank of the Cuckmere River, Litlington is yet another oh-so-charming little downland village complete with flint cottages. On the other side of the valley is a chalk-horse figure carved into the hillside by a certain James Pagden.

The local pub is the *Plough and Harrow* (☎ 01323-870632; food Mon noon-2.30pm, Tue-Thur noon-2.30pm & 6-8.30pm, Fri noon-2.30pm & 6.30-9pm, Sat noon-3pm & 6.30-9 pm, Sun noon-3pm &

6.30-8.30pm) which serves a variety of bar meals ranging from a ploughman's lunch (£7.50) to rabbit & pancetta pie (£10.50). The bar is open all day.

This village is also home to the very popular *Litlington Tea Gardens & Nursery* (☎ 01323-870222; Apr-Nov Tue-Sun & Bank Hols 11am-5pm). It's well worth leaving the path here to stop for a relaxing cup of tea and a scone in the lovely garden.

❏ Smuggling

Smuggling of wool, brandy and gin was rife along the Sussex coast with Cuckmere Haven and Birling Gap being favourite places for gangs of smugglers to load and unload their contraband in the late 18th and early 19th centuries. One of the most infamous groups was the Alfriston Gang who would smuggle goods to and from Cuckmere Haven along the Cuckmere River.

The leader of the Alfriston Gang was Stanton Collins who owned the now aptly named Ye Olde Smugglers Inn from where the group plotted their exploits. These included a raid on a Dutch ship wrecked at Cuckmere Haven. The figurehead of the ship, a red lion's head, still stands next to the Star Inn in the village. Stanton Collins was eventually arrested in 1831 for sheep rustling and was shipped off to Australia.

WESTDEAN & EXCEAT   MAP 43

On the north side of the small wooded ridge of chalk is the wonderfully secluded and secret **Westdean**, a tiny collection of beautiful cottages complete with duck pond, nestled in a wooded fold. On the other side of the ridge is **Exceat**, more a collection of tourist facilities than a village but with a very good information centre. This is the gateway to the **Seven Sisters Country Park** (see box p166) and the spectacular Cuckmere Valley and beach.

If Exceat is an overnight stop on your walk, try to arrive here early in the day to give yourself time to enjoy the area around the beach.

Services

The excellent **information centre** (now staffed by volunteers and open irregular hours) next to the path, has information on wildlife and conservation efforts in the Seven Sisters Country Park. **Bikes** can be hired (£25 a day) next door at Cuckmere

Cycle Co (aka Seven Sisters Cycle Co; ☎ 01323-870310, 🖥 www.cuckmere-cycle .co.uk; summer daily 10am-6pm, winter 10am to dusk). There's a **water fountain** behind the toilet block.

For a **bus**, Brighton & Hove Buses' Nos 12 and 12a pass through Exceat and provide a regular service between Brighton and Eastbourne. Cuckmere Community Bus's No 47 service also stops here; see public transport map and table, pp44-6.

Where to stay and eat

Exceat Farmhouse (☎ 01323-870218; 1D/ 1T, one en suite and the other with private bathroom; ☛; 🐾) is a 17th-century farmhouse with B&B from £80 per room; £50 for single occupancy. Their *restaurant* (mid-Feb to mid-Nov daily 10am-4pm, to 5pm in the main season; mid-Nov to mid-Feb Fri-Mon 10am-4pm) offers lunches, drinks and some delicious home-made cakes; they can also provide packed lunches.

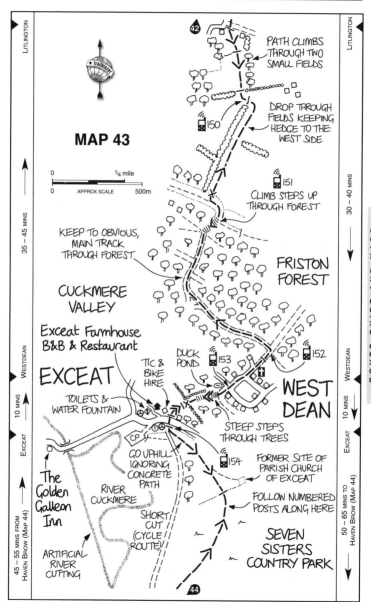

LITLINGTON

PATH CLIMBS THROUGH TWO SMALL FIELDS

DROP THROUGH FIELDS KEEPING HEDGE TO THE WEST SIDE

MAP 43

150

CLIMB STEPS UP THROUGH FOREST

0   ¼ mile
0   APPROX SCALE   500m

KEEP TO OBVIOUS, MAIN TRACK THROUGH FOREST

CUCKMERE VALLEY

FRISTON FOREST

Exceat Farmhouse B&B & Restaurant

DUCK POND

153

152

EXCEAT

TIC & BIKE HIRE

WEST DEAN

TOILETS & WATER FOUNTAIN

STEEP STEPS THROUGH TREES

CP

The Golden Galleon Inn

GO UPHILL IGNORING CONCRETE PATH

154

FORMER SITE OF PARISH CHURCH OF EXCEAT

RIVER CUCKMERE

SHORT CUT (CYCLE ROUTE)

FOLLOW NUMBERED POSTS ALONG HERE

SEVEN SISTERS COUNTRY PARK

ARTIFICIAL RIVER CUTTING

42

44

LITLINGTON

30 – 40 MINS

WESTDEAN

10 MINS

50 – 65 MINS TO HAVEN BROW (MAP 44)

ROUTE GUIDE AND MAPS

35 – 45 MINS

WESTDEAN

10 MINS

EXCEAT

45 – 55 MINS FROM HAVEN BROW (MAP 44)

By the bridge, the large *Golden Galleon Inn* (☎ 01323-892247; food Mon-Sat noon-10pm, Sun noon-9.30pm; WI-FI) has a big garden overlooking the River Cuckmere. Their menu includes salmon and broccoli fishcakes with salad or chips for £7.75. It gets very busy during the sum-mer due to its great location. If staying at Exceat Farmhouse and visiting the pub in the evening, take a torch as the road between the two is unlit.

(Note that **Foxhole Campsite** is now open only to educational groups. For infor-mation ☎ 01273-482670).

❏ **Seven Sisters Country Park**

This extensive country park (🖳 www.sevensisters.org.uk) of rolling coastal down-land includes the spectacular Seven Sisters chalk cliffs over which the South Downs Way passes. There is an excellent visitor centre at Exceat where you can glean all sorts of information from the displays and exhibitions.

Apart from the obvious attraction of the chalk cliffs and downland the park also includes Cuckmere Haven and estuary, one of the only river mouths in the south-east of England that has not been spoilt by development. That is not to say that the estu-ary is untouched. The natural meanders of the river, seen so spectacularly from the ridge above Exceat, have been left to sit as idle ponds thanks to the man-made chan-nel that diverts the flow of the river more swiftly to the sea. Plans were underway to restore the Cuckmere Estuary to its natural state by filling in the man-made channel and allowing the blockade to gradually deteriorate. This would have restored the flow of the river through the meanders and encouraged the natural restoration of the salt-marsh and mudflats. However, by 2006 this plan had been suspended after a 'model-ling miscalculation' by the project's environmental consultant was found.

The country park covers an area steeped in history. Some of the most fascinat-ing stories involve the numerous shipwrecks that litter the seabed below the Seven Sisters cliffs. The most significant of these is that of the Spanish ship *Nympha Americana* which, in 1747, ran aground halfway along the line of chalk cliffs, result-ing in the deaths of thirty crewmen.

BIRLING GAP   **MAP 45, p168**

All that's in this gap is a small line of ter-raced houses that are falling into the sea, a B&B and a café/bar. Considering the beau-tiful position of the hamlet on a low saddle along the line of chalk cliffs, it's a shame that some of the buildings are so ugly and out of place. However, now that the hotel has been closed and been taken over by the National Trust as a café and bar perhaps they can do something to make the place more in keeping with the surroundings. The attractive fish design fence is a good start.

The *Boathouse B&B* (☎ 01323-423073; 2D/1S, all en suite) is perfectly located and the friendly owner offers B&B for £45 for a double, or £30 for the single.

National Trust Café & Bar (☎ 01323-423197, 🖳 www.nationaltrust.org.uk; food daily 11.30am-4pm, breakfasts from 10am) has outside seating and a great range of cakes, salads and light lunches. A bacon roll and a pot of tea/coffee is £4.65, served 10-11.30am. The adjoining bar (same hours) also does lunches.

A 15-20 minute walk from Birling Gap, *Belle Tout Lighthouse* (☎ 01323-423185, 🖳 www.belletoute.co.uk; 6D en suite; ☞; WI-FI) is now a luxury B&B with incredible coastal views. They charge between £145 and £215 for two depending on the room and the season. There's usual-ly a two-night minimum stay policy but if you contact them within a week of your arrival they may be able to offer a single nights. Outside the lighthouse there's a *snack shop* serving drinks and ice-creams.

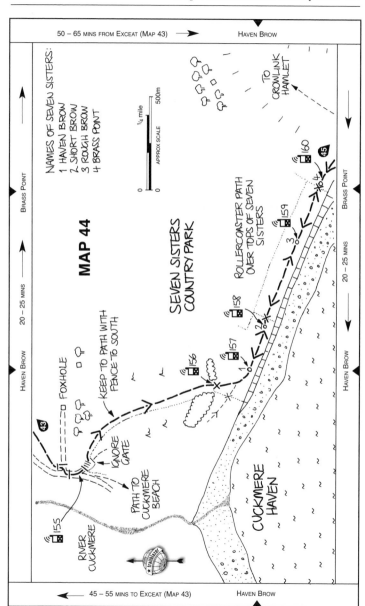

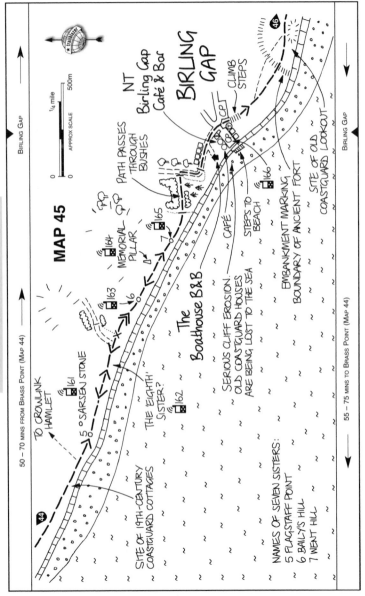

MAP 45

← 50 – 70 MINS FROM BRASS POINT (MAP 44)

BIRLING GAP

APPROX SCALE
¼ mile
500m

TO CROWLINK HAMLET

5 ° SARSEN STONE

SITE OF 19TH-CENTURY COASTGUARD COTTAGES

THE 'EIGHTH' SISTER?

PATH PASSES THROUGH BUSHES

MEMORIAL PILLAR

NT Birling Gap Café & Bar

BIRLING GAP

CLIMB STEPS

The Boathouse B&B

~ CAFÉ

STEPS TO BEACH

SERIOUS CLIFF EROSION. OLD COASTGUARD HOUSES ARE BEING LOST TO THE SEA

EMBANKMENT MARKING BOUNDARY OF ANCIENT FORT

SITE OF OLD COASTGUARD LOOKOUT

BIRLING GAP

55 – 75 MINS TO BRASS POINT (MAP 44)

NAMES OF SEVEN SISTERS:
5 FLAGSTAFF POINT
6 BAILY'S HILL
7 WENT HILL

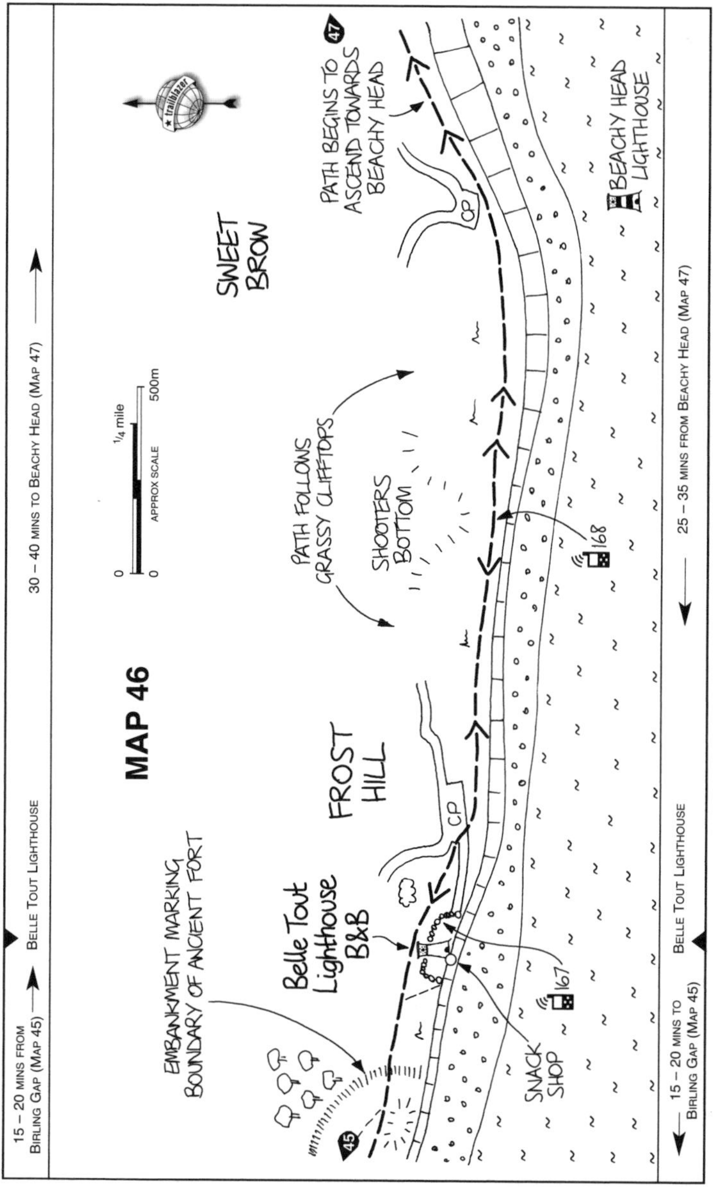
15 – 20 mins from Birling Gap (Map 45)
Belle Tout Lighthouse
30 – 40 mins to Beachy Head (Map 47)
MAP 46
0
0
APPROX SCALE
1/4 mile
500m
trailblazer
EMBANKMENT MARKING BOUNDARY OF ANCIENT FORT
Belle Tout Lighthouse B&B
FROST HILL
CP
PATH FOLLOWS GRASSY CLIFFTOPS
SHOOTERS BOTTOM
SWEET BROW
CP
PATH BEGINS TO ASCEND TOWARDS BEACHY HEAD
47
45
SNACK SHOP
167
168
BEACHY HEAD LIGHTHOUSE
15 – 20 mins to Birling Gap (Map 45)
Belle Tout Lighthouse
25 – 35 mins from Beachy Head (Map 47)

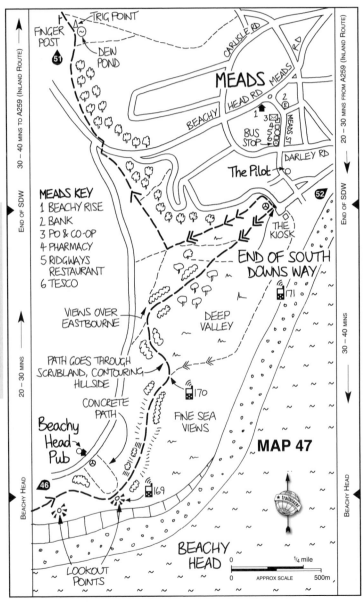

TRIG POINT

FINGER POST

51

DEW POND

CARLISLE RD

MEADS

BEACHY HEAD RD MEADS

MEADS RD

1
2
3
4
5
6

BUS STOP

MEADS ST

DARLEY RD

The Pilot

52

THE KIOSK

MEADS KEY
1 BEACHY RISE
2 BANK
3 PO & CO-OP
4 PHARMACY
5 RIDGWAYS RESTAURANT
6 TESCO

END OF SOUTH DOWNS WAY

171

VIEWS OVER EASTBOURNE

DEEP VALLEY

PATH GOES THROUGH SCRUBLAND, CONTOURING HILLSIDE

170

CONCRETE PATH

FINE SEA VIEWS

MAP 47

Beachy Head Pub

46

169

LOOKOUT POINTS

BEACHY HEAD

0   1/4 mile

0   500m
APPROX SCALE

30 – 40 MINS TO A259 (INLAND ROUTE)

END OF SDW

20 – 30 MINS

BEACHY HEAD

20 – 30 – 30 MINS FROM A259 (INLAND ROUTE)

END OF SDW

30 – 40 MINS

BEACHY HEAD

BEACHY HEAD   MAP 47

Beachy Head is, thankfully, relatively unspoilt with just one large chain pub near the top: *The Beachy Head* (☎ 01323-728060; food Mon-Sat noon-10pm, Sun noon-9.30pm; WI-FI). It's not the best place to celebrate the walk's end but could be useful if you need to shelter from the weather. The food is good value and there's free wi-fi here.

Brighton & Hove's No 12a **bus** service and Eastbourne Buses' No 3 service call here; see public transport map and table, pp44-6.

MEADS VILLAGE   MAP 47

Meads Village is actually the most westerly suburb of Eastbourne. It is a quiet, well-to-do part of town with a genuine village feel. More importantly for South Downs Way walkers, it is positioned right at the official end of the walk, making a stop here a more appealing prospect than the half-hour walk into the hectic centre of Eastbourne.

To reach Meads Village head straight on where the South Downs Way reaches the ice-cream kiosk at the bottom of the hill and turn left at Holywell Rd.

Services

Everything one might need here is centred along one short stretch of Meads St. There is a **Co-op** (Mon-Sat 7.30am-9pm, Sun 8am-9pm) on the corner of Matlock Rd which also incorporates the **post office** (Mon-Fri 9am-5.30pm, Sat 9am-12.30pm), a **Tesco Express** (daily 6am-11pm) and a bank with an **ATM**.

For those requiring attention to blistered feet there's **Meads Pharmacy** (Mon-Fri 9am-1pm & 2-5.30pm, Sat 9am-1pm).

Eastbourne **Buses**' No 3 service is the one to catch into central Eastbourne; see public transport map and table, pp44-6. The bus leaves from the foot of the hill at the end of the path and also from here.

Where to stay and eat

The closest accommodation to the end of the walk – indeed the only option here – is *Beachy Rise* (☎ 01323-639171, ☐ www.beachyrise.com; 2D/1F/2D or T, all en suite; ✆; WI-FI) on Meads Rd with B&B from £25-35 per person.

The Pilot (☎ 01323-723440; food Mon-Fri noon-2.30pm & 6-9pm, Sat noon-9pm, Sun noon-7pm), on a bend on Meads St, is the first pub reached after leaving the end of the South Downs Way. The bar is open all day which makes it convenient for a celebration drink.

If, after 100 miles, you feel the need to treat yourself and push the boat out you can do no better than book a table at the exclusive *Ridgways Restaurant* (☎ 01323-726805, ☐ www.ridgwaysrestaurant.co.uk; Tue-Sat noon-1.45pm & 7pm to late, Sun noon-1.45pm, booking strongly advised). They specialise in traditional English dishes. The 'smart/casual wear only' notice means that the hiking boots will have to be left behind.

EASTBOURNE

For the guide to Eastbourne turn to p178.

❏ **Important note – walking times**
Unless otherwise specified, **all times in this book refer only to the time spent walking.** You will need to add 20-30% to allow for rests, photography, checking the map, drinking water etc.

ALFRISTON TO EASTBOURNE (INLAND ROUTE VIA JEVINGTON)
MAP 42 p161 & MAPS 48-51

This inland **alternative route** is geared towards horse-riders and cyclists but walkers are welcome to use the bridleway too.

Although these **7½ miles (12km, 2¾-3½hrs** – plus another 1½ miles to Eastbourne centre) are not as spectacular as the coastal route there are still plenty of fine downland views to enjoy high up on **Windover Hill** (Map 48, opposite) while a detour to see the famous **Long Man of Wilmington** (see box below) is strongly recommended.

It is a good idea to keep an extra day spare for this section even if you have already walked the coastal route.

MILTON STREET   MAP 48

Milton Street is nothing more than a small collection of scattered houses. There is, however, a good pub here, *The Sussex Ox* (☎ 01323-870840, 🖳 www.thesussexox .co.uk; food served daily noon-2pm & 6-9pm). Although it is closed in the afternoons between 3pm and 6pm, it is worth a visit. The varied menu changes daily but it might feature chilli beef ox burger (£9.50), duck confit (£14), seared calf's liver (£11) or mussels (£10).

WILMINGTON   off MAP 48

Wilmington is best known for the Long Man, a huge chalk figure adorning Windover Hill above the village.

A little way from the South Downs Way on the main road north of the village is *Crossways Hotel* (☎ 01323-482455, 🖳 www.crosswayshotel.co.uk; 1S/4D/2T, all en suite; ➥; WI-FI) with B&B from £135. The single room costs £79. From Tuesday to Saturday (7.30-8.30pm) they serve a four-course set meal including coffee for £36.95 .

❏ The Long Man of Wilmington

No-one is quite sure when or why this large chalk figure appeared on the side of Windover Hill above Wilmington (Map 48, opposite).

Best viewed from the lane leading out of the village, he stands 70m tall and holds a vertical rod in each hand. Although it was only in 1969 that the white blocks were placed along the lines of the figure, suggestions as to when the original was made range from the prehistoric era or the Roman age to just a few hundred years ago.

As for the question of why, well that is even harder to answer. Some say he is a fertility symbol robbed of his genitalia; others claim he was carved out for fun by monks from the nearby Wilmington Priory. Or could it be that a real giant collapsed and died on that very spot?

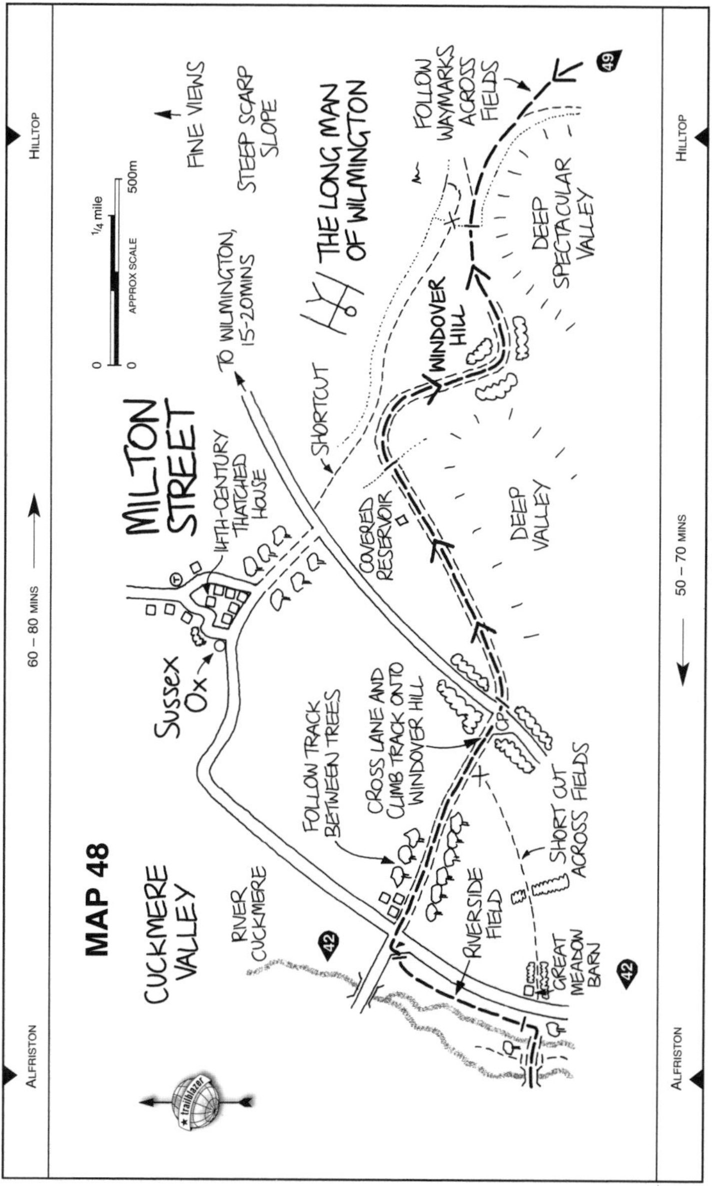

MAP 48

CUCKMERE VALLEY

RIVER CUCKMERE

ALFRISTON ◄

60 – 80 MINS ──────

HILLTOP ►

Sussex Ox

MILTON STREET

14TH-CENTURY THATCHED HOUSE

FOLLOW TRACK BETWEEN TREES

CROSS LANE AND CLIMB TRACK ONTO WINDOVER HILL

COVERED RESERVOIR

TO WILMINGTON, 15-20MINS

SHORTCUT

APPROX SCALE

0   ¼ mile

0   500m

FINE VIEWS

STEEP SCARP SLOPE

THE LONG MAN OF WILMINGTON

WINDOVER HILL

FOLLOW WAYMARKS ACROSS FIELDS

DEEP SPECTACULAR VALLEY

49

RIVERSIDE FIELD

SHORT CUT ACROSS FIELDS

GREAT MEADOW BARN

DEEP VALLEY

42

42

ALFRISTON ◄

50 – 70 MINS ──────

HILLTOP ►

JEVINGTON   MAP 49

Jevington, sitting comfortably in the Cuckmere valley, is another beautiful village that provides a good alternative stop to the somewhat exploited streets of Alfriston.

Where to stay and eat

For accommodation in the village there is *The Paddocks* (☎ 01323-482499, 🖳 www.thepaddockstables.co.uk; 1D/1T, both en suite; ●; 🐾; WI-FI), a comfortable B&B with rooms from £35 per person and the owner can provide packed lunches. They welcome dogs and there is also stabling to keep your horse, should you require it.

Jevington Tea Gardens (☎ 01323-489692; Mar (Mother's Day) to Oct, Wed-Sun, 10.30am-5pm, also open bank hols) at Hawthorne Lodge sell cream teas and coffees indoors or in the garden and they also serve light lunches such as toasties and soups; everything is made on the premises and it's well worth stopping by here.

The village pub, the *Eight Bells* (☎ 01323-484442; food Mon-Sat noon-3pm & 6-9pm, Sun noon-9pm), is a five-minute walk up the lane (the blind bend on the road is very dangerous as there is no pavement for pedestrians – it is safer to use the path by the church). The bar is open all day, every day and they have a wide range of pub meals as well as a pleasant garden, with views over the Downs, in which to eat them.

In the centre of the village, the Hungry Monk Restaurant (🖳 www.hungrymonk. co.uk), which claimed to be the birthplace in 1972 of banoffi pie, has now closed. You can still find the recipe on their website, though.

❏ **Lullington Heath**
This hidden National Nature Reserve near Jevington (see Map 49) is a short detour from the South Downs Way and is a good place to escape the crowds who tend to congregate around the tourist traps of Alfriston, Jevington and Wilmington.

The rough chalk grassland is a good place to see a variety of species of butterfly including the Chalkhill blue. In summer the shallow valley is often ablaze with the yellow flowers of gorse and broom. To the south of Lullington Heath is the expansive cover of **Friston Forest**, another good place to get lost and explore countless forest tracks.

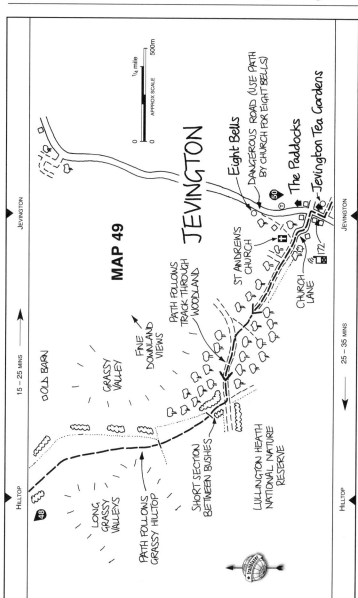

MAP 49

JEVINGTON

HILLTOP ◀ — 15 – 25 MINS — ▶ JEVINGTON

◀ HILLTOP — 25 – 35 MINS — ▶ JEVINGTON

LONG, GRASSY VALLEYS

PATH FOLLOWS GRASSY HILLTOP

48

OLD BARN

GRASSY VALLEY

FINE DOWNLAND VIEWS

PATH FOLLOWS TRACK THROUGH WOODLAND

SHORT SECTION BETWEEN BUSHES

LULLINGTON HEATH NATIONAL NATURE RESERVE

ST ANDREW'S CHURCH

CHURCH LANE

172

Eight Bells

DANGEROUS ROAD (USE PATH BY CHURCH FOR EIGHT BELLS)

The Paddocks

Jevington Tea Gardens

50

0 — ¼ mile

0 — 500m

APPROX SCALE

ROUTE GUIDE AND MAPS

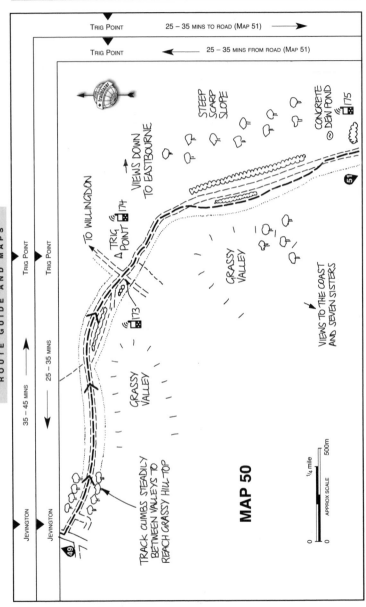

TRIG POINT   25 – 35 MINS TO ROAD (MAP 51) ⟶

TRIG POINT   ⟵ 25 – 35 MINS FROM ROAD (MAP 51)

STEEP SCARP SLOPE

CONCRETE DEW POND 175

VIEWS DOWN TO EASTBOURNE

TO WILLINGDON

TRIG POINT 174

173

GRASSY VALLEY

51

GRASSY VALLEY

VIEWS TO THE COAST AND SEVEN SISTERS

JEVINGTON

TRIG POINT

JEVINGTON

TRIG POINT

35 – 45 MINS

25 – 35 MINS

49

TRACK CLIMBS STEADILY BETWEEN VALLEYS TO REACH GRASSY HILL-TOP

MAP 50

¼ mile

500m

APPROX SCALE

0

0

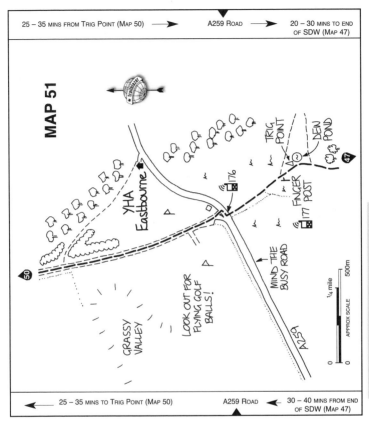

MAP 51

TRIG POINT

DEW POND

FINGER POST

176

177

YHA Eastbourne

MIND THE BUSY ROAD

LOOK OUT FOR FLYING GOLF BALLS!

GRASSY VALLEY

A259

¼ mile

APPROX SCALE

500m

ROUTE GUIDE AND MAPS

EASTBOURNE   MAP 52

Eastbourne is a typical English seaside resort, complete with a grand Victorian pier, though it does have something of a reputation as a retirement town.

Having received a lot of unfair criticism over the years as being one of the least adventurous resorts, particularly when compared to its upbeat neighbour Brighton, Eastbourne has recently undergone something of a revival. The signs on the edge of town shout out 'Welcome to the Sunshine Coast' and certainly this is one of the sunnier corners of the UK. However, whether this really is England's Costa del Sol is open to question.

Love it or hate it, Eastbourne, sprawled out below the hill and stretching along the coast, is a safe and friendly town. It may not have the history and charm of Winchester at the other end of the South Downs Way but Beachy Head, at least, makes for a fitting end to a long walk.

The **Wish Tower** is a Martello Tower, one of a number built along the coast to counter an invasion threat from Napoleon.

Services

The commercial centre is around Terminus Rd and the Arndale Shopping Centre, about 30 minutes' walk from the foot of the South Downs and the end of the Way.

The **tourist information centre** (TIC; ☎ 0871-663 0031, 🖳 www.visiteast bourne.com; May-Sept Mon-Fri 9.15am-5.30pm, Sat 9.15am-5pm, Sun 10am-1pm; Mar-Apr & Oct Mon-Fri 9.15am-5.30pm, Sat 9.15am-4pm, Nov-Feb Mon-Fri 9.15am-4.30pm, Sat 9.15am-1pm) is off the northern end of Terminus Rd on Cornfield Rd. There is plenty of free information here, not only for Eastbourne but also the rest of South-East England and London too.

The **post office** (Mon-Sat 9am-5.30pm) is not far away on the corner of Langney Rd and along the pedestrianised section of Terminus Rd there are also **chemists** and **banks**.

If you need to replace worn-out socks head to **Millets** or **Blacks**, both outdoor shops, on Terminus Rd (both open Mon-Sat 9am-5.30pm, Sun 10.30am-4.30pm).

There is a large Sainsbury's **supermarket** in the Arndale Shopping Centre and another, smaller mini-market (Premier Supermarket) on Seaside Rd which has long opening hours (daily 8am-11pm).

Regular **trains** (see box p42) from Eastbourne go to Lewes, Brighton, Hastings, Gatwick Airport and London Victoria.

Stagecoach's **bus** No 3 runs to Meads Village at the end of the South Downs Way. Renown Coaches' No 126 goes via Alfriston to Seaford while Brighton & Hove Buses have several services to Brighton: the No 12 and 12a go via Seaford and Newhaven, and their No 13X is an open-top service that calls in at such tourist hotspots as Birling Gap and Beachy Head; the bus departs approximately twice an hour in summer at weekends. See the public transport map and table, pp44-6.

Try Eastbourne Taxis (☎ 01323-720720) if you need a **taxi**.

Where to stay

As a major seaside resort Eastbourne is overflowing with hotels and guesthouses. There's a lot of competition and if you're looking for a bargain this is one place where it may not be best to book in advance; the cheaper places will put out signs advertising their prices if they haven't filled their rooms, sometimes as low as £25pp. At more upmarket hotels you can even try bargaining! Listed here are just a few accommodation choices.

YHA Eastbourne (☎ 0845-371 9316, 🖳 eastbourne@yha.org.uk; 30 beds from £13, rooms from £36) has en suite rooms and is self-catering only. It's housed in a new building by the A259 near the golf course on the western edge of Eastbourne. See Map 51, p177.

As you head into town from the end point of the SDW you'll find three good B&Bs in the same area. *Cherry Tree Guesthouse* (☎ 01323-722406, 🖳 www.cherrytree-eastbourne.co.uk; 3S/2T/3D/1D or F, all en suite; ➾; WI-FI) is at 15 Silverdale Rd; it's an Edwardian townhouse with B&B from £36 per person low season to £55 in summer. Just around the corner is *Brayscroft Hotel* (☎ 01323-647005, 🖳

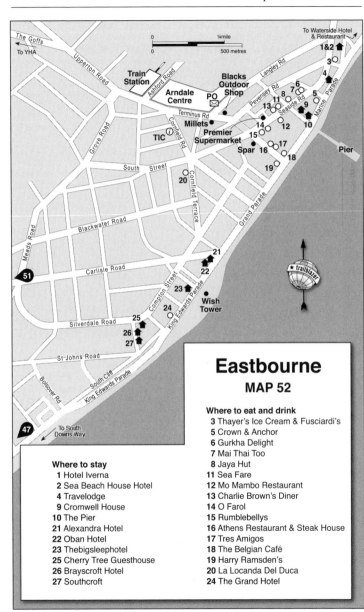

Eastbourne

MAP 52

Where to eat and drink

3 Thayer's Ice Cream & Fusciardi's
5 Crown & Anchor
6 Gurkha Delight
7 Mai Thai Too
8 Jaya Hut
11 Sea Fare
12 Mo Mambo Restaurant
13 Charlie Brown's Diner
14 O Farol
15 Rumblebellys
16 Athens Restaurant & Steak House
17 Tres Amigos
18 The Belgian Café
19 Harry Ramsden's
20 La Locanda Del Duca
24 The Grand Hotel

Where to stay

1 Hotel Iverna
2 Sea Beach House Hotel
4 Travelodge
9 Cromwell House
10 The Pier
21 Alexandra Hotel
22 Oban Hotel
23 Thebigsleephotel
25 Cherry Tree Guesthouse
26 Brayscroft Hotel
27 Southcroft

www.brayscrofthotel.co.uk; 1S/2T/3D, all en suite; ✆; WI-FI) at 13 South Cliff Ave, another Edwardian house with lots of antique furniture and beds for £40 per person; dinners available from £15. Next door at number 15 is *Southcroft* (✆ 01323-729071, 🖳 www.southcrofthotel.co.uk; 2T/3D/1D or T, all en suite; ✆; WI-FI) which charges £68-80 for a double or twin room depending on the time of year; single occupancy is from £44 to £50. Dinners are £14 here.

Along the seafront and King Edward's Parade there's *Alexandra Hotel* (✆ 01323-720131, 🖳 http://alexandrahotel.eastbourne.biz; 11S/10D/17T, all en suite; ✆; 🐾; WI-FI) where B&B is from £35 per person.

There's also *Oban Hotel* (✆ 01323-731581, 🖳 www.oban-hotel.co.uk; 7S/9D/13T/1F, all en suite; ✆; WI-FI), a large establishment with B&B from £85-95 per room in high season, singles from about £50.

The following places are all on the north side of Terminus Rd which means a longer walk to get to them if coming from the end of the South Downs Way. Right opposite the pier is the appropriately named *The Pier* (✆ 01323-649544, 🖳 www.relaxinnz.co.uk; 11S/11D/8T/1F, all en suite; ✆; WI-FI), a place that's not without its charms and is in a great location. Rooms are fair value at around £39-44 for a single, £55-79 for a double.

Also on the seafront are *Hotel Iverna* (✆ 01323-730768, 🖳 www.hotel-iverna .co.uk; 1S/2D/2T/1F, en suite or private facilities; ✆; 🐾), 32 Marine Parade, with beds from £25 to £35 per person; and *Cromwell House* (✆ 01323-725288, 🖳 www.cromwell-house.co.uk; 2S/2T/1D/3D or T en suite; WI-FI), at 23 Cavendish Place, a Victorian townhouse with beds from £33 per person.

The extensive national hotel chain, *Travelodge*, also has a property on Marine Parade (✆ 0871-984 6354, www.travelodge.co.uk; 90D or F , all en suite; ✆; 🐾 £20; WI-FI). If you just walk in off the street the rates are around £48-84, though book in advance and online and they can be as little as £19.

The *Sea Beach House Hotel* (✆ 01323-410458, 🖳 www.seabeachhouse .co.uk; 1S/5D/4T, all en suite; ✆; WI-FI), is at 40 Marine Parade. Most of the rooms have sea views and cost from £35 per person. Princess (later to become Queen) Victoria is said to have stayed here.

Thebigsleephotel (✆ 01323-722676, 🖳 www.thebigsleephotel.com; 50 en suite rooms; ✆; 🐾 £5; WI-FI), is a stylish, thoroughly modern place on the seafront. Curiously pitched somewhere between a hostel and a boutique hotel, the place is packed with facilities including pool and table tennis tables, 12-channel TVs in the rooms and even a bar serving takeaway food. Prices are reasonable: from £65 (£45 for singles) including continental breakfast.

If it's luxury and pampering you require after your walk, try the *Waterside Hotel* (off Map 52; ✆ 01323-646566, 🖳 www.water sidehoteleastbourne.co.uk; 2T/17D en suite rooms; ✆; WI-FI), 11-12 Royal Parade, a boutique spa hotel with a top-class restaurant. Double rooms cost £90 in the high season. Relaxation spa packages including B&B, cocktails and a spa treatment for two people cost from £175.

Where to eat and drink

You'll find a surprisingly eclectic mix of restaurants and cafés, many of which are on or around **Seaside Rd** and **Terminus Rd**.

There are several good Portuguese cafés and restaurants. *O Farol* (✆ 01323-301050; daily 9am-11pm) at 39 Seaside Rd, is an authentic place that has been serving the Portuguese community here for many years. *Bacalhau a farol* (fried cod with potatoes and onions) is £9.75; chicken *piri-piri* is £8.50.

For perhaps more familiar dishes, there's *Charlie Brown's Diner* (✆ 01323-726588; Tue-Sat 6-11pm, Sun & Mon 6-9pm), at 54 Seaside Rd, with wooden floors and pictures of New York skyscrapers all over the walls. There are burgers from £7.75 and steaks from £11.95.

Opposite at No 71 is *Mo Mambo's* (✆ 01323-732832; Mon-Thur 11am-3pm & 5pm-10pm, Fri & Sat 11am-10pm, Sun 5-10pm), an Italian restaurant with pasta dishes from £7.90, pizzas from £6.70 and a good-value lunch menu for just £5.50.

Rumblebellys (☎ 01323-728247; Mon-Fri 5.30-11pm, Sun noon-11pm), at 5-7 Seaside Rd, is a diner with Apache décor, burgers from £6.50, sirloin steak for £14.95 and veggie burgers for £5.95.

Further east at 74 Seaside Rd is *Jaya Hut* (☎ 01323-642775; Mon-Sat noon-2.30pm & 5-11pm, Sun 4-10.30pm), which is a budget Malaysian and Chinese restaurant and takeaway. Chicken satay is £3.50.

At 124 Seaside Rd there's the excellent *Mai Thai Too* (☎ 01323-727169; Mon-Wed 5.30-11pm, Thur-Sat noon-2.30pm & 5.30-11pm). Thai green curry is £5.95 to take away, £6.50 to eat in. Next door is *Gurkha Delight* (☎ 01323-640978; daily noon-2.30pm & 5-11pm). They do momos for £6.50 and their Himalayan curry is £6.95.

At 207 Terminus Rd is the cheerful *Tres Amigos* (☎ 01323-739944; Mon-Fri 5-10pm, Fri, Sat & Sun noon-10pm) with a range of tapas dishes from £3.10, burritos from £8.95 and some special meal deals. There are numerous places to eat along this section of Terminus Rd towards the sea. *Athens Restaurant & Steak House* (☎ 01323-733278; daily 11.30am-2.30pm & 5.30-10.30pm), at No 195, gets excellent reviews. It's efficiently run by three generations of a hospitable Greek family.

In a prime location by the seafront is *The Belgian Café* (☎ 01323-729967; food daily 10am-9pm) where they boast that they offer 50 different ways of eating mussels (including plain old *moules frites*) and you can wash them down with any one of the 50 Belgian beers on offer here. There are set menus from £9.95 to £23.50.

The *La Locana Del Duca* (☎ 01323-737177; daily noon-2.30pm & 5.30-11pm, to 10.30pm on Sun), 26 Cornfield Terrace, is an authentic Italian place offering set menus for £18.50/20.50 for two/three courses as well as traditional favourites à la carte.

There are numerous pubs, some rather rougher than others. The *Crown & Anchor* (☎ 01323-642500; food daily noon-3pm & 5.30-9pm), on the seafront at 15 Marine Parade, often has live music at weekends.

As a seaside town Eastbourne would not be complete without lots of fish and chip shops. *Sea Fare* (☎ 01323-641893; daily 11.30-3.30pm & 4.30-9pm), at 66 Seaside Rd, is a good traditional chippie. Cod and chips is £5.10 in the restaurant and £4.50 to takeaway. There's also a branch of the *Harry Ramsden's* chain (☎ 01323-417454; Sun-Thur 11.30am-9pm, Fri & Sat 11.30am-10pm, winter 11.30am-8pm), on the seafront at the end of Terminus Rd.

For something rather smarter, *Waterside Restaurant* (off Map 52; ☎ 01323-646566, 🖳 www.watersiderestauranteastbourne.co.uk; Tue-Sat 7-10pm), at the hotel of the same name at 11-12 Royal Parade, is recommended. Half a dozen oysters are £9, *escabeche* of sea bream is £6.90 and local fillet of plaice is £15.50.

Another seaside tradition is ice cream. Between Marine Parade and Seaside Rd are two competing outlets, both very good. The cheaper of the two, *Thayer's Ice Cream*, is a small family-run business with 32 different flavours of the stuff. Bigger, brasher *Fusciardi's*, on the seafront, has 18 flavours but also has a sit-down café.

If your walk ends at about tea time and you wish to celebrate in style there can be no better place for a top-of-the-range cream tea than *The Grand Hotel* (☎ 01323-412345, 🖳 www.grandeastbourne.com). You should phone ahead to book. It's served daily from 2.45pm to 6pm when for £22.50 you get a full spread including sandwiches, quiche and cakes. You can push the boat out even further and order the Grand Champagne Tea (£30). The hotel is easy to find: you walk right past it on the way into Eastbourne from the end of the South Downs Way. Splash out – you deserve it!

Moving on

Trains connect Eastbourne with London Victoria, taking approximately 90 minutes. Brighton and Hastings are both about 30 minutes along the coast, west and east respectively. National Express's Nos 24 and 25 **coaches** also travel to London Victoria, while their No 315 travels west all the way along the coast to Helston in Cornwall via Brighton, Portsmouth and Devon.

APPENDIX A – GPS WAYPOINTS

Each GPS waypoint was taken on the route at the reference number marked on the map as below.

MAP	REF	GPS WAYPOINT		DESCRIPTION
Map 2	001	N51° 03.228'	W01° 16.749'	Join road
Map 2	002	N51° 02.862'	W01° 16.146'	Turn left onto track
Map 2	003	N51° 03.006'	W01° 15.865'	Leave track
Map 3	004	N51° 02.813'	W01° 14.842'	Road crossing
Map 3	005	N51° 02.997'	W01° 14.437'	Through gate on track
Map 3	006	N51° 03.433'	W01° 14.089'	Track junction at farmyard
Map 3	007	N51° 02.955'	W01° 12.769'	Crossroads
Map 4	008	N51° 02.727'	W01° 12.399'	Gate into field
Map 4	009	N51° 02.346'	W01° 12.081'	Cross A272 road
Map 4	010	N51° 01.586'	W01° 11.793'	Join lane leading uphill
Map 5	011	N51° 01.041'	W01° 11.358'	The Milbury's
Map 5	012	N51° 00.821'	W01° 10.521'	Gate to Wind Farm
Map 5	013	N51° 00.580'	W01° 09.631'	Track past houses
Map 6	014	N51° 00.059'	W01° 08.913'	Beacon Hill car park
Map 6	015	N50° 59.555'	W01° 08.413'	Stile to cross fields
Map 6	016	N50° 59.342'	W01° 08.227'	Stile to cross track
Map 7	017	N50° 59.040'	W01° 07.728'	The Shoe Inn, Exton
Map 7	018	N50° 59.252'	W01° 07.208'	Bridge over stream
Map 7	019	N50° 59.196'	W01° 06.725'	Cross disused railway
Map 7	020	N50° 58.854'	W01° 05.328'	Hill fort, Old Winchester Hill
Map 8	021	N50° 59.009'	W01° 04.712'	Turn off track
Map 8	022	N50° 59.279'	W01° 04.827'	Car park
Map 8	023	N50° 59.443'	W01° 04.934'	Gate at fork in road
Map 8	024	N50° 59.238'	W01° 04.546'	Join track
Map 8	025	N50° 59.296'	W01° 04.200'	Left turn at farmyard
Map 8	026	N50° 59.446'	W01° 03.153'	Turn onto tree-lined avenue
Map 8	027	N50° 59.066'	W01° 03.085'	Crossroads
Map 9	028	N50° 58.079'	W01° 02.373'	Wetherdown Hostel
Map 9	029	N50° 57.939'	W01° 01.698'	Road junction
Map 10	030	N50° 58.051'	W01° 00.110'	Homelands Farm
Map 10	031	N50° 58.026'	W00° 59.794'	Junction with Hogs Lodge Lane
Map 10	032	N50° 58.465'	W00° 59.274'	Butser Hill car park
Map 10	033	N50° 57.891'	W00° 58.866'	Gate before A3 road crossing
Map 11	034	N50° 57.501'	W00° 58.639'	Car park, QE Country Park
Map 11	035	N50° 57.938'	W00° 58.020'	Benham Bushes BBQ site
Map 12	036	N50° 58.372'	W00° 57.375'	Car park and road crossing
Map 12	037	N50° 58.206'	W00° 56.456'	Track junction
Map 12	038	N50° 58.153'	W00° 55.787'	Road junction
Map 13	039	N50° 57.980'	W00° 54.137'	Road crossing
Map 13	040	N50° 57.611'	W00° 53.213'	Car park, B2146 road crossing
Map 13	041	N50° 57.435'	W00° 52.672'	Car park, B2141 road crossing
Map 14	042	N50° 57.659'	W00° 51.469'	Turn-off to East Harting
Map 14	043	N50° 57.547'	W00° 51.119'	Trig point, Beacon Hill
Map 14	044	N50° 57.535'	W00° 50.447'	Path, not farm track!
Map 14	045	N50° 57.267'	W00° 49.981'	Track junction

MAP	REF	GPS WAYPOINT		DESCRIPTION
Map 15	046	N50° 56.760'	W00° 49.665'	Track crossroads
Map 15	047	N50° 56.999'	W00° 48.587'	Track crossroads
Map 15	048	N50° 56.873'	W00° 47.494'	Path junction, Cocking Down
Map 16	049	N50° 56.759'	W00° 47.002'	Track crossroads
Map 16	050	N50° 56.660'	W00° 46.360'	Junction near ball of chalk
Map 16	051	N50° 56.571'	W00° 45.338'	Car park at A268 crossing
Map 16	052	N50° 56.544'	W00° 45.002'	Water tap
Map 17	053	N50° 56.440'	W00° 44.226'	Fork in track
Map 17	054	N50° 56.463'	W00° 43.706'	Path junction
Map 17	055	N50° 56.466'	W00° 43.258'	Turn-off to Heyshott
Map 18	056	N50° 56.457'	W00° 42.857'	Path junction
Map 18	057	N50° 56.378'	W00° 42.375'	Track junction
Map 18	058	N50° 56.353'	W00° 42.128'	Track junction
Map 18	059	N50° 56.239'	W00° 40.938'	Signpost with memorials
Map 18	060	N50° 56.016'	W00° 39.082'	Track junction
Map 19	061	N50° 55.902'	W00° 39.598'	Track crossroads
Map 19	062	N50° 55.307'	W00° 38.925'	Cross A285 road
Map 19	063	N50° 54.803'	W00° 38.488'	Track junction
Map 20	064	N50° 54.441'	W00° 37.926'	Track junction
Map 20	065	N50° 54.402'	W00° 37.319'	Track junction
Map 20	066	N50° 54.464'	W00° 36.968'	Bignor Hill car park
Map 20	067	N50° 54.587'	W00° 36.157'	Grave
Map 21	068	N50° 54.470'	W00° 35.814'	Track junction
Map 21	069	N50° 53.884'	W00° 34.403'	Cross A29 road
Map 21	070	N50° 53.837'	W00° 33.310'	Cross country lane
Map 22	071	N50° 53.952'	W00° 32.927'	Bridge over River Arun
Map 22	072	N50° 54.025'	W00° 32.358'	Leave B2139 road
Map 22	073	N50° 54.195'	W00° 31.927'	Road junction
Map 22	074	N50° 54.188'	W00° 31.839'	Leave road
Map 22	075	N50° 54.158'	W00° 31.215'	Gate & stile
Map 23	076	N50° 54.190'	W00° 30.413'	Join track
Map 23	077	N50° 54.145'	W00° 29.540'	Track junction
Map 23	078	N50° 54.111'	W00° 28.747'	Track junction
Map 23	079	N50° 54.051'	W00° 28.347'	Turn-off to Storrington
Map 25	080	N50° 53.656'	W00° 26.641'	New barn
Map 25	081	N50° 53.755'	W00° 26.032'	Gate on track
Map 25	082	N50° 53.791'	W00° 25.812'	Turn-off to Washington
Map 25	083	N50° 54.279'	W00° 25.030'	Join track
Map 25	084	N50° 54.251'	W00° 24.885'	Join road into Washington
Map 25	085	N50° 54.304'	W00° 24.306'	Frankland Arms, Washington
Map 25	086	N50° 54.189'	W00° 24.382'	Road junction, Washington
Map 25	087	N50° 53.807'	W00° 24.344'	Steep section of track
Map 26	088	N50° 53.617'	W00° 23.643'	Track junction
Map 26	089	N50° 53.757'	W00° 23.351'	Gate on track
Map 26	090	N50° 53.779'	W00° 22.928'	Chanctonbury Ring
Map 26	091	N50° 53.637'	W00° 22.612'	Gate on track
Map 26	092	N50° 53.409'	W00° 22.421'	Track junction
Map 26	093	N50° 53.269'	W00° 22.001'	Track junction
Map 27	094	N50° 53.219'	W00° 21.675'	Turn-off to Steyning
Map 27	095	N50° 52.669'	W00° 20.972'	Track junction
Map 29	096	N50° 52.403'	W00° 17.958'	Turn-off A283 road

MAP	REF	GPS WAYPOINT		DESCRIPTION
Map 29	097	N50° 52.430'	W00° 17.094'	Car park
Map 29	098	N50° 52.881'	W00° 15.991'	Join road to Truleigh Hill YH
Map 30	099	N50° 52.919'	W00° 15.461'	Truleigh Hill
Map 30	100	N50° 53.063'	W00° 13.763'	Turn-off to Fulking
Map 30	101	N50° 52.937'	W00° 13.213'	Gate
Map 31	102	N50° 53.092'	W00° 12.744'	Devil's Dyke Pub
Map 31	103	N50° 52.978'	W00° 12.254'	Gate on path
Map 31	104	N50° 53.309'	W00° 11.663'	Road crossing
Map 31	105	N50° 53.349'	W00° 11.466'	Gate into woodland
Map 31	106	N50° 53.410'	W00° 10.968'	Gate on path
Map 32	107	N50° 53.743'	W00° 10.001'	Join road
Map 32	108	N50° 53.923'	W00° 09.837'	Crossroads, Pyecombe
Map 32	109	N50° 54.056'	W00° 09.593'	Car park at golf club
Map 32	110	N50° 54.026'	W00° 08.687'	Track crossroads
Map 32	111	N50° 54.227'	W00° 08.718'	Track junction
Map 33	112	N50° 54.027'	W00° 07.845'	Turn-off to Dower Cottage
Map 33	113	N50° 54.146'	W00° 07.327'	Dew pond
Map 33	114	N50° 54.046'	W00° 06.278'	Car park, Ditchling Beacon
Map 33	115	N50° 53.940'	W00° 05.814'	Turn-off to Ditchling
Map 34	116	N50° 53.910'	W00° 04.709'	Road crossing
Map 34	117	N50° 53.876'	W00° 04.387'	Turn-off to Plumpton
Map 34	118	N50° 53.759'	W00° 03.198'	Turn-off to Lewes
Map 35	119	N50° 53.259'	W00° 03.666'	Gate at track junction
Map 35	120	N50° 53.000'	W00° 03.295'	Leave track through gate
Map 35	121	N50° 52.505'	W00° 02.808'	Through gate & stile
Map 35	122	N50° 52.426'	W00° 03.190'	Small hut and pylon
Map 35	123	N50° 51.977'	W00° 03.268'	Steps
Map 35	124	N50° 51.977'	W00° 03.487'	Bridge over A27 road
Map 35	125	N50° 51.872'	W00° 02.952'	Pass under railway
Map 36	126	N50° 51.548'	W00° 03.227'	Through gate
Map 36	127	N50° 51.224'	W00° 03.463'	Through gate
Map 36	128	N50° 51.025'	W00° 03.266'	Through gate, follow fence
Map 36	129	N50° 51.278'	W00° 02.526'	Through gate by dew pond
Map 36	130	N50° 51.032'	W00° 01.876'	Join track
Map 37	131	N50° 50.673'	W00° 01.557'	Track, Swanborough Hill
Map 37	132	N50° 50.086'	E00° 00.479'	Leave track through gate
Map 38	133	N50° 50.009'	E00° 00.149'	Through gate, cross track
Map 38	134	N50° 49.566'	E00° 00.315'	Through gate onto track
Map 38	135	N50° 49.795'	E00° 01.061'	Road junction, Southease
Map 38	136	N50° 49.805'	E00° 01.562'	Bridge over River Ouse
Map 38	137	N50° 49.888'	E00° 01.849'	Level crossing
Map 38	138	N50° 49.804'	E00° 02.228'	Gate after bridge over A26
Map 39	139	N50° 49.875'	E00° 03.090'	Trig point & dew pond
Map 39	140	N50° 50.092'	E00° 03.667'	Gate onto track
Map 39	141	N50° 50.063'	E00° 04.114'	Masts, Beddingham Hill
Map 39	142	N50° 50.069'	E00° 04.468'	Gate on path
Map 40	143	N50° 50.018'	E00° 04.987'	Car park, Firle Beacon
Map 40	144	N50° 50.029'	E00° 06.497'	Trig point, Firle Beacon
Map 40	145	N50° 49.527'	E00° 07.208'	Gate, Bo Peep
Map 41	146	N50° 49.108'	E00° 07.823'	Gate on path

MAP	REF	GPS WAYPOINT	DESCRIPTION
Map 41	147	N50° 48.659' E00° 08.550'	Track junction
Map 42	148	N50° 48.405' E00° 09.581'	Church, Alfriston
Map 42	149	N50° 48.689' E00° 09.581'	Plough & Harrow, Litlington
Map 43	150	N50° 47.440' E00° 09.628'	Through stile on path
Map 43	151	N50° 47.098' E00° 09.471'	Steps up through forest
Map 43	152	N50° 46.707' E00° 09.699'	Track junction
Map 43	153	N50° 46.398' E00° 09.559'	Crossroads, Westdean
Map 43	154	N50° 46.499' E00° 09.244'	Road crossing, Exceat
Map 44	155	N50° 45.905' E00° 09.085'	Turn off track
Map 44	156	N50° 45.909' E00° 09.508'	Stile on path
Map 44	157	N50° 45.376' E00° 09.578'	Haven Brow
Map 44	158	N50° 45.310' E00° 09.793'	Short Brow
Map 44	159	N50° 45.198' E00° 10.139'	Rough Brow
Map 44	160	N50° 45.143' E00° 10.376'	Brass Point
Map 44	161	N50° 44.995' E00° 10.792'	Sarsen stone
Map 45	162	N50° 44.957' E00° 11.020'	The 'Eighth' Sister
Map 45	163	N50° 44.910' E00° 11.284'	Baily's Hill
Map 45	164	N50° 44.570' E00° 11.462'	Memorial pillar
Map 45	165	N50° 44.766' E00° 11.667'	Went Hill
Map 45	166	N50° 44.585' E00° 12.075'	Car park, Birling Gap
Map 46	167	N50° 44.302' E00° 12.901'	Belle Tout Lighthouse
Map 46	168	N50° 44.112' E00° 13.870'	Path near Shooters Bottom
Map 47	169	N50° 44.335' E00° 15.220'	Lookout point
Map 47	170	N50° 44.634' E00° 15.478'	Fork in path
Map 47	171	N50° 45.113' E00° 16.027'	End of SDW coastal route
Map 49	172	N50° 47.518' E00° 12.825'	Jevington Tea Gardens
Map 50	173	N50° 47.222' E00° 14.083'	Turn-off to Willingdon
Map 50	174	N50° 47.196' E00° 14.162'	Trig point
Map 50	175	N50° 46.658' E00° 14.575'	Concrete dew pond
Map 51	176	N50° 45.901' E00° 14.776'	Road crossing
Map 51	177	N50° 45.729' E00° 15.000'	Finger post

APPENDIX B – TAKING A DOG

TAKING DOGS ALONG THE WAY

Many are the rewards that await those prepared to make the extra effort required to bring their best friend along the trail. However, because the South Downs is a prime sheep-farming area your dog may have to be on a lead for much of the walk.

You shouldn't underestimate the amount of work involved, though. Indeed, just about every decision you make will be influenced by the fact that you've got a dog: how you plan to travel to the start of the trail, where you're going to stay, how far you're going to walk each day, where you're going to rest and where you're going to eat in the evening etc.

If you're also sure your dog can cope with (and will enjoy) walking 10 miles or more a day for several days in a row, you need to start preparing accordingly. Extra thought also needs to go into your itinerary. The best starting point is to study the town & village facilities table on pp30-1 (and the advice below), and plan where to stop and where to buy food.

Looking after your dog

To begin with, you need to make sure that your own dog is fully **inoculated** against the usual doggy illnesses, and also up to date with regard to **worm pills** (eg Drontal) and **flea preventatives** such as Frontline – they are, after all, following in the pawprints of many a dog before them, some of whom may well have left fleas or other parasites on the trail that now lie in wait for their next meal to arrive. **Pet insurance** is also a very good idea; if you've already got insurance, do check that it will cover a trip such as this.

On the subject of looking after your dog's health, perhaps the most important implement you can take with you is the **plastic tick remover**, available from vets for a couple of quid. These removers, while fiddly, help you to remove the tick safely (ie without leaving its head behind buried under the dog's skin).

Being in unfamiliar territory also makes it more likely that you and your dog could become separated. For this reason, make sure your dog has a **tag with your contact details on it** (a mobile phone number would be best if you are carrying one with you); you could also consider having it **microchipped** for further security.

When to keep your dog on a lead

● **On cliff tops** It's a sad fact that, every year, a few dogs lose their lives falling over the edge of the cliffs. It usually occurs when they are chasing rabbits (which know where the cliff-edge is and are able, unlike your poor pooch, to stop in time).
● **When crossing farmland**, particularly in the lambing season (around May) when your dog can scare the sheep, causing them to lose their young. Farmers are allowed by law to shoot at and kill any dogs that they consider are worrying their sheep. During lambing, most farmers would prefer it if you didn't bring your dog at all. The exception is if your dog is being attacked by cows. A couple of years ago there were three deaths in the UK caused by walkers being trampled as they tried to rescue their dogs from the attentions of cattle. The advice in this instance is to let go of the lead, head speedily to a position of safety (usually the other side of the field gate or stile) and call your dog to you.
● **On National Trust land**, where it is compulsory to keep your dog on a lead.
● **Around ground-nesting birds** It's important to keep your dog under control when crossing an area where certain species of birds nest on the ground. Most dogs love foraging around in the woods but make sure you have permission to do so; some woods are used as 'nurseries' for game birds and dogs are only allowed through them if they are on a lead.

What to pack

You've probably already got a good idea of what to bring to keep your dog alive and happy, but the following is a checklist:

● **Food/water bowl** Foldable cloth bowls are popular with walkers, being light and take up little room in the rucksack. You can get also get a water-bottle-and-bowl combination, where the bottle folds into a 'trough' from which the dog can drink.

● **Lead and collar** An extendable one is probably preferable for this sort of trip. Make sure both lead and collar are in good condition – you don't want either to snap on the trail, or you may end up carrying your dog through sheep fields until a replacement can be found.

● **Medication** You'll know if you need to bring any lotions or potions.

● **Tick remover** See above

● **Bedding** A simple blanket may suffice, or you can opt for something more elaborate if you aren't carrying your own luggage.

● **Poo bags** Essential.

● **Hygiene wipes** For cleaning your dog after it's rolled in stuff.

● **A favourite toy** Helps prevent your dog from pining for the entire walk.

● **Food/water** Remember to bring treats as well as regular food to keep up the mutt's morale. That said, if your dog is anything like mine the chances are they'll spend most of the walk dining on rabbit droppings and sheep poo anyway.

● **Corkscrew stake** Available from camping or pet shops, this will help you to keep your dog secure in one place while you set up camp/doze.

● **Raingear** It can rain!

● **Old towels** For drying your dog.

What to pack

When it comes to packing, I always leave an exterior pocket of my rucksack empty so I can put used poo bags in there (for deposit at the first bin we come to). I always like to keep all the dog's kit together and separate from the other luggage (usually inside a plastic bag inside my rucksack). I have also seen several dogs sporting their own 'doggy rucksack', so they can carry their own food, water, poo etc – which certainly reduces the burden on their owner!

Cleaning up after your dog

It is extremely important that dog owners behave in a responsible way when walking the path. Dog excrement should be cleaned up. In towns, villages and fields where animals graze or which will be cut for silage, hay etc, you need to pick up and bag the excrement.

Staying with your dog

In this guide we have used the symbol 🐕 to denote where a hotel, pub or B&B welcomes dogs. However, this always needs to be arranged in advance and some places may charge extra. Hostels (both YHA and independent) do not permit them unless they are an assistance (guide) dog; smaller campsites tend to accept them, but some of the larger holiday parks do not. Before you turn up always double check whether the place you would like to stay accepts dogs and whether there is space for them; many places have only one or two rooms suitable for people with dogs.

When it comes to eating, most landlords allow dogs in at least a section of their pubs, though few restaurants do. Make sure you always ask first and ensure your dog doesn't run around the pub but is secured to your table or a radiator.

Henry Stedman

INDEX

Page references in bold type refer to maps

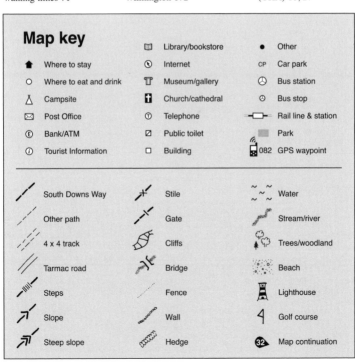

Map key

♠	Where to stay
○	Where to eat and drink
△	Campsite
⊠	Post Office
ⓔ	Bank/ATM
ⓘ	Tourist Information
📖	Library/bookstore
Ⓢ	Internet
🏛	Museum/gallery
✝	Church/cathedral
ⓣ	Telephone
☑	Public toilet
□	Building
●	Other
CP	Car park
⊘	Bus station
⊙	Bus stop
—▭—	Rail line & station
	Park
082	GPS waypoint

/	South Downs Way
/	Other path
/	4 x 4 track
/	Tarmac road
/	Steps
↗	Slope
↗	Steep slope
✗	Stile
✗	Gate
Cliffs	Cliffs
Bridge	Bridge
Fence	Fence
Wall	Wall
Hedge	Hedge
~ ~ ~	Water
Stream/river	Stream/river
Trees/woodland	Trees/woodland
Beach	Beach
🗼	Lighthouse
⚑	Golf course
32	Map continuation

TRAILBLAZER'S LONG-DISTANCE PATH (LDP) WALKING GUIDES

We've applied to destinations which are closer to home Trailblazer's proven formula for publishing definitive practical route guides for adventurous travellers. Britain's network of long-distance trails enables the walker to explore some of the finest landscapes in the country's best walking areas. These are guides that are user-friendly, practical, informative and environmentally sensitive.

● **Unique mapping features** In many walking guidebooks the reader has to read a route description then try to relate it to the map. Our guides are much easier to use because walking directions, tricky junctions, places to stay and eat, points of interest and walking times are all written onto the maps themselves in the places to which they apply. With their uncluttered clarity, these are not general-purpose maps but fully edited maps drawn by walkers for walkers.

● **Largest-scale walking maps** At a scale of just under 1:20,000 (8cm or 3¹/₈ inches to one mile) the maps in these guides are bigger than even the most detailed British walking maps currently available in the shops.

● **Not just a trail guide – includes where to stay, where to eat and public transport** Our guidebooks cover the complete walking experience, not just the route. Accommodation options for all budgets are provided (pubs, hotels, B&Bs, campsites, bunkhouses, hostels) as well as places to eat. Detailed public transport information for all access points to each trail means that there are itineraries for all walkers, for hiking the entire route as well as for day or weekend walks.

Coast to Coast *Henry Stedman*, 5th edition, £11.99
ISBN 978-1-905864-47-8, 256pp, 110 maps, 40 colour photos

Cornwall Coast Path (SW Coast Path Pt 2) 4th edition, £11.99
ISBN 978-1-905864-44-7, 352pp, 130 maps, 40 colour photos

Cotswold Way *Tricia & Bob Hayne* 2nd edition, £11.99
ISBN 978-1-905864-48-5, 192pp, 60 maps, 40 colour photos

Dorset & South Devon (SW Coast Path Pt 3) *Stedman & Newton*, £11.99
ISBN 978-1-905864-45-4, 192pp, 60 maps, 40 colour photos – due early 2013

Exmoor & North Devon (SW Coast Path Pt 1) *Stedman & Newton*, £11.99
ISBN 978-1-905864-43-0, 192pp, 60 maps, 40 colour photos

Hadrian's Wall Path *Henry Stedman*, 3rd edition, £11.99
ISBN 978-1-905864-37-9, 224pp, 60 maps, 40 colour photos

North Downs Way *John Curtin*, 1st edition, £9.99
ISBN 978-1-873756-96-6, 192pp, 80 maps, 40 colour photos

Offa's Dyke Path *Keith Carter*, 3rd edition, £11.99
ISBN 978-1-905864-35-5, 240pp, 98 maps, 40 colour photos

Peddars Way & Norfolk Coast Path *Alexander Stewart*, £11.99
ISBN 978-1-905864-28-7, 192pp, 54 maps, 40 colour photos

Pembrokeshire Coast Path *Jim Manthorpe*, 4th edition, £11.99
ISBN 978-1-905864-51-5, 224pp, 96 maps, 40 colour photos – due early 2013

Pennine Way *Keith Carter & Chris Scott*, 3rd edition, £11.99
ISBN 978-1-905864-34-8, 272pp, 138 maps, 40 colour photos

The Ridgeway *Nick Hill*, 3rd edition, £11.99
ISBN 978-1-905864-40-9, 192pp, 53 maps, 40 colour photos

South Downs Way *Jim Manthorpe*, 4th edition, £11.99
ISBN 978-1-905864-42-3, 192pp, 60 maps, 40 colour photos

West Highland Way *Charlie Loram*, 4th edition, £9.99
ISBN 978-1-905864-29-4, 192pp, 60 maps, 40 colour photos

'The same attention to detail that distinguishes its other guides has been brought to bear here'.

THE
SUNDAY TIMES

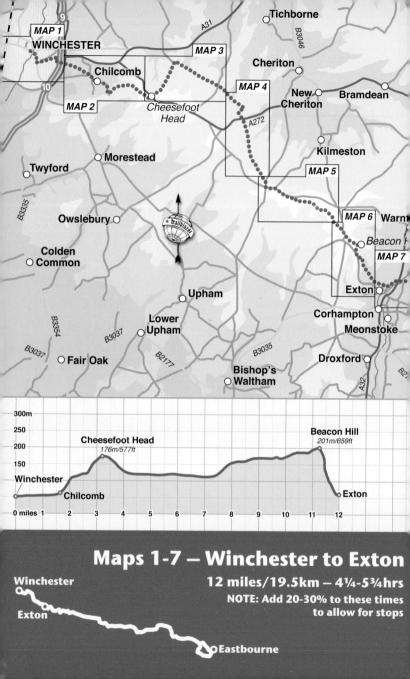

Maps 1-7 – Winchester to Exton

12 miles/19.5km – 4¼-5¾hrs
NOTE: Add 20-30% to these times
to allow for stops

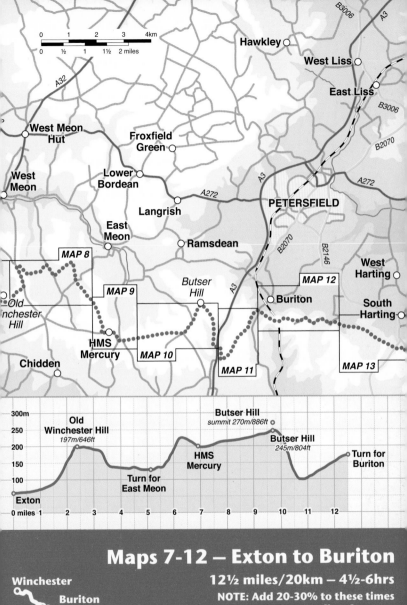

Maps 7-12 — Exton to Buriton

12½ miles/20km – 4½-6hrs

**NOTE: Add 20-30% to these times
to allow for stops**

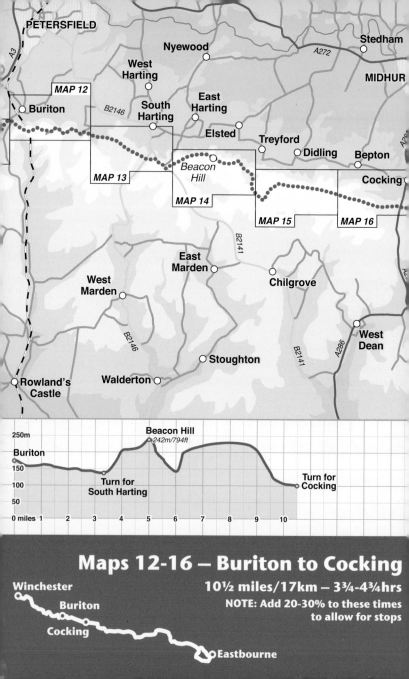

PETERSFIELD

Stedham

Nyewood

West
Harting

A272

MIDHUR

MAP 12

Buriton

B2146

South
Harting

East
Harting

Elsted

Treyford

Didling

Bepton

Cocking

MAP 13

*Beacon
Hill*

MAP 14

MAP 15

MAP 16

B2141

East
Marden

Chilgrove

West
Marden

West
Dean

B2146

B2141

A286

Rowland's
Castle

Walderton

Stoughton

250m

Beacon Hill
242m/794ft

Buriton

150

Turn for
South Harting

Turn for
Cocking

100

50

0 miles 1   2   3   4   5   6   7   8   9   10

Maps 12-16 – Buriton to Cocking

10½ miles/17km – 3¾-4¾hrs

**NOTE: Add 20-30% to these times
to allow for stops**

Winchester

Buriton

Cocking

Eastbourne

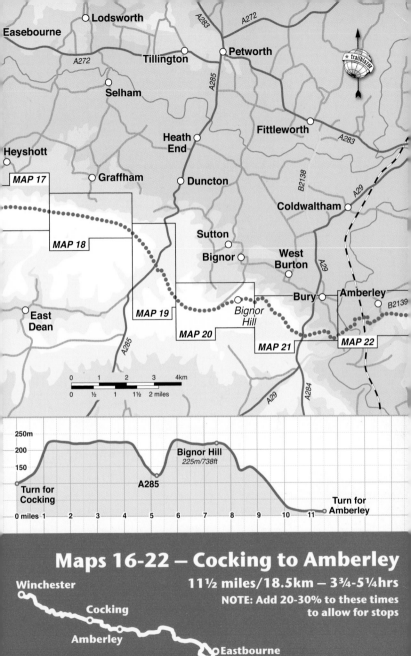

Maps 16-22 – Cocking to Amberley
11½ miles/18.5km – 3¾-5¼hrs
NOTE: Add 20-30% to these times to allow for stops

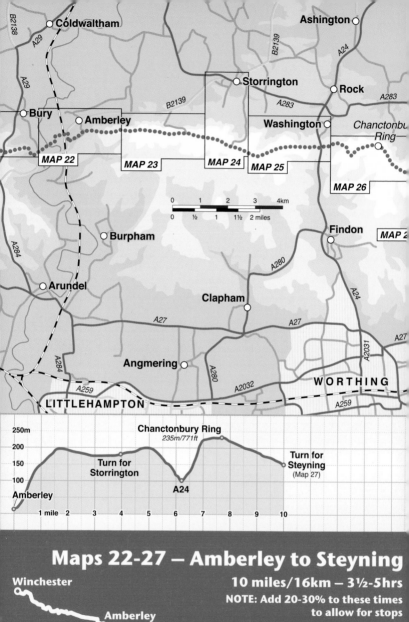

Maps 22-27 — Amberley to Steyning

10 miles/16km – 3½-5hrs
NOTE: Add 20-30% to these times to allow for stops

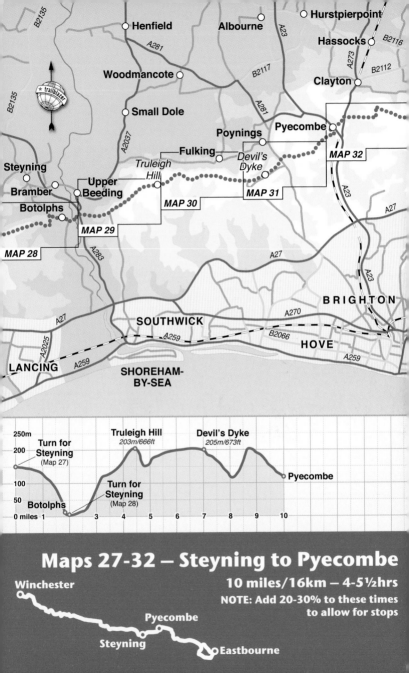

B2135

Hurstpierpoint

Henfield

Albourne

A281

Hassocks

B2116

A23

B2117

Woodmancote

A273

B2112

A281

Clayton

B2135

Small Dole

Pyecombe

A2037

Poynings

MAP 32

Fulking

Devil's
Dyke

Steyning

Truleigh
Hill

MAP 31

A23

Bramber

Upper
Beeding

MAP 30

Botolphs

A27

MAP 29

A283

MAP 28

A27

SOUTHWICK

A270

B R I G H T O N

A27

A2025

A259

B2066

HOVE

A23

LANCING

A259

A259

SHOREHAM-
BY-SEA

250m

Truleigh Hill
203m/666ft

Devil's Dyke
205m/673ft

200

**Turn for
Steyning**
(Map 27)

150

100

**Turn for
Steyning**
(Map 28)

Pyecombe

50

Botolphs

0 miles 1   3   4   5   6   7   8   9   10

Maps 27-32 – Steyning to Pyecombe

10 miles/16km – 4-5½hrs

**NOTE: Add 20-30% to these times
to allow for stops**

Winchester

Pyecombe

Steyning

Eastbourne

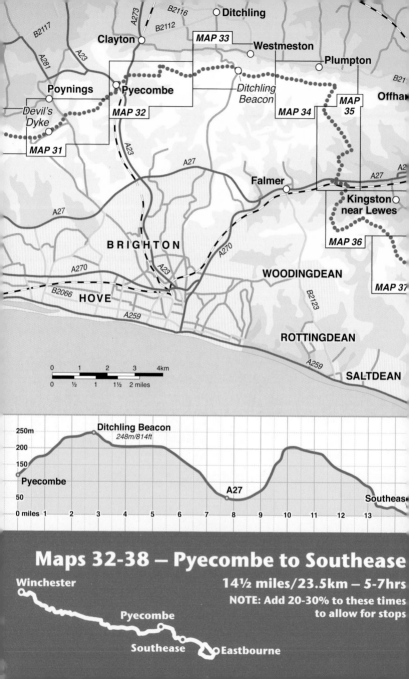

Maps 32-38 – Pyecombe to Southease

14½ miles/23.5km – 5-7hrs

NOTE: Add 20-30% to these times to allow for stops

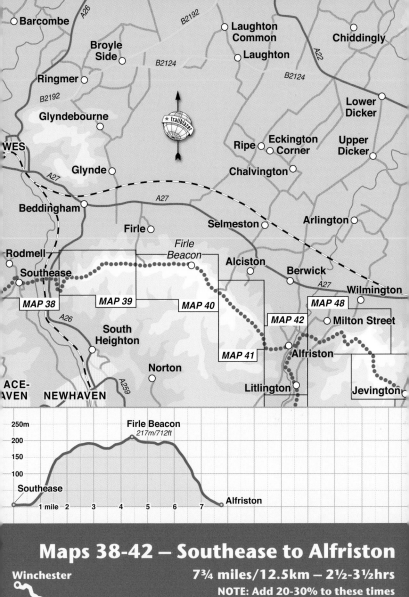

Barcombe

A26

B2192

Laughton
Common

Chiddingly

Broyle
Side

B2124

Laughton

A22

Ringmer

B2192

B2124

Lower
Dicker

Glyndebourne

Ripe

Eckington
Corner

Upper
Dicker

WES

A27

Glynde

Chalvington

Beddingham

A27

Selmeston

Arlington

Firle

Rodmell

Firle
Beacon

Alciston

Berwick

Southease

A27

Wilmington

MAP 38

MAP 39

MAP 40

MAP 48

A26

MAP 42

Milton Street

South
Heighton

MAP 41

Alfriston

Norton

A259

Litlington

Jevington

ACE-
AVEN

NEWHAVEN

250m

Firle Beacon
217m/712ft

200

150

100

Southease

Alfriston

1 mile 2   3   4   5   6   7

Maps 38-42 – Southease to Alfriston

7¾ miles/12.5km – 2½-3½hrs

**NOTE: Add 20-30% to these times
to allow for stops**

Winchester

Southease

Alfriston

Eastbourne

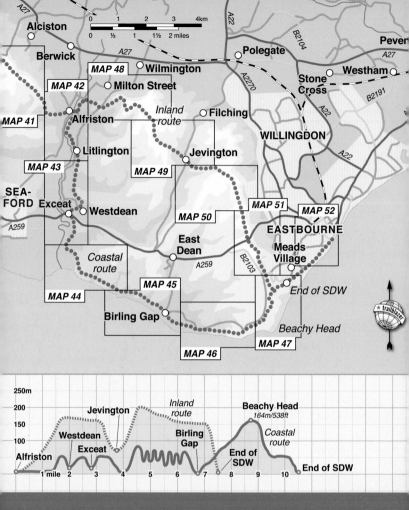

Maps 42-52 – Alfriston to end of SDW

COASTAL ROUTE – 10½ miles/17km – 4¼-5¾hrs
INLAND ROUTE – 7½ miles/12km – 2¾-3½hrs
NOTE: Add 20-30% to these times to allow for stops
Add 1½ miles for end of SDW to Eastbourne centre

Winchester

Alfriston ⚬ Eastbourne

TRAILBLAZER TITLE LIST

For more information about Trailblazer and our
expanding range of guides, for guidebook updates or
for credit card mail order sales visit our website:

www.trailblazer-guides.com

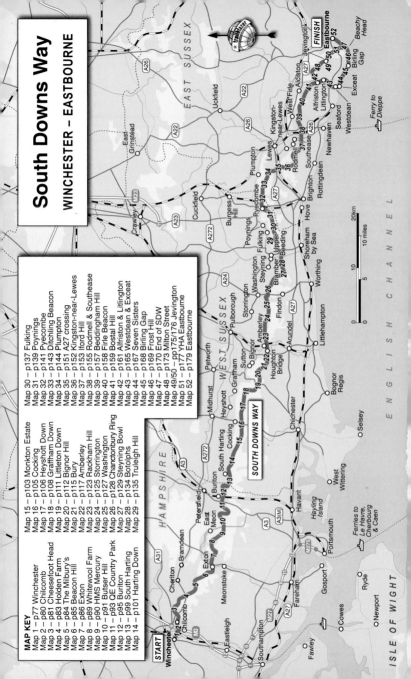

South Downs Way

WINCHESTER – EASTBOURNE